The River of History

The River of History

TRANS-NATIONAL AND TRANS-DISCIPLINARY
PERSPECTIVES ON THE IMMANENCE OF THE PAST

Edited by Peter Farrugia

UNIVERSITY OF
CALGARY
PRESS

© 2005 Peter Farrugia

Published by the
University of Calgary Press
2500 University Drive NW
Calgary, Alberta, Canada T2N 1N4
www.uofcpress.com

No part of this publication may be reproduced, stored in a retrieval system or transmitted, in any form or by any means, without the prior written consent of the publisher or a licence from The Canadian Copyright Licensing Agency (Access Copyright). For an Access Copyright licence, visit www.accesscopyright.ca or call toll free to 1-800-893-5777.

We acknowledge the financial support of the Government of Canada, through the Book Publishing Industry Development Program (BPIDP), and the Alberta Foundation for the Arts for our publishing activities. We acknowledge the support of the Canada Council for the Arts for our publishing program.

The publication of this manuscript was made possible by the generous support of Laurier Brantford, Wilfrid Laurier University and the Wilfrid Laurier Special Initiatives Fund.

LIBRARY AND ARCHIVES CANADA CATALOGUING IN PUBLICATION

The river of history : trans-national and trans-disciplinary perspectives on the immanence of the past / edited by Peter Farrugia.

Papers from a conference titled The lessons of history: an interdisciplinary approach to past, present and future, held in Brantford, Ont., Sept. 30, 2002.
Includes bibliographical references and index.
ISBN 1-55238-160-9

1. History – Philosophy. 2. History – Methodology. 3. Historiography.
I. Farrugia, Peter, 1965–

D13.R53 2005   901   C2005-902628-6

Cover design, Meika West.
Cover photograph, National Geographic.
Internal design & typesetting, zijn digital.

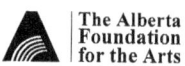

For Liisa, always the brightest light that shines

Table of Contents

List of Contributors   ix
Acknowledgments   xi

Introduction: Navigating the River of History   1
Peter Farrugia

Section 1: Whither History? Professional Historians, Specialization and Popularization

1 The Way We Were?: History as Infotainment in the Age of *History Television*   35
   Robert Wright
2 Teaching History: The Future of the Past   59
   Leo Groarke

Section II: "Sharper than Any Two-Edged Sword": History, Colonialism and Land

3   The Memory of Property: The Challenge of Using the Past to Enlighten the Lawyers of the Future   79
    John McLaren

4   Reading the Past: The Dispossession of the Poor and the Aborigines in Colonial New South Wales   103
    Nancy E. Wright

5   Understanding Property in Australian History   125
    A. R. Buck

Section III: Past, Present and Future Tense: How Do We Own the Past?

6   Historical Fictions: The Invention of Historical Events for Political Purposes   149
    John S. Hill

7   Being Present, Owning the Past, and Growing into the Future: Temporality, Revelation and the Therapeutic Culture   173
    Jeffrey Scott Brown

8   *Travessao*: African Diasporic Migratory Subjectivity and the Making of History   195
    Carol B. Duncan

Section IV: Future History: Technological Development and Historical Change

9   Canada's Lost Tradition of Technological Criticism   217
    James Gerrie

10 Linking the Past to the Future   247
    M. Carleton Simpson

11 Predictions of Global Catastrophe: Just Another Chicken Little?   269
    Stephen F. Haller

Index   285

Contributors

A.R. Buck	Senior lecturer, Department of Law, Division of Law, Macquarie University, Sydney, Australia
Jeffrey Scott Brown	Assistant professor, Department of History, University of New Brunswick, Fredericton, NB
Carol B. Duncan	Assistant professor, Department of Culture and Religion, Wilfrid Laurier University, Waterloo, ON
Peter Farrugia	Assistant professor, Contemporary Studies Program, Wilfrid Laurier University, Brantford, ON

James Gerrie	Instructor, Department of Philosophy, University of Guelph, Guelph, ON
Leo Groarke	Dean of the Brantford campus, Wilfrid Laurier University, Brantford, ON
Stephen F. Haller	Assistant professor, Contemporary Studies Program, Wilfrid Laurier University, Brantford, ON
John McLaren	Professor, Faculty of Law, University of Victoria, Victoria, BC
John S. Hill	Professor and chair, Department of History, Immaculata College, Immaculata, PN
M. Carleton Simpson	Instructor, Department of Philosophy, University of Guelph, Guelph, ON
Robert Wright	Assistant professor, Department of History, Trent University, Peterborough, ON
Nancy E. Wright	Director of the Centre for the Interdisciplinary Study of Property Rights, University of Newcastle, Newcastle, Australia

Acknowledgments

This volume grew out of papers presented at the inaugural Laurier Brantford interdisciplinary conference entitled "The Lessons of History: An Interdisciplinary Approach to Past, Present and Future," which took place from 28–30 September 2000 in Brantford, Ontario. There are a number of people whose assistance proved invaluable in the organization of this conference and the production of this volume. Dr. Art Read, the first dean of the Brantford campus, allowed a young and inexperienced faculty member to try and realize his dream of organizing an international, interdisciplinary conference. Wilfrid Laurier University's former vice president academic, Dr. Rowland Smith, was, from the beginning, supportive of that dream and generously contributed funds to see that our vision became reality. Finally, The Bell Homestead National Historic Site, the Brant Museum and Archives, the Brantford Downtown Business Improvement Area, the City of Brantford Planning Department, Tourism Brantford and the Woodland Cultural Centre all provided technical expertise and/or financial support for the conference.

While it is true that the more immediate impetus for this anthology lay in Laurier Brantford's inaugural interdisciplinary conference, it is equally true that the deeper roots of this project were formed as a result of my own studies in history and three men in particular deserve thanks for providing a model of breadth of learning, intellectual curiosity and humane scholarship that attracted me to the discipline of history: Drs. Christopher Greene, Stuart Robson and John Syrett.

As the project of a book advanced, a number of people played vital roles in shaping the emerging manuscript. Philip Cercone at the McGill-Queen's University Press was a source of valuable information, and the current dean of the Brantford campus, Dr. Leo Groarke, provided welcome support throughout the process. I appreciated the constructive criticism of Dr. Doug Lorimer of the Wilfrid Laurier University history department as I worked on my own contribution to the volume and both Tracy Arabski and Dr. Gary Warrick provided much needed encouragement at critical moments in the manuscript's development.

I would be remiss if I did not thank Walter Hildebrandt and the team at the University of Calgary Press for their support. They saw the potential in this manuscript and moved quickly to indicate their interest. They also responded speedily, thoroughly and cheerfully to the many questions asked by a first-time editor, which made the necessary revisions throughout the editing process that much easier to complete.

Finally, I would like to thank my family for their support and patience as I worked on this project. If there is a lesson to be drawn from the history of this particular enterprise, it is that our loved ones help us to forget past frustrations, to avoid getting too caught up in future plans and to derive as much pleasure as possible from the present.

Brantford, Ontario, August 2004

Introduction: Navigating the River of History

PETER FARRUGIA

"History" is a Greek word which means, literally, just "investigation."
– Arnold Toynbee

What else can history teach us? Only the vanity of believing we can impose our theories on history. Any philosophy which asserts that human experience repeats itself is ineffectual.
– Jacques Ellul

¶ The River of History

This collection of essays is the work of a number of academics active in a wide variety of disciplines, seeking to understand the relationship between the past, present and future. It is valuable, not only because it examines that complex interplay, but because it underlines the importance of history and historical consciousness across time, cultures and disciplinary borders. Given the confusion surrounding terms such as "past," "memory" and "history," it would perhaps be advisable to begin with some rudimentary definitions. The past is simply those events – real or imagined – reputed to have taken place previously. Memory is the recollection of these events held either by individuals or collectives. And history is the study – whether based on oral testimonies or textual records – of these events.[1]

The organizers of the conference out of which this volume grew chose the theme "Lessons of History," expecting that those presenting would, for the most part, set themselves up in opposition to this notion of history providing a roadmap for future generations.[2] However, one of the more interesting things that emerged from the papers presented was that, despite a widespread reluctance to draw "lessons" from history among professional historians, the idea of history providing a blueprint for future action persists. Another theme – perhaps not unrelated – that emerged during the course of the gathering was widespread suspicion of professional historians. There has been a "Lutheran" movement questioning the priestly role of historians as the true interpreters of history. Finally, the conference revealed that, notwithstanding both the occasionally outlandish claims made on behalf of history as a guide to the future, and increased scepticism vis-à-vis the practitioners of history, most people continue to acknowledge that history has a bearing on a variety of questions in realms as disparate as indigenous studies, psychology, and environmental science. This anthology is a testament to that influence.

The relevance of history to contemporary concerns – so clearly embodied in the disciplinary breadth of the contributors to this volume – suggests that perhaps we have been too rigid in our delineation of past, present and future. Perhaps in our efforts to separate, distinguish and analyze, we have not always been alive to their interconnection. In this regard, the analogy of a river might be helpful. The Greek philosopher,

Heraclitus of Ephesus, was the first to discuss the notion of history as a river. He is commonly translated as having stated that "No man can cross the same river twice, because neither the man nor the river are the same." This image accords nicely with Heraclitus' theory of eternal flux, in which the only constant is change.

However, this statement is not entirely satisfying. While most with any familiarity with history would agree that it does not, as the old saw runs, "repeat itself," neither do we seem to be wholly independent of the past. The past is, in a sense, immanent in the present. Some of the pebbles on which Heraclitus' man stepped, upon entering the river the first time, remain in the same place on the river bed. And some of those same water molecules that rushed past him *en route* to the river's mouth have since evaporated, condensed again, been precipitated and flowed past the same bend in the river once more. As it happens, Heraclitus was aware of this possibility. A more literal translation of what he wrote reads: "On those stepping into rivers staying the same other and other waters flow."[3] It is on this conception of the river of history – at once new and familiar – that the essays which follow will build.

¶ The Impossibility of Poetry, The Possibility of History

Most are aware of Theodor Adorno's assertion that, in the wake of the Second World War, with its staggering human and material cost and the resulting questions raised about the nature of humanity, it was impossible to write poetry. Yet that did not preclude a longing for some attempt to make sense of what had transpired. In fact, there was a widespread yearning for certainties after 1945. The world found an eager purveyor of such certainties in the English historian, Alan John Percivale Taylor. Even before the war, Taylor had carved out a reputation as a pungent writer, willing to make bold claims and unafraid of controversy. He achieved an even higher degree of notoriety in 1961 with publication of *The Origins of the Second World War*, which, even today, must be addressed by any serious student of the period. In fact, one respected analyst has gone so far as to assert that Taylor continues to hold a sort of first mortgage on the question of the causes of World War II, such was the influence of his book.[4]

Taylor epitomized the professional historian of the first half of the twentieth century. He began the second edition of *Origins* by maintaining that "I do not come to history as a judge." He steadfastly maintained that he was the dispassionate, even scientific, observer, attempting to get at root causes and pursuing no other agenda.[5] Taylor made this claim despite challenging much of the prevailing orthodoxy surrounding the outbreak of the war. For example, he refused to see a grand design in Hitler's foreign policy, characterizing him instead as a rank opportunist. He declared "statesmen are too absorbed by events to follow a preconceived plan. They take one step, and the next follows from it. The systems are created by historians ... and the systems attributed to Hitler are really those of Hugh Trevor-Roper, Elizabeth Wiskemann and Alan Bullock."[6]

Whatever Taylor's ultimate intent, there can be no question that to publish so controversial a book on so sensitive a topic as the origins of the recent war required great confidence in his own skills. This alone would make him a fitting symbol of his profession at the time. Yet, while Taylor may have embodied the professional historian of the mid-twentieth century, supremely confident in his ability to objectively weigh various factors and arrive at an unbiased opinion, he was at the same time emblematic of one of the developments that most profoundly influenced history: the growing influence of media.

¶ History and the Rise of Media

In the contemporary era, film, television and now the Internet are playing an ever-expanding role in shaping the historical consciousness of people. It is no surprise, for example, that when he discerned a lack of knowledge about the Holocaust, director Stephen Spielberg felt it incumbent upon himself to produce a film exploring this event and was convinced that he could help eliminate the ignorance he found so shocking.[7]

More than one observer has noted that, in an era when fewer people are engaged by the work of professional historians, there is still a mounting interest in depictions of historical events in literature, film and television. This seeming paradox is addressed by Anne-Louise Shapiro in an issue of *History and Theory* dealing with the production of the past. She contends:

> We seem to be living in a ... moment when there is both considerable worry about historical illiteracy, cultural amnesia and intractable presentism – the loss of meaningful history – and an equally powerful sense of history as everywhere present: the high profile subject of films, museum exhibits, and theme parks; the source of struggle and recrimination in domestic and international politics; the center of controversies over school curricula; the focus of multiplying civic ceremonies and memorials; and the object of intense debate in the electronic media.[8]

But well before we reached this stage, the new media were starting to exert influence on historical perceptions. A.J.P. Taylor epitomized this trend.

Taylor grew to be the century's prototypical historian/celebrity.[9] His popularity began to swell as a result of his radio work during the Second World War. His appearance on "The World at War – Your Questions Answered" in March 1942 marked his debut on BBC Forces' radio. By the end of the war Taylor had delivered in excess of twenty radio broadcasts on various subjects related to foreign affairs.[10] Even at this early stage in his career, Taylor was demonstrating some of the qualities that often make professional historians suspicious of radio and television work. He seemed opinionated and prone to sweeping generalizations.

These qualities were even more in evidence in 1946, when Taylor was drafted to create a four-program series on "The Roots of British Foreign Policy" for the BBC's new venture, the Third Programme. Taylor decided to discuss the need for controversy in public discussion of foreign policy in the first episode and then move on to address Britain's relations with the United States, the USSR and Europe respectively in the remaining programs. Taylor's sharp criticism of the United States and his insistence that Britain's best hope lay in close future relations with the Soviets stirred up tremendous anger, both within the BBC and among the political elite. Taylor was taken to task in speeches made in the House of Commons and he later wrote in his autobiography that the controversy had much to do with his inability to win honours from either the Crown or government later in life.[11] Regardless of its impact on his chances for honours, this incident highlights the problems posed by the new media for historians. Now, in addition to maintaining the traditional virtues of accuracy and balance, they were expected to turn a clever phrase; now, in addition to informing, they were expected to entertain and provoke.

¶ The Emergence of Social History

Another important development in the historical profession had a tremendous impact on history generally but especially that branch of history to which Taylor's *Origins* belongs: international relations. This was the rise of social history, which can be defined as the study of ordinary life, including family relations, work, leisure, education, and demographic trends.[12]

It is safe to say that, until fairly recently, history did focus on the words and actions of the most influential elements in society. In part, this was a function of our reliance on written records, which tend to record only the deeds of the powerful. However, it also reflected choices made by historians, who privileged some documents – proclamations, laws, learned treatises, biographies – over others – baptismal records, death certificates – that might shed light, even in an indirect manner, on the "lower orders." The perceived need to teach and/or inspire through the lives of the great took precedence over any notion of recovering the experiences of all members of society. Today, few would argue that our understanding of the past has not been deepened and broadened by social historians' use of a wider array of sources and their exploration of the lives of a wider range of people. To select but one of the more arresting examples, our understanding of the French Revolution has only been enriched by pioneering studies into the peasantry and the urban poor; names like Soboul, Lefebvre, Cobb and Rudé have become forever linked with 1789 and its consequences.[13]

A number of factors converged to fuel the interest in social history. The decade of the 1960s was instrumental in this process because it ushered in a new consciousness of the precariousness of modern society. As Georg Iggers has pointed out, it was in the 1960s that the "conditions created by World War II bec[a]me obvious, among them the end of the colonial empires and a greater awareness that non-Western peoples also had a history."[14] But the repositioning of our collective gaze on the formerly ignored elements in society was not just a matter of adding colour. As Shapiro rightly points out, the worries about whether we are inundated with too much history or are, in fact, starved for it are "not two different sets of problems, but aspects of the same larger concern: that the wrong kind of history ... is producing an unfortunate kind of historical consciousness."[15] It all comes down to a debate about what constitutes *good* history.

¶ The Post-Modernist Critique

In the discussion surrounding the nature of history, it is not unusual for commentators to label those calling for fundamental reform as post-modernists. In reality, what is termed "the post-modernist critique" owes a great deal to various theories of literary criticism. While recognizing that the opponents of History with a capital H are by no means monolithic in their approach, the following sketch of more recent debates will follow common practice in speaking of a "post-modernist critique" that has challenged certain fundamental assumptions about history and prompted interesting responses from within the discipline.

If social historians attacked the way in which historical research had previously been conducted, post-modernists questioned the whole historical enterprise. Interestingly, they heaped scorn on the notion of a significant difference between "bourgeois" and "proletarian" varieties of history. To quote one recent contributor to the debate, both versions:

> ... articulated as key elements in their respective ideologies, a shared view of history as a movement with a direction immanent within it – a history which was purposefully going somewhere – differing only in the selection of "its" ultimate destination and the "essentialist" dynamics which would get "it" there.[16]

While the engines believed to be driving history were different, both bourgeois and proletarian forms of history were based on the belief that there *was* an engine and that the vehicle was being propelled along some sort of clear route towards a destination. History was linear.

One critic who questioned this supposition was Hayden White. His rejection of linearity – whether labelled bourgeois or proletarian – drew its inspiration from his sense of the sublime purpose of history. In an influential 1982 essay he wrote:

> It seems to me that the kind of politics that is based on a vision of a perfected society can compel devotion to it only by virtue of the contrast it offers to a past that is understood in the way Schiller conceived it, that is, as a "spectacle" of "confusion," "uncertainty" and "moral anarchy." Surely this is the appeal of those eschatological religions that envision a "rule of the saints" that is the very antithesis of the spectacle of sin and corruption that the history of a fallen humanity displays to the eye of the faithful.... But modern ideologies seem to me to differ crucially from eschatological religious myths in that they impute a meaning to history that renders its manifest confusion comprehensible to either reason, understanding or aesthetic sensibility. To the extent that they succeed in doing so, these ideologies deprive history of the kind of meaninglessness that alone can goad living human beings to make their lives different for themselves and their children, which is to say, endow their lives with a meaning, for which they alone are responsible.[17]

History is not devoid of meaning – as some opponents of post-modernism have accused their adversaries of claiming – but that meaning lies in each individual's personal struggle to make sense of the past.

The post-modernist revolution has had a profound impact on the practice of history. This variegated movement has questioned a number of fundamental assumptions and suggested correctives. However, its most important contentions have been: 1) that truth is, if not unattainable, then, at the very least, personal and provisional; 2) that history has traditionally favoured the text over the spoken word, though the text withholds as much as it reveals; and 3) that grand narratives in the old style are attempts at totalization that marginalize or erase altogether minority groups. These claims are, of course, very serious and have sometimes prompted a rearguard action on the part of opponents.

¶ The Rejection of the Post-Modernist Critique

Many historians have taken umbrage at the allegations made by the post-modernists. Arguably the most frequently levelled counter charge has been that the post-modernist approach leads inevitably to relativism. Richard Evans has claimed that to accept the post-modernist critique would be to:

… surrender to the hyper-relativism of the postmodernists and admit that in the end no kind of objective knowledge about the past, in the sense of the patterns of interconnectedness that makes it history rather than chronicle, can ever be possible.… The fundamental problem with this kind of relativism is, as we have already seen, that it inevitably falls foul of its own principles when they are applied to itself … in practice, even the most extreme deconstructionists do not really accept that their own theories can be applied to their own work. They wish, on the contrary, to retain their own identity as authors and their own control over the interpretations to which their own texts are subject.[18]

This interpretation of post-modernism reduces post-modernist history to the bald statement "There is no Truth, save our Truth."

In this country, the debate over the nature and possible uses of history became front-page news as a result of the intervention of one of Canada's best known historians, J. L. Granatstein. In the provocatively titled *Who Killed Canadian History?*, Granatstein pillories the historical profession for failing Canadians. After complaining that the halls of academe are peopled with individuals who "study whatever they choose without fear of losing their jobs,"[19] he describes the struggle for control of history departments around the country:

As the old white males rallied themselves and fought back, the resulting war produced heavy casualties, much bloodshed, and vast expenditures of time and effort. The political historians believed that narrative was important, that chronology mattered, and that the study of the past could not neglect the personalities of the leaders and the nations they led. The social historians had no interest in the history of the "elites" and almost none in political history, except to denounce the repressiveness of Canadian governments and business. It was far more important to study how the workers resisted industrialization, the Marxist historians claimed; to investigate how birth control was practised before the Pill, feminist historians maintained; or to document gay men's experiences in Toronto's bath houses, than to study the boring lives of prime ministers, the efforts of the Canadian Corps in the Great War, or the Quiet Revolution in

Quebec. Blame had to be allocated. Canada was guilty of genocide against the Indians, the bombing of Germany, the ecological rape of the landscape, and so on.[20]

According to Granatstein, one of the most regrettable consequences of the triumph of the new breed of historians has been the rejection of narrative. This has left history devoid of all that is truly worthwhile. It should hardly be a surprise, therefore, that a generation of citizens has grown up with little interest in or knowledge of Canadian history.

Interestingly enough, the CBC's ambitious project, *Canada: A People's History* may have thrown Granatstein's conclusions into question. The series garnered mixed critical reviews, but audience numbers seemed to show that many Canadians were willing to tune in to learn more about their past. The documentary also aroused considerable academic discussion. For example it was discussed in a specially organized forum "Canadian History in Film," that took place at the 2000 meeting of the Canadian Historical Association in Edmonton.[21] Even Robert Wright, who elsewhere in this volume expresses deep concern about the growing influence of popular media and corporations in shaping public perceptions of the past, admits that the series was, in a number of ways, "impressive."[22]

¶ Accommodating the Post-Modernist Critique

While there has unquestionably been an angry backlash against postmodernism in some quarters, it is clear that the emergence of this approach has had a profound impact on the study of history. As a result of the critique, many historians have reconsidered a number of assumptions about their discipline. Joyce Appleby, Lynn Hunt and Margaret Jacob are among them. Their collective work, *Telling the Truth About History*, reveals their concern. "Is history supposed to create ethnic pride and self-confidence?" they ask:

[o]r should history convey some kind of objective truth about the past? Must history be continually rewritten to undo the perpetuation of racial and sexual stereotypes? Or should it stand above the tumult of present day political and

social concerns? Is the teaching of a coherent national history essential to democracy? Is the attack on traditional history another sign of an insidious new barbarism at the gates, one that devalues knowledge and denies the possibility of truth?[23]

These questions are all the more relevant in an age of globalization, when certain groups are retreating into a walled ethnic nationalism, fortified by shared language, religion and/or history.[24]

In the end, Appleby et al. reject the charge that, in taking on board some of the post-modernists' criticisms, they are necessarily besmirching the reputations of important figures, promoting the elevation of relativism over judgment, or proclaiming the impossibility of objective truth. They maintain:

> The realist never denies that the very act of representing the past makes the historian an agent who actively molds how the past is to be seen.... Our version of objectivity concedes the impossibility of any research being neutral ... and accepts the fact that knowledge seeking involves a lively, contentious struggle among diverse groups of truth-seekers. Neither admission undermines the viability of stable bodies of knowledge that can be communicated, built upon, and subjected to testing.[25]

The fallibility of the seeker does not preclude the possibility of the existence of Truth with a capital T. And, while historians may be deeply flawed individuals, they can still contribute to the gradual creation of a historical record that approaches that Truth.

For these historians, intent matters. It is enough that the historian strives to the best of her ability to reach the truth. Still, they warn that while it is true that democracy "thrives on a passion for establishing and communicating the truth ... history always involves power and exclusion, for any history is always someone's history, told by that someone from a partial point of view.... All histories are provisional; none will have the last word."[26] It would seem that, emerging out of the twentieth century, we have learned a degree of modesty, though at a terribly high price. The crowds in Vienna, Berlin, Paris and London who thought along with Rupert Brooke that they were "into cleanness leaping"[27] instead endured four years of troglodyte existence on the battlefields of Europe. The

Bolsheviks who promised "Bread, Peace, Land" set in motion a series of events that produced instead famine, civil war and forced collectivization. The "lesson" that appeasement was at least partially responsible for the rise of Hitler led to a fifty year standoff between the superpowers during which the world was poised on a knife's edge.

¶ History and Memory

There is one final factor that has contributed to the transformation of history in the late twentieth and early twenty-first centuries. That is the growing preoccupation with memory. History and memory have frequently been depicted as at odds with one another. Any instructor who has had to lecture on the Second World War with veterans in attendance will instantly appreciate the diplomacy necessary to ensure that both are given their due in the classroom. The reasons for the alleged conflict between history and memory are suggested by John Tosh in his *The Pursuit of History*. Tosh begins by pointing out the complexities of the individual's memory. "We know," he says, "from personal experience that memory is neither fixed nor infallible: we forget, we overlay early memories with later experience, we shift the emphasis, we entertain false memories and so on. In important matters we are likely to seek confirmation of our memories from an outside source."[28] Reliability has always been a concern for historians trying to figure out what to make of memory, particularly in those instances where the historian concerned has worked under the assumption that strict objectivity must be maintained; memory was, thus, always suspect.

After assuring the reader that what applies to the individual also holds true for entire societies, Tosh touches on another contentious point. He declares that "it would be a mistake to suppose that social memory is the preserve of small-scale, pre-literate societies. In fact the term itself highlights a universal need: if the individual cannot exist without memory, neither can society, and that goes for large-scale technologically advanced societies too."[29] The need for memory reminds us of the fundamental similarity of human beings across cultures. It is not difficult to imagine that this was a less than palatable truth in societies which viewed themselves as superior to the "backward" cultures they dominated thanks to empire.[30]

Today, we are much more conscious of the need to acknowledge both memory and history. The recollections of the witness and the analysis of the professional historian both have an important place in shaping our understanding of the past. But it was not always so. In the early decades of the twentieth century the historian still reigned triumphant. As John Hill points out,[31] it was not the release of an anthology of veterans' observations about their experiences but the release of tomes of official documents that aroused excitement in the wake of the Great War.

The war itself was as a major watershed in the gradual emergence of memory in the twentieth century. A rich vein of material was opened up by Paul Fussell and explored further by George Mosse, Samuel Hynes and Jay Winter; while these historians did not necessarily agree on either the nature or the extent of the changes wrought by the First World War, all agreed that memory was critical after 1918.[32] The most tangible reminders of the necessity of remembering were the monuments erected to mark the conflict and those who served in it.[33] For example, at Thiepval we find Edward Luytens' Monument to the Missing of the Battle of the Somme, noteworthy for its emphasis on each and every missing soldier and for the absence of heroic statuary adorning the structure. The Vimy memorial, designed by Walter Allward, though including some sculptures reminiscent of earlier monuments, is similarly simple in its construction and features the names of those killed in the battle, carved on its sides. Across the countryside or northeastern France, meanwhile, scores of monuments of various shapes and sizes commemorate particular battles, regiments or even individuals.[34] Of course, the most obvious example of the new ethic of commemoration was the creation of tombs dedicated to unknown soldiers. In 1920 the British created such a memorial in Westminster Abbey and the French did the same under the Arc de Triomphe. The next year the United States, Belgium, Italy and Portugal took similar steps. In the French case, great emphasis was laid on ensuring that the identity of the soldier remained unknown. Bodies from six key battle sites were brought to Ypres where a blindfolded officer selected the remains to be interred beneath Napoleon's self-aggrandizing monument.[35]

The decades after the Great War contributed to a further intensification of the influence of memory. Recognition of the immense cost of the Second World War led to an increased sensitivity to anniversaries. In addition, the horrors of the Final Solution resulted in a greater value being placed on testimonies of the kind provided by Holocaust survivors like Primo Levi and Elie Wiesel.[36] In a little over thirty years, more than 50 million people had been killed, and between 1939 and 1945 a significant portion of the casualties had been civilians. Offering a nod in the direction of those average citizens who had sacrificed much in the world wars, the ruling elites encouraged rites of commemoration.

But the elites themselves could not entirely manage this process of democratization that was underway. Developments arose too rapidly for them to control. The emergence of social history and post-modernism, like the new forms of remembering the dead, were underpinned by the idea that acknowledging individuals previously overlooked would help us to arrive at a fuller understanding of the past. And so, today, the influence of memory is ever present. It is manifested in the seemingly daily anniversaries solemnly marked by governments, interest groups and news outlets and in the spontaneous memorials that mark the passing of public figures like Princess Diana or even average individuals like the victims of the attacks on the World Trade Center.

¶ History Matters

Despite the many challenges that it has been forced to confront, it is clear that history still matters. A number of contemporary debates illustrate this point admirably. In Germany, controversy has arisen over the reclaiming of Germany's past in its totality. The writer and critic W. G. Sebald has contended that:

> The recurrent complaint that no one, to the present day, has written the great German epic of the wartime and postwar periods is not unconnected with this failure.... In spite of strenuous efforts to come to terms with the past, as people like to put it, it seems to me that we Germans today are a nation strikingly blind to history and lacking in tradition. We do not feel any passionate interest in our earlier way of life and the specific features of our own civilization.... And when

we turn to take a retrospective view, particularly of the years 1930 to 1950, we are always looking and looking away at the same time."[37]

This is what motivates Sebald to explore the repressed memories of German suffering during World War II, most notably those associated with the campaign of area bombing launched by the Allies beginning in 1942.

There are others who would agree with Sebald's assessment of the situation. In 1998 the novelist Martin Walser found himself at the centre of a conflict following a speech he made in accepting the Peace Prize of the German Book Trade. Walser had just written a critically acclaimed novel, *Ein springender Brunnen*, an autobiographical work recounting the life of a young Catholic who joins the army late in the war. Interestingly, Walser's narrator states that "[w]hat people may think of as the objectively true past ... is in fact a construction which they have created for their own purposes in the present. Every past, inasmuch as it is told in the present, is therefore at least partly a fiction. 'Geschichte' as history is always also 'Geschichte' as story."[38]

In the acceptance speech Walser concentrated his attacks on those writers and thinkers who were too eager in his opinion to criticize their own country. He declared that they had cloaked themselves in an air of spiritual mindedness and appointed themselves the national conscience. But Walser found their attempts "empty, pompous [and] comic" because "conscience cannot be delegated." Thus, there was a fundamental difference between Walser's novel and his speech: while the former asserted that "the attempt to tame the past was doomed to failure," the latter argued the opposite, suggesting that, in fact, "the past is being successfully instrumentalized by self-hating Germans – and perhaps also by Germany's international rivals – for political reasons."[39] The implications of this battle over German history are obvious. Until the telling of the full story of the German people – including both the suffering they perpetrated and the suffering they endured – is permissible, Germany will remain in a kind of enforced adolescence, unable to act independently on the international stage for fear that any assertiveness might signal the recrudescence of fascism.

Meanwhile, back in Canada, the public debate launched by Jack Granatstein's *Who Killed Canadian History?* seemed to suggest that history mattered to a great many people. But Granatstein's assertion that history was dead seemed confirmed by a series of surveys conducted by the Dominion Institute beginning in 1997. The survey results revealed a lack of self-knowledge on the part of Canadians. The 2001 survey found that almost 50 per cent of the 1,003 Canadians polled could not name Canada's first prime minister, nor could they differentiate between the American motto "life, liberty and the pursuit of happiness" and its Canadian counterpart, "peace, order and good government." An editorial in the *Globe and Mail* suggested that:

Some will dismiss these results as the product of cultural difference. It should be no surprise, they will say, that the flag-waving, chest-beating Americans boast of their historical achievements more readily than we modest Canadians. Nonsense. Americans know their history because they have been taught to believe that it is vitally important.... Others will say Americans know their history better because it is more exciting, more memorable. That is true to a point. Canada had no violent revolution, no bloody civil war; no Abraham Lincoln, no Martin Luther King. But as the CBC showed last year in its absorbing *People's History of Canada*, there is drama enough in our relatively peaceful history to stir the heart. Just go to the Canadian War Museum in Ottawa and gaze at the tunic of Isaac Brock. A neat hole marks the passage of the bullet that killed him at Queenston Heights. Now that's drama for you.[40]

There are a number of assumptions that strike the reader in this assessment of the relative familiarity of Canadians and Americans with their national histories. One of the most interesting is that "bloody revolutions" and "violent civil wars" are the stuff of entertaining history. In this approach, the study of social movements, of difference along class or gender lines, even of the progress of particular ideas can be relegated to the footnotes. Another assumption that seems to undergird this view is that only the larger-than-life figures, the Great Men, are important and warrant special consideration when reflecting upon the past. The more difficult job of separating myth from reality, and of sorting out the often-mixed legacies of these giant figures is presumed to be of little interest. The problem with this notion of history is that it presupposes that we can all agree on one storyline. It reduces history to little more than "the lie agreed upon" to borrow Napoleon's famous encapsulation.

¶ From Lessons of History to Making History

The powerful pull of history – so clear in the recent controversies documented above – was also suggested by the diversity of backgrounds and approaches evident among the delegates at the interdisciplinary conference out of which this anthology arose. Participants came from points across North America as well as Australia and worked in fields such as political science, English literature, philosophy, religious studies and law. Despite this diversity, however, common concerns were apparent in their papers and these have become the four themes around which the essays in this volume have been clustered: 1) assessing the health of professional history and determining the extent to which popularization and specialization pose threats to its future; 2) discussing the manner in which divergent historical traditions have produced conflicting visions of land, most strikingly revealed under colonialism; 3) exploring the way an individual's conscious or unconscious framework of time profoundly influences the history she/he produces; and 4) studying historical approaches to technological change in order to better understand contemporary problems posed by technology. All of these themes are founded upon the notion – a truism for all graduate students in history departments around the world but perhaps still elusive to some who are less well acquainted with the discipline – that human beings are active agents in making history.

To return to our organizing themes, in Section 1 both contributors – Robert Wright and Leo Groarke – acknowledge the value of history. However, they share the fear that, as Wright phrases it, "history has largely ceased to provide the social, cultural, economic and political architecture within which Canadians contextualize their lived experience."[41] Although both men see similar symptoms presenting, their diagnoses and prescriptions differ markedly. For Wright the problem is the tinsel-glow of the entertainment industry. He laments the growing influence of profit-driven corporations on public perceptions of history and argues that it is time for the professionals to reclaim the past. For Groarke the cause of the "decline" of history is the failure of members of the profession to engage a wider audience. He advocates less specialization and greater emphasis on the relevance of history to contemporary concerns in order to rehabilitate the profession.

Perhaps some further light can be shed on this vexing question by the philosopher, Isaiah Berlin, who famously noted that "The fox knows many things, but the hedgehog knows one big thing."[42] It is not unreasonable to apply this metaphor to those who study history. Groarke worries that "It is especially difficult to see how the specialization which characterizes history as a discipline can be employed as a methodology which can inform a broad discussion of periods of the past that may shed light on our lives today."[43] While it is true that history – like all academic disciplines – must guard against becoming too inward looking, there are a couple of difficulties with the remedies he proposes.

First of all, without those specialists who are on the cutting edge of any particular historical debate, we would never move beyond the current orthodoxy, even if that orthodoxy is ultimately false. As John Hill documents in his contribution to this collection, after 1918 well-meaning British and American historians – taking at face value the work of revisionist German historians – came to accept that the world had simply "slid into war" in 1914.[44] It was the work of Fritz Fischer that undermined this interpretation and laid out evidence that Imperial Germany was pursuing an aggressive foreign policy in part because senior military men felt that they could win a limited war.[45] It would be nice if history could be written without recourse to dusty archives. However, there is no substitute for research and it requires a certain degree of specialization to have an inkling of where to look and how to use the raw data collected. The second problem with Groarke's plans to sweep away specialization is clear when he suggests that it is the ability to "shed light on our lives today" that truly gives weight to history. If we accept this proposition, we are engaging in a form of presentism that sees value only in those aspects of the past with "clear" utility in our world. We are back to the old conception of history, requiring only an oracle to divine the lessons intended for those alive in the present.

If the Scylla of specialization is not entirely to blame for the perceived decline of history, then neither is the Charybdis of popularization solely responsible. While there is undoubtedly some questionable programming on stations like History Television, as Robert Wright points out, this does not justify a wholesale dismissal of the project of creating a commercial network dedicated to historical inquiry. Equally importantly, if professional historians have somehow lost control of perceptions of history, must this be attributed either to their failure or the hatching of some nefarious plot by venture capitalists? Could it not be that, as Anne Louise Shapiro suggests, the new forms of conveying visions of history – popular literature, film, museums, commemorations, the Internet – are appealing, especially among young people, and are here to stay? If so, academics had best accommodate themselves to the new reality.

Some of the problem can be attributed to the age-old tension between the "popular" and the "scholarly." At one time popular historical works – of the kind written by Pierre Berton in Canada – were at the centre of the controversy. More recently, the chief irritant for academics has been history on television and in film. While vigilance is not unwarranted, moderation is also required. Ken Burns' documentary on the American Civil War attracted the largest PBS audience ever recorded and earned the director kudos for his extensive use of archival material, while Jay Winter's history of the First World War, likewise, garnered critical praise and strong audience numbers.[46] Even when it comes to works of fiction, we must be prepared to acknowledge their utility in certain circumstances. Films like *Schindler's List* and *Saving Private Ryan* may have done more to open people's eyes to the horrors of the Holocaust and the D-Day landings in Normandy than a legion of excellent but weighty tomes.

Section II in this anthology explores the battle between the dominant and the marginalized in history. Focussing on the specific issue of native and non-native conceptions of property, John McLaren, Nancy Wright and Andrew Buck approach the issue from the perspectives of law, literature and political science respectively. McLaren highlights the visions of property that have been operative in European and aboriginal culture, visions whose differences are most starkly visible in the way they have mapped the land. He lays out these differences in the hope of educating a generation of lawyers who might well be litigating future land claims. Wright builds a "local reading" of colonial culture as it pertains to aboriginal land rights by tracing the various discourses discernible in parliamentary debates, legal decisions and popular literature. Andrew Buck – once again using parliamentary records, legal treatises and newspaper articles – contrasts the settler conception of property, which was based on the commodification of land and on the notion of "improvement," with the aboriginal conception, founded on the idea of communal use.

Under colonialism the colonizers deployed political power, literature and the law to dispossess aboriginal groups. And since the end of colonial rule the process has not ceased. Indigenous peoples still find themselves in a dominant culture that is, at best, foreign and, at worst, openly hostile to their own culture. Fortunately, as the law course highlighted by John McLaren in his essay illustrates,[47] there are innovative perspectives on history, law and culture being advanced by some academics. These prove that the weight of the past, while never to be underestimated, need not incapacitate us.

Section III focuses on conscious and unconscious assumptions about the relationship between past, present and future and how these can shape the purposes to which history is put. The essays in this section also explore particular aspects of the human agency in history. John Hill looks at the deliberate fabrications designed to explain German and American involvement in World War 1. In so doing, he reveals how these fabrications were foisted on people in order to promote a contemporary political agenda and how these fabrications often had historical implications that ran contrary to the will of the manipulators. Jeffrey Brown undertakes a re-evaluation of the "therapeutic turn," which emphasizes the immanence of the past in the present. He suggests that this mode of thought was more a response to than a reflection of the strains of contemporary life. Carol Duncan examines *trevassao* consciousness, a way of viewing the past that discards all pretense of linear time. She sees its spiritual and literary manifestations – in which the author is simultaneously subject and actor – as very helpful in understanding how history functions.

Each of these papers, in one way or another, examines the subtle interplay between past, present and future that shapes history. One of the best examinations of how this works can be found in Paul Cohen's *History in Three Keys: The Boxers as Event, Experience and Myth*. As the title suggests, Cohen sets himself the task of understanding the Boxer Rebellion of 1898–1900 as an event recorded, an experience lived and a myth used to serve purposes in the present. This last phenomenon is particularly interesting. Cohen charts the various interpretations of the rebellion, each determined, in large measure, by contemporary concerns. In the early part of the twentieth century, the Boxers were seen in the West as the incarnation of the "Yellow Peril" and Chinese commentators prior to 1920 also associated them with backwardness. During the 1920s, when anti-foreign feeling flared up in China, the Boxers were recast as patriots fighting against western imperialism. This interpretation reached its peak during the Cultural Revolution of 1966–76, when the Communists were attempting to rid Chinese culture of all western influences.[48]

After laying out how the view of the Boxers shifted in accordance with contemporary external and internal political agendas, Cohen concludes:

> The Boxers as *event* represent a particular reading of the past, while the Boxers as *myth* represent an impressing of the past into the service of a particular reading of the present. Either way a dynamic interaction is set up between present and past, in which the past is continually being reshaped, either consciously or unconsciously, in accordance with the diverse and shifting preoccupations of people in the present.[49]

Whether through a deeper understanding of how selective editing of archival material works to promote specific agendas in the present, a heightened awareness of how the twelve-step model might allow us to "own" our past or a greater sensitivity to other forms of consciousness in which the past, present and future are less rigidly defined, the chapters in this section help us to better comprehend the dynamic interaction of which Cohen speaks.

In Section IV the dividing line between past, present and future is also scrutinized closely under the rubric of the history of technology. Jim Gerrie looks at three of Canada's most respected critics of technology – Marshal McLuhan, George Grant and Harold Innis. He sees in their reluctance to offer detailed prescriptions for action a useful example of how to react to technology in a non-programmatic manner. Carl Simpson offers a cautionary tale that explores a specific instance of technological "progress." He discusses the building of a new highway during which the past was obliterated to make way for the future. Stephen Haller examines the pressing issue of global climate change and suggests that, even though it is, strictly speaking, not a scientific principle, the precautionary principle offers the most satisfactory method of dealing with the challenges that technology poses.

Issues of the kind explored by Haller in his essay place the problems engendered by technology in stark relief. It is hardly surprising then that there are now dozens of books warning of the risks we are running as a result of our careless treatment of the environment. The litany of concerns is familiar to most of us: the depletion of the ozone layer; the increase in acid rain; the destruction of rain forests; the loss of some twenty thousand species each year; and continued massive population growth. Given these alarming trends, some scientists have suggested that "The assumptions that we've made about how the natural world operates and what our relationship is to it are no longer tenable."[50] There have been prophets of doom before; meanwhile, there remain some who believe that irrefutable evidence of a connection between environmental degradation and human actions has yet to be found. That is why we must strive to retain our flexibility. As Stephen Haller suggests, if we are faced with potentially catastrophic consequences, and the only indisputably safe response requires an overhaul of the scientific method, then so be it. The use of the precautionary principle would allow us to follow the example of intellectuals like McLuhan, Innis and Grant, who studiously avoided advocating programmatic responses to technological change.[51] Once again, as in the previous section, we are moving towards a more fluid conception of past, present and future. Long-held views about the benefits inevitably attaching to technological change and knowledge of previous dire warnings that ultimately proved unfounded shape, to some degree, our view of current challenges posed by technology. At the same time, concern for future generations and willingness to consider even statistically improbable though potentially disastrous outcomes must also be weighed in our deliberations.

¶ Conclusions

What, on the basis of the essays in this collection, can we conclude? First of all, *the past is always with us*. Whether we recognize its influence or not, the past exercises great power over individuals and collectives alike. Never was this more clearly in evidence than in the wake of the attacks on the United States in 2001. People struggled to make sense of what had happened. They reached out for historical references that placed the tragedy in some sort of context. *The Washington Post* was typical when it stated that "Not since Dec. 7, 1941, has the U.S. homeland sustained such an aggression."[52]

The danger of groping after historical analogies was illustrated by the resurgence of interest in the W. H. Auden poem "September 1st, 1939." After 9/11 the Internet was awash in excerpts from the poem, whose memorable first stanza runs: "I sit in one of the dives / On Fifty-second Street / Uncertain and afraid / As the clever hopes expire / Of a low dishonest decade: / Waves of anger and fear / Circulate over the bright / And darkened lands of the earth, / Obsessing our private lives; / The unmentionable odour of death / Offends the September night."[53] Whether the 1990s were as "low" a decade as the 1930s were reputed to have been was left to readers to sort out for themselves. Appropriately or not, our perceptions of the past often provide the vehicle for making sense of the present.

A second conclusion we can draw based on the evidence presented in this volume is that we need to *reconsider our linear view of time*. The heavily guarded borders we have created between past, present and future do not serve us well. An interesting corrective is the idea of the "Long Now." As explained by Stewart Brand, co-chairman of the board of "The Long Now" Foundation, "'Now' is the period in which people feel they live and act and have responsibility. For most of us, 'now' is about a week, sometimes a year. For some traditional tribes in the American northeast and Australia, 'now' is seven generations back and forward. Just as the Earth photographs gave us a sense of 'the big here,' we need things which give people a sense of 'The Long Now.'" In order to reinforce this new awareness, Brand proposes a number of projects, including scientific studies requiring prolonged periods for data collection, institutions meant to last not fade away, systems of reward for slow responsible behaviour and education that instills "feeling for the span of history."[54] All are aimed at expanding people's sense of time beyond the cost-benefit horizon and encouraging people to make connections between the past, present and future.

Finally, in attempting to come to grips with history, *we cannot own the past, though we must seek to own it*. We cannot own the past in the sense of controlling it. Rather, we must seek to own the past in the sense that we take responsibility for it and move forward. A perfect example of how this can be accomplished has been provided in the life of Nelson Mandela. Released from prison after twenty-seven years in captivity, he harboured no bitterness towards his captors. On the day he was released he could embrace his warders, recognizing "the essential humanity even of those who had kept me behind bars."[55] Later, in his first press conference as a free man, he took great pains to assure the people of South Africa that he bore no ill will to the whites of the country. As he recalled: "I knew that people expected me to harbour anger towards the whites. But I had none. In prison, my anger towards whites decreased, but my hatred for the system grew.... I wanted to impress upon the reporters the critical role of whites in any new dispensation. I have tried never to lose sight of this."[56] That Mandela was sincere was revealed when he launched South Africa's Truth and Reconciliation Commission. This commission was a courageous attempt to face the past squarely, without equivocation but without rancour also.[57] Mandela made no attempt to control the outcome of the committee but recognized that all South Africans had to accept their share of the burden of the past if the country were ever going to move ahead.

Mandela's decision not to seek vengeance but to seek truth and reconciliation is highlighted by Erna Paris in her fascinating book, *Long Shadows*.[58] Her study records a number of successful and failed recent attempts to deal with the past. She concludes that the grand gesture is not always necessary:

There are other ways. In the deep place where memory lives, simple actions can speak of a national commitment to turn the historical page: official acknowledgements; apologies, if necessary; memorials to the victims; restitution; permanent museums that tell a factual story; the teaching of children about the origins of hatred. All potent symbolic acts.

The Germans call it *Vergangenheitsbewältigung*: Mastering or overcoming the past. A lofty ideal that is doomed to failure, not just because of the immensity of the Nazi crimes. For the past, it seems, can never be overcome. It lurks forever in memory. It loiters in cemeteries. It shelters behind beautifully painted movable screens.

The past can only be managed. With remembrance. With accountability. With justice – however frail, however inadequate, however imperfect.[59]

Perhaps even the choice of the word "manage" – with its corporate overtones and its implications of near or complete control – is too strong. The term "cope" better captures our efforts to deal with the past and build a fuller and fairer account of it.

Coping is all the more difficult because the past remains elusive. Perhaps what the twentieth century has really taught us is that we ignore at our own peril the powerful irony of history.[60] Whenever human beings have thought themselves capable of extracting useful lessons from history or discerning underlying patterns in it, events have proven them wrong. Confidently predicted outcomes rarely materialize. The Church sought to prevent the spread of Galileo's heresy of a heliocentric solar system; its treatment of the scientist only spread word of his theories more quickly. Napoleon longed to conquer Moscow; he took the city but, in the process, lost the war and his throne. The world rejoiced at the destruction of the Berlin Wall; now we inhabit a world full of uncertainty, in which ethnic nationalism looms menacingly.

The difficulty given this reality is that it is all too easy to slip into despondency. We look at the past and see a litany of failed social experiments and ideas, left like so many empty oxygen canisters on the slopes of Mount Everest. We despair. But our inability to fully comprehend what has gone before or predict what lies in store does not discredit the enterprise of trying to gain new insights. To return to Heraclitus, we may not know what lies beyond the next bend in the river but that does not make the journey along its course to create a rudimentary map any less valid an undertaking. A view of history that: has room for both popular and scholarly practitioners; understands how history has been wielded all too often as a weapon to erase or enslave others; avoids the trap of linearity; and, finally, encourages the individual to take ownership for what has gone before while contemplating what might lie ahead will be indispensable in accomplishing the urgent tasks that we face in the new century. It will help us appreciate a river whose turns and rapids challenge and fascinate us.

Endnotes

1. These definitions may seem at first glance to be cursory. However, the difficulty of pinning down these terms is suggested by the *Canadian Oxford Dictionary*'s singularly unhelpful definition of the past as "what has happened in past time." See *The Canadian Oxford Dictionary*, ed. Katherine Barber (Toronto: Oxford University Press, 1998), 1063.
2. The issue is addressed most admirably in Michael Howard, *The Lessons of History* (New Haven, CT: Yale University Press, 1991).
3. DK22B12. This rather cryptic reference (a Diels-Kranz number) is a result of the fact that the works of the Presocratic philosophers only survived as excerpts found in the writings of others or the subjects of reports or reviews. The numbers are named for Hermann Diels, the creator of *Die Fragmente der Vorsokratiker: griechisch und deutsch* (Dublin: Weidmann, 1967–70), which became a standard in ancient philosophy, and Walther Kranz, who refined his colleague's work.
4. Gordon Martel, "Introduction: The Revisionist as Moralist – A.J.P. Taylor and the Lessons of European History," in Gordon Martel, ed., *The Origins of the Second World War Reconsidered: The A.J.P. Taylor debate after twenty-five years* (New York: Routledge, 1986), 2.
5. A.J.P. Taylor, *The Origins of the Second World War* (London: Penguin, 1964), 7. By no means do I wish to suggest that Taylor was the originator of the idea of objectivity in history. That notion can be traced back all the way to the father of history, Thucydides, and found arguably its most forceful expression in the writings of the nineteenth-century Prussian historian, Leopold von Ranke (for an interesting examination of how contemporary thinkers may have misinterpreted Ranke, see Peter Novick, *That Noble Dream: The 'Objectivity Question' and the American Historical Profession* [Cambridge: Cambridge University Press, 1988], 25–30).
6. Taylor, *Origins*, 98. The naming of colleagues in this passage is typical of Taylor, who was often accused of courting controversy. See especially Benjamin Carter Hett, "'Goak Here': A.J.P. Taylor and *The Origins of the Second World War*," *Canadian Journal of History* 31:2 (August 1996): 257–80, in which the author notes Taylor's delight in playing devil's advocate.
7. A fascinating – though by no means comprehensive – analysis of the impact of *Schindler's List* can be found in Yosefa Loshitzky ed., *Spielberg's Holocaust: Critical Perspectives on Schindler's List* (Bloomington, IN: Indiana University Press, 1997).
8. Anne-Louise Shapiro, "Whose (Which) History Is It Anyway?", *Producing the Past: Making Histories Inside and Outside the Academy*, special issue of *History and Theory* 36:4 (December 1997): 1.
9. A number of historians – Voltaire, Carlyle, Treitschke and Toynbee, for example – gained varying degrees of popularity with a wider audience. However, the profound impact of radio and television on shaping popular perceptions of history in the twentieth century gave Taylor a special influence. It is also worth noting that the role of historian/celebrity was one to which Taylor was temperamentally very well suited.
10. Kathleen Burk, *Troublemaker: The Life and History of A.J.P. Taylor* (New Haven, CT: Yale University Press, 2000), 375–76.
11. Ibid., 378–79. For Parliamentary reaction to the series, see Hansard, *House of Commons Debates*, vol. 431, cols. 1237–40, 1285. For Taylor's assessment of the situation, see A.J.P. Taylor, *A Personal History* (London: Hamish Hamilton, 1983), 181.

12 Prior to this development, international relations could be characterized as "the record of what one clerk said to another clerk." (See Zara Steiner, "On Writing International History: Chaps, Maps and Much More," *International Affairs* 73:3 [1997]: 533.)

13 Albert Soboul, *Paysans, San-Culottes et Jacobins* (Paris, Librairie Clavreuil, 1966); Georges Lefebvre, *The Great Fear of 1789: Rural Panic in Revolutionary France* (New York: Vintage Books, 1973); Richard Cobb, *The Police and the People: French Popular Protest, 1789–1820* (Oxford: Clarendon Press, 1970); and Georges Rudé, *The Crowd in the French Revolution* (Oxford: Clarendon Press, 1960).

14 Georg G. Iggers, *Historiography in the Twentieth Century: From Scientific Objectivity to the Postmodern Challenge* (London: Wesleyan University Press, 1997), 6.

15 Shapiro, "Whose (Which) History Is It Anyway?", 1.

16 Keith Jenkins, *On What Is History? From Carr and Elton to Rorty and White* (New York: Routledge, 1995), 8.

17 Hayden White, "The Politics of Historical Interpretation: Discipline and Desublimation," in *The Content of the Form* (Baltimore: Johns Hopkins University Press, 1987), 72. White's is a particularly instructive case. Though an unrepentant structuralist in outlook, his work has frequently been included under the rubric of "the post-modernist critique," particularly by traditionalists on the defensive.

18 Richard J. Evans, *In Defence of History* (London: Granta Publications, 1997), 231–32.

19 J. L. Granatstein, *Who Killed Canadian History?* (Toronto: Harper Collins, 1998), 52–53.

20 Ibid., 58–59. The martial language is not simply hyperbole but a deliberate attempt to wave the red cape of military history, one of the sub-disciplines often derided by post-modernists.

21 For signs of academic interest, see the *Canadian Historical Review* 82:2 (June 2001). For a positive review, see Peter Steven, "Canada's History Unfolds," *The Beaver*, December 2000/January 2001, 46–47 and for a less glowing appraisal see Robert Fulford's column in the *National Post*, 16 January 2001.

22 Wright's concerns are enumerated in his essay for this anthology, "The Way We Were?: History as 'Infotainment' in the Age of *History Television*" (especially 49–51). His assessment of *A People's History* was offered in personal correspondence with the author (Tuesday, 24 October 2000). Wright did add that "No doubt about it, the $20 million budget...was utterly necessary to rescue the series form the charge that it 'looked Canadian' (i.e., cheap and plodding)!" and finished off by asserting that "I still believe ... that few among the young were tuned in unless they were stranded in front of Grandma's TV," a conclusion perhaps borne out by the fact that only 3.3 per cent of viewers were under the age of twenty-five (see <http://www.carleton.ca/ historycollaborative/> [30 August, 2004]).

23 Joyce Appleby, Lynn Hunt & Margaret Jacob, *Telling the Truth about History* (New York: W. W. Norton, 1994), 5–6.

24 See Michael Ignatieff, *Blood and Belonging: Journeys into the New Nationalism* (New York: Farrar, Straus, Giroux, 1993).

25 Appleby et al., *Telling the Truth*, 249, 254.

26 Ibid., 11.

27 The expression is from the poem "Peace," written by Rupert Brooke and published in 1914 (cited in Brian Gardner, ed., *Up the Line to Death: The War Poets, 1914–1918* [London: Methuen, 1987], 10–11).

28 John Tosh, *The Pursuit of History*, 3rd ed. (Toronto: Longman, 2000), 1.
29 Ibid., 3.
30 Thus the dismissive attitude toward oral history on the part of Europeans, underlined forcefully by Nancy Wright in her chapter "Reading the Past: The Dispossession of the Poor and the Aborigines in Colonial New South Wales" 140–72 (especially 103–4).
31 John Hill, "Historical Fictions: The Invention of Historical Events for Political Purposes," 154–56.
32 Paul Fussell, *The Great War and Modern Memory* (Oxford: Oxford University Press, 1975); George Mosse, *Fallen Soldiers. Reshaping the Memory of the World Wars* (New York: Oxford University Press, 1990); Samuel Hynes, *A War Imagined. The First World War and English Culture* (London: Bodley Head, 1991); Jay Winter, *Sites of Memory, Sites of Mourning: The Great War in European Cultural History* (Cambridge: Cambridge University Press, 1995). Though it ranges far beyond the Great War, Pierre Nora ed., *Realms of Memory: The Construction of the French Past*, trans. Arthur Goldhammer (New York: Columbia University Press, 1998), is a treasure trove of material on the influence of memory.
33 I have discussed the central role played by the Great War in promoting memory in "Remembering the Dead: the Democratization of Grief in the Twentieth Century," paper delivered at the interdisciplinary conference "Grave Concerns: The Ethics of the Dead," Brantford, ON, 30 November 2001.
34 Antoine Prost has determined that fewer than 1 per cent of French communes do not possess a memorial to the Great War (see Antoine Prost, "Monuments to the Dead" in Nora, *Realms of Memory*, vol. II, *Traditions*, 307).
35 Adrian Gregory, *The Silence of Memory: Armistice Day 1919–1946* (Oxford: Berg, 1994), 25.
36 See Primo Levi, *Moments of Reprieve* (New York: Penguin Books, 1995) and Elie Wiesel, *Night* (Toronto: Bantam Books, 1982), for example.
37 W. G. Sebald, *On the Natural History of Destruction*, trans. Anthea Bell (New York: Random House, 2003), viii–ix.
38 Stephen Brockmann, "Martin Walser and the Presence of the German Past," *The German Quarterly* 75:2 (Spring 2002), 128.
39 Ibid., 135, 138 (my translation). Another voice raised in favour of recovering all of German history has been that of Nobel Laureate Günter Grass. His novel *Crabwalk* tells the story of the sinking of the *Wilhelm Gustloff*, a German ship crowded with refugees. Grass concludes, as one reviewer has astutely observed, that it is crucial to remember the *Gustloff* because "unless moderates do, as part of a full picture of the past, then only extremists will – and they will use the story to keep the wounds of history open." (See Adam Mars-Jones, "Review of *Crabwalk*," *The Observer*, Sunday, 23 March 2003; <http://books.guardian.co.uk/reviews/generalfiction/0,6121,919823,00.html>).
40 "Our neglected national past," *Globe and Mail*, 30 June 2001, A14.
41 Wright, "The Way We Were?", 52.
42 Isaiah Berlin, *The Hedgehog and the Fox: An Essay on Tolstoy's View of History* (New York: Clarion Books, 1970), 1.
43 Leo Groarke, "Teaching History: The Future of the Past," 69.
44 The phrase was made famous by Sidney B. Fay in *The Origins of the World War*, 2 vols. (New York: Macmillan, 1930).

45 Fischer's work began with *Germany's Aims in the First World War* (New York: W. W. Norton, 1967) and continued with *War of Illusions: German Policies From 1911 to 1914* (London: Chatto & Windus, 1975) and *From Kaiserreich to Third Reich: Elements of Continuity in German History, 1871–1945* (London: Allen & Unwin, 1986). More recently, Niall Ferguson has challenged the orthodoxy established by Fischer and subsequent authors in his work, *The Pity of War* (New York: Basic Books, 1999).
46 For an assessment of Burns' documentary, see Michael A. Morrison and Robert E. May, "The Limitations of Classroom Media: Ken Burns' Civil War Series As a Test Case, *Journal of American Culture* 19 (Fall 1996): 39–49; a typical evaluation of Winter's documentary and book can be found in Stanley Hoffman, "Review of *The Great War and the Twentieth Century*," *Foreign Affairs* 80:2 (March/April 2001) 180. Perhaps it is not coincidence that two of the most successful recent documentaries from both a popular and scholarly perspective have been on the theme of war.
47 See McLaren, "The Memory of Property." The image of the hunting grounds of the Beaver nation, provided by McLaren (90) is a truly fitting representation of history: seemingly random but with a much deeper meaning.
48 Paul Cohen, *History in Three Keys: The Boxers as Event, Experience, and Myth* (New York: Columbia University Press, 1997), xiii.
49 Ibid.
50 Anita Gordon and David Suzuki, *It's a Matter of Survival* (Toronto: Stoddart, 1990), 3, 1. For a fuller treatment of the advantages of the precautionary principle, see Stephen F. Haller, *Apocalypse Soon?: Wagering on Warnings of Global Catastrophe* (Montreal: McGill-Queen's University Press, 2002).
51 James Gerrie, "Canada's Lost Tradition of Technological Criticism," especially 237.
52 "Editorial," *The Washington Post*, 12 September 2001, A30.
53 W. H. Auden, "September 1st, 1939" in *Another Time* (New York: Random House, 1940).
54 Stewart Brand, "Reframing the Problems" (Paper invited by the David and Lucille Packard Foundation, 1996) <http://www.longnow.org/about/articles/ArtReframe.html> (30 August 2004).
55 Nelson Mandela, *Long Walk to Freedom* (Toronto: Little Brown & Co., 1994), 490.
56 Ibid., 495.
57 Opinions on the efficacy of the Commission have varied. See for example Alex Boraine, *A Country Unmasked* (New York: Oxford University Press, 2000); Antjie Krog, *Country of My Skull: Guilt, Sorrow, and the Limits of Forgiveness in the New South Africa* (New York: Times Books, 1998); Martin Meredith and Tina Rosenberg, *Coming to Terms: South Africa's Search for Truth* (New York: Public Affairs, 1999); Dorothy Shea, *The South African Truth Commission: The Politics of Reconciliation* (Washington, DC: United States Institute of Peace Press, 2000).
58 Erna Paris, *Long Shadows: Truth, Lies and History* (Toronto: Alfred A. Knopf, 2000), 240–309.
59 Ibid., 464.
60 I first encountered this term as an undergraduate at Trent University in the lectures of Prof. Stuart Robson. Essentially, he argued that the "accidental century" was no more accidental than any of its predecessors and that human beings – bound and determined to learn lessons from history – simply committed new and improved errors in their day.

Peter Farrugia

Bibliography

Appleby, Joyce, Lynn Hunt, and Margaret Jacob. *Telling the Truth About History.* New York: W. W. Norton, 1994.
Berlin, Isaiah. *The Hedgehog and the Fox: An Essay on Tolstoy's View of History.* New York: Clarion Books, 1970.
Boraine, Alex. *A Country Unmasked.* New York: Oxford University Press, 2000.
Brand, Stewart. "Reframing the Problems." <http://www.longnow.org/about/articles/ArtReframe.html>.
Brockmann, Stephen. "Martin Walser and the Presence of the German Past." *The German Quarterly* 75:2 (Spring 2002): 127–43.
Burk, Kathleen. *Troublemaker: The Life and History of A.J.P. Taylor.* New Haven, Conn: Yale University Press, 2000.
Cobb, Richard. *The Police and the People: French Popular Protest, 1789–1820.* Oxford: Clarendon Press, 1970.
Cohen, Paul. *History in Three Keys: The Boxers as Event, Experience and Myth.* New York: Columbia University Press, 1997.
Evans, Richard J. *In Defence of History.* London: Granta Publications, 1997.
Fay, Sidney B. *The Origins of the World War.* 2 vols. New York: Macmillan, 1930.
Ferguson, Niall. *The Pity of War.* New York: Basic Books, 1999.
Fischer, Fritz. *Germany's Aims in the First World War.* New York: W. W. Norton, 1967.
———. *War of Illusions: German Policies From 1911 to 1914.* London: Chatto & Windus, 1975.
———. *From Kaiserreich to Third Reich: Elements of Continuity in German History, 1871–1945.* London: Allen & Unwin, 1986.
Fussell, Paul. *The Great War and Modern Memory.* Oxford: Oxford University Press, 1975.
Gordon, Anita, and David Suzuki. *It's A Matter of Survival.* Toronto: Stoddart, 1990.
Granatstein, J. L. *Who Killed Canadian History?* Toronto: Harper Collins, 1998.
Gregory, Adrian. *The Silence of Memory: Armistice Day 1919–1946.* Oxford: Berg, 1994.
Haller, Stephen F. *Apocalypse Soon?: Wagering on Warnings of Global Catastrophe.* Montreal: McGill-Queen's University Press, 2002.
Hansard. *House of Commons Debates*, vol. 431, cols. 1237–40, 1285.
Hett, Benjamin Carter. "'Goak Here': A.J.P. Taylor and *The Origins of the Second World War*." *Canadian Journal of History* 31:2 (August 1996): 257–80.
Hoffman, Stanley. "Review of *The Great War and the Twentieth Century*." *Foreign Affairs* 80:2 (March/April 2001): 180.
Howard, Michael. *The Lessons of History.* New Haven: Yale University Press, 1991.
Hynes, Samuel. *A war imagined. The First World War and English Culture.* London: Bodley Head, 1991.
Iggers, Georg G. *Historiography in the Twentieth Century: From Scientific Objectivity to the Postmodern Challenge.* London: Wesleyan University Press, 1997.
Ignatieff, Michael. *Blood and Belonging: Journeys into the New Nationalism.* New York: Farrar, Straus, Giroux, 1993.
Jenkins, Keith. *On What Is History? From Carr and Elton to Rorty and White.* New York: Routledge, 1995.
Krog, Antjie. *Country of My Skull: Guilt, Sorrow, and the Limits of Forgiveness in the New South Africa.* New York: Times Books, 1998.

Lefebvre, Georges. *The Great Fear of 1789: Rural Panic in Revolutionary France*. New York: Vintage Books, 1973.

Levi, Primo. *Moments of Reprieve*. New York: Penguin Books, 1995.

Loshitzky, Yosefa, ed. *Spielberg's Holocaust: Critical Perspectives on Schindler's List*. Bloomington Indiana: Indiana University Press, 1997.

Mandela, Nelson. *Long Walk to Freedom*. Toronto: Little Brown & Co., 1994.

Mars-Jones, Adam. "Review of *Crabwalk*." *The Observer*, Sunday, 23 March 2003. <http://books.guardian.co.uk/reviews/generalfiction/0,6121,919823,00.html>

Martel, Gordon, ed. *The Origins of the Second World War Reconsidered: The A.J.P. Taylor Debate after Twenty-five Years*. New York: Routledge, 1986.

Martin, Meredith, and Tina Rosenberg. *Coming to Terms: South Africa's Search for Truth*. New York: Public Affairs, 1999.

Morrison, Michael A., and Robert E. May. "The Limitations of Classroom Media: Ken Burns' Civil War Series As a Test Case." *Journal of American Culture* 19 (Fall 1996): 39–49.

Mosse, George. *Fallen soldiers. Reshaping the memory of the world wars*. New York: Oxford University Press, 1990.

Nora, Pierre, ed. *Realms of Memory: The Construction of the French Past*. Trans. Arthur Goldhammer. New York: Columbia University Press, 1998.

Novick, Peter. *That Noble Dream: The 'Objectivity Question' and the American Historical Profession*. Cambridge: Cambridge University Press, 1988.

Paris, Erna. *Long Shadows: Truth, Lies and History*. Toronto: Alfred A. Knopf, 2000.

Rudé, Georges. *The Crowd in the French Revolution*. Oxford: Clarendon Press, 1960.

Sebald, W. G. *On the Natural History of Destruction*. Trans. Anthea Bell. New York: Random House, 2003.

Shapiro, Anne-Louise. "'Whose History Is It Anyway?' Producing the Past: Making Histories Inside and Outside the Academy." Special Issue of *History and Theory* 36:4 (December 1997): 1–3.

Shea, Dorothy. *The South African Truth Commission: The Politics of Reconciliation*. Washington, DC: United States Institute of Peace Press, 2000.

Soboul, Albert. *Paysans, San-Culottes et Jacobins*. Paris, Librairie Clavreuil, 1966.

Steiner, Zara. "On Writing International History: Chaps, Maps and Much More," *International Affairs* 73:3 (July 1997): 531–46.

Steven, Peter. "Canada's History Unfolds." *The Beaver* (December 2000/January 2001): 46–47.

Taylor, A. J. P. *The Origins of the Second World War*. London: Penguin, 1964.

———. *A Personal History*. London: Hamish Hamilton, 1983.

Tosh, John. *The Pursuit of History*. 3rd ed. Toronto: Longman, 2000.

White, Hayden. *The Content of the Form*. Baltimore: Johns Hopkins University Press, 1987.

Wiesel, Elie. *Night*. Toronto: Bantam Books, 1982.

Winter, Jay. *Sites of Memory, Sites of Mourning: The Great War in European Cultural History*. Cambridge: Cambridge University Press, 1995.

I

Whither History? Professional Historians, Specialization and Popularization

When you work in the archives ... you're bored, you're in a hurry.... You're bound to make mistakes.
– Lawrence Stone

History, to be above evasion or dispute, must stand on documents, not on opinions.
– Lord Acton

I

The Way We Were? History as "Infotainment" in the Age of *History Television*[1]

ROBERT WRIGHT

To judge from the scholarly literature, the rise of history television – which now reaches millions of Canadian television viewers every week and tens of millions in the United States – has not been of much formal concern to historians. I find this surprising, partly because such cable services are enjoying enviable success but also because history television executives now routinely take credit for doing what academic historians are no longer thought capable of: making history interesting, entertaining, relevant and popular. History television ought to interest us for any number of reasons,[2] but I shall limit myself to an exploration of the discursive means by which it legitimizes itself as the last best hope for the historically challenged. In the end, I must say that, although my research has not tempered my opinion that corporate-controlled, profit-driven history television is a poor – and sometimes dangerous – surrogate for professional historiography, it has certainly added a curious twist to my understanding of the current crisis in Canadian history. If J. L.

Granatstein really believes that there are no longer "heroes in our past to stir the soul, and no myths on which a national spirit can be built," at least one inescapable conclusion may be drawn: J. L. Granatstein does not have cable.[3]

According to *American History Illustrated*, the idea of a cable channel devoted entirely to history was inspired by the "immense popularity" of Ken Burns' 1991 television series on the U.S. Civil War, which was viewed by roughly 14 million people. In the fall of 1993 two "competing cable companies" announced that they were planning to launch history channels: the Liberty/Cox/Advance-owned *Discovery Channel* proposed a service called *The History Network*, while the Hearst/ABC/NBC-owned *Arts & Entertainment* organization proposed *The History TV Network*. Both groups were said to be planning schedules of "documentaries, miniseries, and movies with historical themes" – a generic programming menu virtually guaranteeing that only one of these proposed services would make it to air.[4] For reasons that are not entirely clear, *A&E* prevailed: *The History TV Network* was re-christened *The History Channel* and launched on 1 January 1995, with an initial audience of one million cable subscribers. The service has since exceeded even its own executives' initial projections; by the spring of 1996 *The History Channel* had 16 million subscribers; by July 2000 it had in excess of 62 million subscribers.[5]

That *The History Channel* was an idea whose time had come had been suggested both by polling data on Americans' historical knowledge and by *A&E*'s own market research. In April 1994, for example, the Gallup organization published data showing that for 21 per cent of Americans "television was their primary source of historical information." Books scored only slightly higher, at 23 per cent. Roughly half of those Gallup had polled said that they were "somewhat or very interested" in history, and fully two-thirds said that "television had not done enough to promote an interest in history." *A&E* was said to be "buoyed by the [Gallup] findings" as it prepared to launch *The History Channel*.[6] According to Dan Davids, senior vice president and general manager at *History*, "focus groups and quantitative research" had revealed the same trend: "Americans are more interested in history now than they were five years ago."[7]

From the outset, *The History Channel* was conceived as a cable service that would be both educational and entertaining, making it a leading exemplar of the 1990s trend in televisual mass media towards "infotainment." As *History* vice president Charles Maday put it in 1995, just a month after launch, the new channel provided "viewer-friendly, original historical programming that stimulates the mind and creates a level of historical awareness in an entertaining and informative way."[8] With respect at least to this imperative to "stimulate the mind," *The History Channel* may be said to bear a greater resemblance to "public" television than to its myriad commercial competitors. Unlike *The Learning Channel*, for example, which has abandoned any pretence of pedagogical value in favour of highly sensationalised natural disaster footage and paramedical reportage, *The History Channel* is predicated on the twin notions that history is a weighty business and that its programming cannot be "dumbed down" *ad infinitum* to appeal to a mass audience.

History is thus a "niche" service in the strictest sense, with strong appeal to a *minority* viewership; practically, this means subsidizing the "hard core" historical content – particularly documentaries – with more popular fare, most notably feature films with "historical themes." This has, in fact, turned out to be a winning strategy. Within a year of its launch, *The History Channel* ranked as "the network most [cable] operators intended to add," beating *ESPN2, Home and Garden, TLC, the Cartoon network* and the *Sci-Fi Channel*. When asked about their intentions to add the *History Channel*, cable executives cited the channel's "program quality." As Jack Myers, Chairman and CEO of Myers Communications, put it: "There's a strong perception of the brand from its marketing. And it has a high perceived value in terms of revenue potential for operators."[9] More significantly perhaps, anecdotal evidence suggests that *The History Channel* was making converts. Writing in 1997, Mark Vittert praised *History*'s appeal to "folks just like us, the ones who 'don't know much about.' It's a reprieve for goof-offs like me who sat through Mr. Alverson's history class drawing mazes. It's also a second chance for those of us who thought the Gettysburg Address was too long and drawn out. All of a sudden, I like history – a lot."[10]

However much this infotainment strategy has fattened the bottom line at *The History Channel*, and even helped to attract "goof-offs" like

Vittert, it has not resolved the deep tensions inherent in its efforts to be both a thinking person's pastime, on the one hand, and a competitive commercial broadcaster, on the other. From the outset, for instance, *History* was intended to feature blockbuster Hollywood movies. But because Hollywood filmmakers have been known to be cavalier about the historical accuracy of their work, the network inaugurated après-film panels of "guest historians and journalists whose commentary will provide historical context, reveal any dramatic license taken by the director, and explore myths that may surround the subject being presented."[11] This is, of course, a case of having one's cash-cow and eating it too! Still, a more serious challenge to the integrity of *The History Channel* has been the perception that its relationship to its own corporate sponsors is too cosy. In late 1996, for example, *History* commissioned a documentary series called *The Spirit of Enterprise*, which was to have profiled the growth of American corporations. When it came to light that the series' corporate underwriters – Boeing, Du Pont and AT&T – were to be given control over the content appearing in their own profiles, a media furore ensued and *History* quickly cancelled the series.[12] In the press release that followed, the network justified its decision by reminding people that "Our mission at the *History Channel* is to adhere to the highest programming standards which our viewers have come to expect."[13]

History Television, the Canadian cable service launched in October 1997, was not only conceptually derivative of the U.S. *History Channel* but also owed much of its early success to the cross-border promotion of its American forebear via *A&E*.[14] In the fall of 1996, the CRTC approved the addition of twenty-eight new specialty channels to Canadian cable television. Of these, only four were granted "immediate priority," namely *CTV News One*, *History Television*, the *Comedy Network* and *Teletoon*; the others were reported as having to wait "until new digital-compression technology expands the potential of the cable universe."[15] Originally a partnership between Alliance Broadcasting and CTV, *History Television* was tagged from the outset as "a Canadian version of *A&E*'s *The History Channel*," though in true Canadian broadcasting fashion network executives were at pains both to differentiate their service from the American and to imbue this differentiation with ideological import. Asked prior to launch how *History Television* would differ from *The History*

Channel, Janet Eastwood, vice president of marketing and communications at Alliance, observed: "It's going to be less jingoistic than the U.S. service in that it will be less focused on wars. The focus is going to be on the real people who made a difference in the lives of Canadians."[16] Notwithstanding the fact that *History Television* had adopted the same sort of "branding" strategy that had made *The History Channel* such a success in the United States, it was a matter of some pride to Alliance executives that their service was "all Canadian" and especially that they had "bought nothing from the American *History Channel*."[17]

In truth, like both *A&E* and *The History Channel* before it, *History Television* was dominated at the outset by World War II programming. Norm Bolen, vice president of programming, said unapologetically in early 1998: "We are doing a lot of World War II. And a lot of people are watching.... When people don't want to watch war, we won't run those programs." Bolen added: "If we only ran war, we might do very well with older men. Whereas we need the 25 to 49 age group which is most attractive to advertisers. And we are getting them as well."[18]

World War II documentaries may have been delivering *History Television*'s primary audience in its inaugural phase, but such programming had already gone a long way towards alienating viewers and critics who had harboured high hopes for the new channel. In the spring of 1998, *The Beaver*, a popular Canadian historical magazine, asked its readers "What should lovers of history make of *History Television*?" and invited them to submit their comments.[19] The *History Television* schedule "struck them as too predictable, too foreign, and particularly too militaristic – an endless diet of old war footage." Some women respondents noted that *History Television* was "hugely dominated by men and by male views of history." Meanwhile, Peter McFarlane, a Montreal journalist, was quoted as saying, "The impression I have gotten is that history began in the summer of 1945." He added suggestively: "Even the non-World War II stuff tends to treat the past as a simple known thing that has been adequately recorded and only need to be assembled and related. Coming to grips with our history, it has always seemed to me, is a struggle."[20]

For *History Television*, as for all private sector interests operating within Canada's heavily regulated broadcasting environment, decisions about "the kind of content we want to offer" are never as straight forward as Bolen's comment might imply. In this country, television and radio broadcasting licences are subject to the myriad conditions imposed by the federal regulator, the CRTC; they include powerful provisions for the maintenance and promotion of "Canadian content." Television licensees in Canada must make explicit commitments, not only to a specified quantity of Canadian programming, but also to the expenditure of a fixed proportion of revenue on its production. The CRTC is empowered by the *Broadcasting Act* to make licences subject to strict limits on vertical integration, allowing it to mandate that a fixed percentage of the programming *broadcast* by a licensee be *produced* at "arms' length" from it or its parent company.

Whether this seemingly strenuous regulatory apparatus in Canada is as heavy-handed in practise as it appears in law has been the subject of considerable debate over the years. Whatever one's position on this question, it is important to note that the mere existence of the federal regulatory apparatus has fashioned a unique "civic" broadcasting discourse in this country, one which centres on the rather earnest question of whether or not the programs aired by licensees *edify* Canadians. Needless to say, this discourse tends to sit uneasily alongside other, competing discourses, most notably those which are oriented towards the bottom line. In fact, what is aired on *History Television* is understood differently by different constituencies, and these discursive differences are carefully managed by those whose task it is to fashion a history channel that must appear to be all things to all people.

One of the most important constituencies to which any publicly traded commercial broadcaster must appeal is its corporate shareholders and the "investment community." From an investment perspective, it is important to note that *History Television* is but one small element – albeit a profitable one – within a highly diversified film and television empire, one which is openly attempting to transcend its national origins and join the ranks of the global entertainment giants. In the spring of 1999, *History Television*'s parent company, Alliance Communications, was granted regulatory approval to merge with its erstwhile domestic rival, Atlantis Communications.[21] With a market capitalization of roughly US$370 million as of July 2000, the merged company, Alliance Atlantis Communications Inc., trades on both the Toronto Stock Exchange and the Nasdaq. The corporation's operations now encompass virtually every phase in the production and distribution of "filmed entertainment," hence its organization into three broad operating groups: Television, Motion Pictures and Broadcasting.

What, then, does Alliance Atlantis tell investors about *History Television*? Here is an introduction that was available at the corporation's online *Investors' Overview* site in June 2000:

History Television, launched in October 1997, features an entertaining and informative blend of movies, biographies and original historical documentary programming from Canada and around the world.

History Television reaches 60% of English Canadian cable households, with 4.14 million paid subscribers. *History Television* reaches almost 4 million Canadian viewers each week. The network's programming spans a wide range of time periods as is evident by its theme nights: *20th Century Mondays, Ancient History Tuesdays, Canadian History Wednesdays* and *History of War Thursdays*. Three nights a week, viewers turn to *History Television* for some of the greatest stories ever brought to film. *History on Film* delivers top-notch entertainment with a fascinating historical perspective.

History Television is ranked among the top 5 Canadian Specialty networks in Average Minute Audience. *History Television*'s audience has grown a dramatic 73% for Adults 25–54 Winter 2000 over Winter 1999.[22]

Clearly, Alliance Atlantis is interested in impressing upon investors the solid performance and especially the growth potential of one of its flagship broadcasting properties. Here, the news is all good. Reduced to its performance statistics, *History Television* is an unmitigated success story, reaching *four million* Canadians weekly and almost doubling its viewership in the lucrative 25–54 age group in the last year. Whatever J. L. Granatstein may think, to the international investor the case is clear: Canadians are fanatical about their history!

According to the Specialty Board of the Canadian Association of Broadcasters – a lobby which bills itself "the representative of the majority of Canadian programming services, including private television and radio stations, and networks, and specialty television services" – the news is not nearly so good. In a detailed presentation to the CRTC in

November 1998, the Specialty Board painted a grim picture of precariously situated Canadian specialty channels besieged by foreign competition, technological change and even regulatory indifference. Indulging heavily in the "civic" Canadian broadcasting discourse noted above, the Board prefaced its remarks by reminding the Commission that "specialty and pay services play an increasingly important role in the Canadian broadcasting system," by providing jobs, by making available "new resources for Canadian program production" and, above all, by "providing Canadians with access to niche programming that speaks to them, tells their stories, and reflects their realities."[23]

The Board emphasized that the Commission must be vigilant in safeguarding the specialty channels' access to cable subscribers because nothing less than Canadian *culture* hangs in the balance:

Fair and equitable access is of central concern to Canadian specialty channels. Cable is the dominant distributor of television services, and will remain so for at least the next five years and probably beyond. Broad, fair, and equitable carriage on high-penetration tiers is thus essential to the success of Canadian specialty services, and to their ability to contribute to Canadians' demand for more and better programming. *If they are to continue to play a role in supporting Canadian cultural objectives, fair and reasonable access to cable subscribers is essential.*[24]

Fear-mongering over Canadian cultural independence was a major feature of the Specialty Board's presentation.

Under the ominous heading of "Competition from Non-Contributing U.S. Service," the Board told the CRTC bluntly that "once U.S. services 'occupy the turf,' it is almost impossible for a competitive Canadian service to launch." This is because, as "highly-specialized niche services, [specialty channels] focus on meeting the viewing needs of a particular audience, whose attention can be fickle" and because they face increasing competition from "non-Canadian satellite services, and even the Internet." The Board concluded:

The most meaningful contributions specialty services make to the system is through expanding diversity, increasing the number of hours of available Canadian programming, viewing to Canadian programming, and the resources available for producing such programming, particularly in niche areas. The

CRTC must continue to ensure that Canadian specialty services are able to offer distinctive programming in well-defined niches, that is complementary to the programming offered by other services, and that Canadian specialty services 'occupy the turf' in as many niches as possible.[25]

When *History Television* executives appear before the CRTC, they tell a similar story and, moreover, they indulge in precisely the same sorts of discourses as the CAB.

In stark contrast to the rosy picture the company places before investors, the version to which the federal regulator is subjected takes the form of a long-suffering but absolutely vital national institution, one whose selfless mission it is to shepherd Canadians out of the historical darkness and into the grandeur that is their own past. Consider, for example, *History Television*'s presentation to the CRTC's Television Policy Review in October 1998. Appearing before the Commission on behalf of *History Television* were Phyllis Yaffe, then President and CEO of the service, Norm Bolen, vice president of programming, and Jennifer Fong, in-house regulatory counsel. It fell to Bolen to bring the Commissioners up to date on the important work the channel was doing, and he did so in superlatives, emphasizing the contribution *History Television* was making in the realm of independent Canadian film production and in the lives of ordinary Canadians:

We believe that the type of programming shown and originated by History Television is of tremendous value or quality. Our programs give a voice to the stories that make up our heritage, which we have all too often ignored.

We are particularly proud of series, such as *The Canadians*. *The Canadians* is a *History Television* original biography series which presents real stories of the men and the women who built this country and established its character. Another series is the award winning *A Scattering of Seeds*. This series documents the lives of ordinary immigrants who came to Canada to make a better life for themselves, from the Schumiatcher family in Calgary who gave us Alberta's famous white cowboy hat to Mary Ann Shadd, the first black woman to edit a newspaper in North America.

A program entitled *Our House* is a unique documentary presentation about the story of the Canadian House of Commons hosted by the Honourable Gilbert Parent, Speaker of the House of Commons. *Our House* was broadcast proudly on July 1st this year as part of *History Television*'s special all-Canadian Canada Day schedule. These are just a few examples of how *History Television* attracts viewers with quality Canadian programming.[26]

Commissioner Andrew Cardoso then prefaced a question for Bolen by emphasizing that *A Scattering of Seeds* was important because it addressed "the absence of cultural diversity being aired on our airwaves" and countered the claim that "our diverse history is not shown and, indeed, most of our history books don't do that, either." He went on to laud *Our House* as well for its ability to "popularize our political history."[27]

This exchange between Bolen and Cardoso raises any number of fascinating questions. Firstly, what is one to make of the total absence of reference to non-documentary programming at *History Television*? Although no formal content analysis of *History Television* programming has yet been undertaken, it appears that programs aired on the channel are of four general sorts. The most popular fare consists in imported movies and popular series, which presumably reach large, broadly based audiences with neither a particular investment in history nor loyalty to *History Television*. The second could be characterized as filler. Shows like *Rat Patrol* and *Combat!* are inexpensive re-runs lacking a significant viewership or appeal to advertisers. The third consists in prime-time light fare, typified by Canadian-made shows like *It Seems Like Yesterday* and *History Bites*. The fourth are the documentaries – serious, fact-based programs which clearly constitute the "hard core" historical content at *History Television* and undoubtedly attract the service's most dedicated history aficionados. That nothing whatsoever was said in this ostensibly broadly based review of Canadian television policy about *History Television*'s regularly scheduled airing of American patriotic chestnuts or blockbuster Hollywood movies illustrates something of the power of the civic discourse I described above.

Of the four *genres*, it is clearly the documentaries that carry the lion's share of the channel's obligatory "Canadian content" – a strategy calculated not only to demonstrate *History Television*'s commitment to Canada's indigenous film industry but to draw symbolically upon Canada's pedigree in documentary film-making.[28] The channel's airing of documentaries also gives it a high degree of intellectual credibility in the low-common-denominator world of commercial broadcasting. It may well be that, given the historic domination of the Canadian broadcasting market by American shows, neither regulators nor licensees perceive any great need to dwell upon the obvious, namely that cheap American programming has always been a cash-cow for Canadian broadcasters. It is also true, moreover, that the discursive means by which *History Television* couches its appeals to the CRTC have been fashioned by network executives in such a way as to maximize their perceived contribution to the nationalist "goals" of the *Broadcasting Act* – a strategy for which they can hardly be faulted. What *is* striking, however, is the extent to which the regulator itself appears to have accommodated to this discourse. That Commissioner Cardoso should grant *History Television* the absurd but symbolically invaluable virtue of being the only bulwark against total historical ignorance in Canada, for example, speaks volumes about the ways in which this discourse works to marginalize other sites of historical inquiry. Indeed, the Commissioner's remarks give credence to the notion that "most of our history books" are inadequate, particularly when it comes to the question of Canadian "diversity" – a comment which constitutes a wholesale indictment of the historical profession.

A second, related question is what to make of the extraordinary emphasis in the exchange between Bolen and Cardoso upon independent documentary film-making generally and on *A Scattering of Seeds* in particular. Transcripts of the hearings reveal that Bolen's comments were meant largely as a prologue to *History Television*'s main lobbying effort, aimed at persuading the Commission that, as CEO Phyllis Yaffe put it, the existing conditions of Alliance's broadcasting licenses put "conventional broadcasters ... at a considerable competitive advantage over *Showcase* and *History*."

Yaffe's remarks centred on the relationship between state-funded production subsidies, in the form of grants from Telefilm's Equity Investment Program, and the Commission's prohibition on vertical integration – or what is known in industry shorthand as "self-dealing between broadcasters and producers." Three questions now faced the Commissioners, she argued:

First, should conventional broadcasters be able to access Telefilm's Equity Investment Program for their own drama or under-represented category productions; second, should specialty services owned by producers continue to be prohibited from triggering Telefilm's Equity Investment Program for its owners' productions; and, furthermore, should these same services continue to be prohibited from running their owners' productions in first window regardless of whether Telefilm money is involved[?]

The essence of Yaffe's argument seems to have been that, as long as the CRTC continued to be vigilant in thwarting the vertical integration of its specialty channel licensees and Canadian content providers, conventional broadcasters – who have always been allowed to "produce for themselves" – should have no claim on TEIP financing. On the matter of vertical integration itself, however, Yaffe was prepared to be ambiguous. Having explicitly questioned whether specialty services ought to "continue to be prohibited from running their owners' productions," she then assured the Commissioners that "Regardless of this difference in regulatory treatment, *Showcase* and *History Television* are prepared to live with the current self-dealing rules. Under the current situation, we accept the self-dealing rules because they continue to be a necessary protection to ensure that Canada's independent production industry remains strong."[29]

Clearly, while Alliance executives' repeated claims of support for independent documentary film-making in Canada can be read as a function of Canada's civic broadcasting discourse, they also constitute a crucial *strategic* element in the corporation's more broadly gauged approach to regulatory politics. It is no great stretch of the imagination to suppose that executives within vertically integrated conglomerates such as Alliance Atlantis would much prefer to privilege the airing of their own companies' productions to the purchase of others.' After all, this is practically a working definition of the currently fashionable idea of "synergy" that inspired the rash of entertainment industry mergers in the Time Warner/AOL vein. Within the Canadian regulatory environment, however, as Yaffe's comments attest, concessions on vertical integration constitute a sort of *quid pro quo*, in which broadcasters are favoured by other, sometimes less obvious material benefits; these include the highly profitable pricing schedules the regulator grants cable providers and the protection of the specialty channels' content monopolies in the domestic market. Ingratiating themselves with CRTC commissioners on the question of the regulator's strict "self-dealing" rules was especially important to Alliance executives in October 1998, moreover, since formal application to merge with Atlantis was filed with the CRTC the following month. Indeed, as the Commission's published account of its decision to allow the merger shows, the onus on Alliance Atlantis to avoid *even the appearance* of favouring its own productions was made a condition of the regulator's acquiescence.³⁰

None of this is to suggest that *History Television* is disingenuous in its commitment to independent Canadian documentary film-making. However, this commitment can only be understood in the discursive context of Canada's regulatory broadcasting environment. The truth is that, however exemplary they might be with respect to the stated goals of the *Broadcasting Act*, Canadian-made documentaries are extremely expensive to produce and notoriously difficult to "sell" on commercial television. *A Scattering of Seeds: The Creation of Canada*, one of the documentary series venerated by Bolen in his remarks before the Commission, is an especially noteworthy case in point. Its production was chronically underfunded and, when finally aired, the program failed to recoup its costs. According to a document filed with CRTC by the Canadian Independent Film Caucus in June 1998, the producers were still scrambling to "recoup [their] investment through international sales," most notably by selling single episodes "to the mother countries of several immigrant groups whose stories are told in the series."³¹ Indeed, the "best distribution news" had come, not from television at all, but from "the educational market." Jerry McNabb of McNabb and Connolly, the series' educational distributor, was quoted as saying that the sales of the series were "great! The best thing since *The Kids of Degrassi Street* series." According to McNabb the series "meets a great need in the education system for Canadian historical material," hence his expectation that "one million children a year for the next three years will see at least one episode of the series in the classroom."³² *A Scattering of Seeds* was, at the time of the CIFC presentation, said to be "ready to begin production of its much-anticipated second season but it is in crisis. Despite its critical success, its proven popularity, and its importance to the educational system, the series may not be able to raise its budget."³³

Whatever else may be said about *A Scattering of Seeds*, the salient point is that this account of the series is a far cry from the confident, self-aggrandizing language of *History Television*'s *Investor Relations* précis. It is true that this description of *A Scattering of Seeds* was intended – as were three other similarly styled "case studies" – to persuade the federal regulator to decisively "increase the quantity of documentary programming available in the schedules of both private, conventional broadcasters and specialty services."[34] But even so, there remains a great discursive gulf between the Cardoso/Bolen exchange, in which the series was said by the latter to represent "the very essence of what we are about at *History Television*," and this rather more troubled rendering by the CIFC. The case of *A Scattering of Seeds* also shows that the Canadian regulatory apparatus itself makes strange bedfellows. At one level, the interests of independent Canadian film-makers are quite at odds with those of commercial entertainment giants like Alliance Atlantis: not only are the broadcasters largely prevented from airing their own productions, but they are required by the federal regulator to capitalize the films of the independents and later to air them – often to relatively small, unprofitable, even "fickle" audiences. Yet the CIFC insisted in its brief to the CRTC that "[d]ocumentary programs are a prominent part of many broadcasters' schedules and *the primary reason for the success of Canadian specialty services Discovery, History Television, and Vision TV.*" The fact remains that, however much Canadian-made documentaries may serve to edify *History Television*, they do not reach large numbers of viewers and they do not pay the bills. Therein lies the deep, perhaps irreconcilable tension between the civic discourse with which the channel conducts its business with the federal regulator and the bottom-line discourse with which it placates its shareholders.

At present, the arbiters of these competing pressures at *History Television* are Sydney Suissa, vice president of programming, and Cindy Witten, director of independent programming. Given their control over programming at *History Television*, – which does, after all reach four million Canadians weekly – Suissa and Witten may be said to exercise an extremely important gatekeeping function with respect to what passes for history in Canadian popular culture.[35] Suissa holds an honours BA in history from the University of Calgary, as well as a Master's degree in journalism. In my correspondence with him I was impressed, not only by the seriousness with which he takes his responsibility for delivering historical content to Canadian television viewers, but with his keen sense of the relationship of *History Television* to the academic study of history. Indeed, I was struck by his confident, unapologetic conviction that a profit-driven history-based television service has an extremely important contribution to make in the lives of Canadians, not least because professional historians have abandoned the field.

I opened our correspondence by asking him to elaborate on *History Television*'s mandate to enhance Canadians' understanding of their own history. He did not mince his words:

> By and large I agree with Jack Granatstein: the political and social agendas that have weighed history down have made it boring and comatose. The greatest contribution *History Television* can make is to revive Canadians' interest in our history. That is the true mandate and it can only be done through well researched, well told stories that are rich in narrative, drama, and character."[36]

History Television employs no historians but Suissa affirmed that they are "used extensively on nearly all the documentaries we commission" and also that they are regularly invited "to discuss movies after they've been aired." He added: "In a more informal way, I have a circle of historians that I feel free to consult with on specific historical questions or issues."[37] Like Norm Bolen and Andrew Cardoso, Suissa subscribes to the notion that *History Television* is the solution to the problem evident in Canadian history. That *History Television* was one of the sponsors, along with Angus Reid and the Dominion Institute, of the famed November 1998 history quiz – in which "60% of respondents failed a 15-question test about basic historical facts" – speaks directly to this claim.[38]

Ought historians to take this usurpation personally? Frankly, I think not. As Suissa himself put the case to me: "*History Television* is not a school, it is a television channel."[39] That professional historians play a strictly adjunct role at *History Television* does, however, bring one back to the decisive issue of programming. Given that the living rooms of Canadians are no place for the "political and social agendas" of professional historians, nor for the "boring and comatose" products of their labours, the question arises as to what kind of "history" *History Television* actually offers. Here, too, Suissa is dauntless. When asked whether "decision-makers at *History Television* distinguish between entertainment and educational content," he replied, evincing yet again the discursive ease with which documentaries are made the standard-bearers for *History Television*: "The distinction is in the treatment, in the way the documentary is told. I avoid pedantic styles, where the emphasis is on explanation and analysis rather than on dramatic storytelling. Any well told story is educational, though its primary objective is not necessarily educational." When asked whether the bulk of his audience share derives from the screening of Hollywood films, Suissa conceded that blockbuster movies are popular because of their "marquee value" but insisted that "there is also great appetite for documentaries from Canada and the rest of the world." He did admit, however, that "documentaries will always be a harder sell, and will draw a smaller audience than movies. This is the reality throughout television and is not specific to *History Television*."[40] Lastly, when invited to comment on the "popular" series *History Bites* and *It Seems Like Yesterday*, he anticipated my scepticism regarding their historical worth, volunteering: "Their mandates are to look at history with a sense of humour and satire, to give viewers a sense that human history at times can be silly, random, and absurd."[41]

In fairness to Suissa and his colleagues at *History Television*, it is important to recall the vote of confidence the CIFC gave the channel as a dedicated programmer of Canadian-made documentaries. Moreover, there is evidence to suggest that *History Television*'s reputation for airing the best international documentaries is deserved. In February 1998, for example, when the Oscar documentary nominees were announced, the channel was in the enviable position of having scheduled two of the nominated films for the period before the award show, namely Spike Lee's *4 Little Girls* and Mark Jonathan Harris' *The Long Way Home*.[42] That *History Television* does indeed have its moments of profundity is undeniable. I would cite, for example, its extensive programming in "remembrance" of Hiroshima as a most impressive case in point.

As Canadian media mogul Moses Znaimer once remarked, however, what matters on television is not the show but the flow – an aphorism that seems to me to carry special import for *History Television*. Having taken so much credit for broadcasting the sublime, surely the channel's executives may be taken to task for also airing the ridiculous. What is one to make, for example, of its four-part "soap" on the life of British fascist Oswald Mosley, in which the subject's love life figured more prominently than his politics?[43] What about the weekly spectacle of having Ann Medina – formerly one of the CBC's most respected foreign correspondents – say the words "Hello there. I'm Ann Medina. Welcome to *History on Film*, a discovery of our past through the movies"?[44] What about Rick Mercer's "hope that his reference to Adolf Hitler having one testicle will one day make it to air" on *It Seems Like Yesterday*?[45] What about *History Television* underwriting the Credo documentary *Pioneer Quest: A Year in the Real West*, in which two couples were paid $100,000 each to "build and share a shelter where they have to live off the land without any modern conveniences, including running water, for one full year"?[46] For that matter, what about *Rat Patrol* and *Combat!*?

In short, in spite of Sidney Suissa's confident claims about the pedagogical and civic virtues of *History Television*, I am not persuaded. Nor do I believe that my calling into question the channel's mix of documentary versus more popular programming is a case of academic hair-splitting. There is a vast difference between *History Television*'s enormously profitable overall market penetration and the modest audience it generates for indigenous documentary programming. According to data published by the CIFC, the largest first-run English-language audience for *A Scattering of Seeds*, never exceeded 135,000 viewers, and some "episodes" did not even reach this number. This is a mere fraction of the 4.14 million paid subscribers *History Television* boasts in its *Investor Relations* précis, a ratio which seems to speak for itself. While it is the Canadian-made documentaries that *History Television* executives privilege when speaking to the federal regulator and academic historians, it is clearly other kinds of programming that constitute the channel's most popular – and profitable – fare. *History Television* may even be said to be a commercial success in spite of – rather than because of – its commitment to indigenous documentary film-making. In the absence of harder data on audience share and especially advertising revenue, I can only conclude that the channel's extraordinary emphasis on Canadian-made documentaries constitutes a discursive and ultimately a strategic valorization of a cable service whose real bread and butter consists, like most of its competitors,' in delivering historically inconsequential programming to an undiscriminating mass audience.

I have not taken Sidney Suissa *et al.* to task because I believe them to be disingenuous. On the contrary, one can hardly blame *History Television* executives for indulging Canada's longstanding civic broadcasting discourse, nor especially for spinning their programming schedule for maximum regulatory and critical effect. My point is that, ironically perhaps, Suissa and the historians he claims to be usurping today find themselves in precisely the same boat, trying to keep history alive and vital in an age in which – as the Swedish poet Kjell Espmark put it – "we have quietly accepted the disappearance of the past."[47] The most telling line in my correspondence with Suissa, arguably, is that "the greatest challenge is not coming up with stories [from our past] or making them, but rather in getting Canadians to watch them." This seems to confirm my view that history is indeed a hard sell these days, whether in the classroom or on television. This is evidence of a far deeper, essentially *cultural* dislocation in public life, in which history has largely ceased to provide the social, cultural, economic and political architecture within which Canadians contextualize their lived experience.[48]

As for Canadian-made documentaries like *A Scattering of Seeds*, perhaps the heirs to the historiographical throne in our televisual age, it is heartening to discover that they continue to reach *millions* of Canadians in the classroom but only tens of thousands in prime time. The subtext of so much of the politicking that takes place in front of the CRTC appears to be that – to paraphrase the American philosopher Kevin Costner – if you air it, they will watch. Yet, for all of their goodwill and civic rectitude, the combined weight of *History Television*, the CRTC and even the CIFC cannot draw more than a handful of television viewers to even the most celebrated of Canadian-made productions. I conclude from this pattern that the rumoured usurpation of historians and history teachers by commercial television broadcasters has been greatly exaggerated.

The CBC series *Canada: A People's History* has been heralded as a revolutionary breakthrough in historical television programming since its launch in October 2000, and it has clearly struck a chord with large numbers of Canadians. Only Canada's public broadcaster could have realized such an ambitious and lavish project, which sets *A People's History* well apart from anything that Canada's independent documentarists and private-sector broadcasters could together deliver. Even so, in the absence of consistent data on the series' market penetration, it is not easy to gauge its true impact among Canadian television viewers. In early 2001, CBC publicity claimed, for example, that "[e]pisodes 1–5 of the series, produced in both English and French, attracted audiences of roughly 2.3 million Canadians to CBC and its French-language counterpart Radio-Canada" in its inaugural season.⁴⁹ Later the same year the CBC made the even more grand boast that *A People's History* was "the most watched documentary in Canadian history: one of every two Canadians watched some part of the series."⁵⁰ Given the enormous publicity that accompanied the launch – and hence the likelihood that some viewers tuned in simply to see what all the fuss was about – it is impossible to gauge the extent of Canadian viewers' episode-over-episode loyalty to the series or, more pointedly, to get any sense of the impact these programs have had on their understanding of Canadian history. What does seem noteworthy, however, is that the strongest market for *A People's History* is expected to be, as it has been for most of its predecessors, in the schools. By the autumn of 2001, according to the CBC, "approximately 80% of schools across the country are expected to have access to the series, either from purchasing the series themselves or through their School Board's licensing of duplication rights."⁵¹

Certainly Mark Starowicz, the much-celebrated executive producer of *A People's History* and director of the CBC's Canadian History Project, envisages a grand future for historical programming at CBC-TV. Working from the premise that "[j]ournalism is a sub-set of the historical profession," he intends to "establish the Project as a permanent history department [at the CBC], similar to that which is maintained at the BBC."⁵² Such a development would without question be good for Canadians and good for Canadian history, but many questions remain. Of these, the most compelling is whether *A People's History* was in fact the harbinger of a revolution in television broadcasting or something far more ephemeral.

Endnotes

1. The following essay has previously appeared in Robert Wright, *Virtual Sovereignty: Nationalism and the Making of Modern Canada* (Toronto: Canadian Scholars' Press, 2004).
2. On this at least, Leo Groarke and I agree. However, we disagree on much else. While he castigates the historical profession for specialization, which "implies a process of reduction and compartmentalization" and operates "by reducing broader questions to narrower ones which are said to be more tractable" (see Leo Groarke, "Teaching History: The Future of the Past," 69 in this volume, I contend that it is

precisely this attention to detail and this reluctance to view history as a blueprint for the future that make the work currently being undertaken in history departments valuable.

3   J. L. Granatstein, *Who Killed Canadian History?* (Toronto: Harper Collins, 1998), 3. See also Ken Osborne, "Review of Granatstein, *Who Killed Canadian History?*", *Canadian Historical Review* 80:1 (March 1999) 114–18; A. B. McKillop, "Who Killed Canadian History? A View from the Trenches," *Canadian Historical Review* 80:2 (1999): 269–99; and Bryan D. Palmer, "Of Silences and Trenches: A Dissident View of Granatstein's Meaning," *Canadian Historical Review* 80:4 (1999): 676–86.

4   "Cable Companies Plan History Networks" *American History Illustrated* 28:4 (September/October 1993): 15.

5   John Flynn, "It's All History Now" *Brandweek* 46:18 (29 April 1996): 6; "History Channel to Debut," *History Today* 29:6 (February 1995): 12.

6   "History Channel to Debut," 12.

7   Dan Davids, cited in Flynn, "It's All History Now," 6.

8   Charles Maday, cited in "*History Channel* to Debut," 12.

9   Jack Myers, cited in Flynn, "It's All History Now," 6.

10 Mark Vittert, "Thankful for History" *Triangle Business Journal* 13:13 (28 November 1997): 39. <http://triangle.bizjournals.com/triangle/stories/1997/12/01/editorial3.html> (5 August, 2004).

11 "*History Channel* to Debut," 12.

12 "*History Channel* Dumps Corporate Profile Series" *Advertising Age* 67:24 (10 June 1996): 2.

13 Cited in "History Plan Rewritten" *Advertising Age* (7 June 1996).

14 Alliance executives acknowledge that they benefitted greatly from *The History Channel*'s US$10 million dollar ad campaign spearheaded by the New York firm Moss/Dragoti and centring on the slogan "Where the past comes alive."

15 John McKay, "Four New Cable Outlets Getting Ready to Launch" *Canadian Press* (11 May 1997).

16 Janet Eastwood, cited in John McKay, "Four New Cable Outlets Getting Ready to Launch."

17 Norm Bolen, cited in Christopher Moore, "*History Television*: Stay Tuned" *Beaver* 78:1 (February/March 1998): 50.

18 Ibid.

19 Ibid.

20 Peter McFarlane, cited in ibid.

21 See *Decision CRTC 99–106* (19 March 1999).

22 Alliance Atlantis Communication Inc., *Investors' Overview*; <http://www.allianceatlantis.com/corporate/inv_relations> (1 November 2000).

23 Canadian Association of Broadcasters, *A Submission to the Canadian Radio-television and Telecommunications Commission with Respect to Public Notice CRTC 1998-44* (30 June 1998) [emphasis added]. This document is available at the Canadian Association of Broadcasters website, at <http://www.cab-acr.ca/english/esearch/98/sub_jun3098.shtm> (15 October 2000).

24 Ibid.

25 Ibid.

26 Norm Bolen, cited in *Transcript of Proceedings for the Canadian Radio-Television and Telecommunications Commission Canadian Television Policy Review* 14:9 (14 October

27 1998) [emphasis added]. This document is posted in full at the CRTC website at <http://www.crtc.gc.ca/eng/transcripts/1998/tb1014.htm> (15 October 2000).
27 Andrew Cardoso, cited in ibid.
28 In its 1998 presentation at the CRTC's Canadian Television Policy Review, The Canadian Independent Film Caucus lauded the work of John Grierson and the National Film Board, which "... led the world in the development of compelling new documentary film making techniques – styles which became renowned as 'cinema direct' and 'candid eye.'" See *A Level Playing Field for the Documentary* (29 June 1998) at <http://www.cab-acr.ca/english/research/1998.shtm> (15 October 2000).
29 Phyllis Yaffe, cited in *Transcript of Proceedings for the Canadian Radio-Television and Telecommunications Commission Canadian Television Policy Review* 14:9 (14 October 1998).
30 See *CRTC Public Notice 1999–48* (20 May 1999) at <http://www.crtc.gc.ca/archive/eng/Notices/1999/PB99-48.htm> (15 October 2000). It is also worth noting that the merger was conditional on increased "Canadian content" provisions. Sydney Suissa, Vice-President of Programming at *History Television*, told me that this minimum content requirement is likely to be exceeded by Alliance Atlantis over the term of its licenses.
31 According to the CIFC's "case study" of *A Scattering of Seeds*, the initial capitalization of this thirteen-part series was so precarious that the producers "had to defer their entire fee." *A Scattering of Seeds* went on to enjoy both great critical acclaim and "popular success," winning top prize (the Gold Medal for Best Documentary Television Series) at the Worldfest in Houston, Texas. In Canada, the series was said to have been "well publicized," translating into "excellent" ratings on both *History Television* and *Historia* (see *A Level Playing Field*).
32 Jerry McNabb, cited in *A Level Playing Field*.
33 Cited in ibid.
34 Cited in ibid.
35 It is perhaps testimony to the mystique of televisual media that Suissa's name appears nowhere in recent Canadian historiography, even though he is clearly one of the country's most influential historical popularisers. It is worth recalling in this connection that an earlier generation of popularisers – most importantly Pierre Berton and Peter C. Newman – enjoyed no such anonymity.
36 Sydney Suissa, Interview by author, June 2000.
37 Ibid.
38 Jason Botchford, "Canadians Flunk Out in War History: Poll," *Toronto Sun*, 11 November 1998.
39 Suissa, Interview by author, June 2000. As for the criteria by which documentaries are selected for broadcast on *History Television*, Suissa listed the following: "i) the quality of the storytelling; ii) the quality and originality of the research; iii) the production values; iv) and the subject."
40 Suissa, Interview by author, June 2000.
41 Ibid.
42 Claire Bickley, "Nominated Documentaries Air Before Oscars," *Toronto Sun*, 17 February 1998.
43 Claire Bickley, "Fascist Immersed in Soapy Froth," *Toronto Sun*, 13 November 1998.

44 Christopher Moore correctly observed that most of *History Television*'s on-screen personalities were "refugees from the bloodlettings of recent years in CBC and CTV current affairs departments" and noted "a painful hint of Ted Baxter about them when they suddenly became historians." See *"History Television:* Stay Tuned," 50.
45 Rick Mercer, cited in Claire Bickley, "Shedding a Little Lite on the Past" *Toronto Sun*, 3 December 1997. Recounts Mercer, of *History Television*'s refusal to sanction this bit of historical speculation: "They say, 'You can't say that,' and I'm saying, 'Why? Is the Hitler family going to get upset?' [They say to me] 'Is that true? This is the History channel and we want to be accurate.' [I say] 'For the point of this show, he only had one ball, okay?' Then we picture the Grade Eight student writing the paper, 'Hitler only had one ball. Footnote: *History Television*.'"
46 Pat St. Germain and Bill Brioux, "Sex Charge Kills Pioneer Dream," *Sun Media*, 7 June 2000. See also Robert Williams, "Pioneers Press On," *Winnipeg Sun*, 27 June 2000.
47 Kjell Espmark, cited in John Ralston Saul, *Reflections of a Siamese Twin: Canada at the End of the Twentieth Century* (Toronto: Penguin, 1998), 30.
48 See Robert Wright, "Historical Underdosing: Pop Demography and the Crisis in Canadian History," *Canadian Historical Review* 81:4 (December 2000): 646–67.
49 CBC Press Release "CBC Delighted by Response to Canada: A People's History" (2 January 2001). <http://history.cbc.ca/history/?MIval=PressContent2.html&press_id =4978> (4 August 2004).
50 CBC Press release "CBC Announces BCE Sponsorship of Season Two of Canada: A People's History" (7 August 2001). <http://history.cbc.ca/history/?Mival= PressContent2.html&press_id=6246> (4 August 2004).
51 CBC Press Release "Season Two Fact Sheet" (1 September 2001). <http://history. cbc.ca/history/?Mival= PressContent2.html&press_id=6246> (4 August 2004).
52 Tod Hoffman, "Making History," *McGill News Alumni Quarterly* (Fall 2001).

Bibliography

Bickley, Claire. "Shedding a Little Lite on the Past." *Toronto Sun*, 3 December 1997.
———. "Nominated Documentaries Air Before Oscars." *Toronto Sun*, 17 February 1998.
———. "Fascist Immersed in Soapy Froth." *Toronto Sun*, 13 November 1998.
Botchford, Jason. "Canadians Flunk Out In War History: Poll." *Toronto Sun*, 11 November 1998.
Canadian Association of Broadcasters. *A Submission to the Canadian Radio-television and Telecommunications Commission with Respect to Public Notice CRTC 1998–44.* <http://www.cab-acr.ca/english/research/98 /sub_nov1898.shtm>.
CBC Press Release. "CBC Announces BCE Sponsorship of Season Two of Canada: A People's History." <http://history.cbc.ca/history/?Mival= PressContent2.html& press_id=6246>.
———. "CBC Delighted by Response to Canada: A People's History." <http://history. cbc.ca/history/?MIval=PressContent2. html&press_id=4978>.
———. "Season Two Fact Sheet." <http://history.cbc.ca/history/?MIval=PressContent2 html&press_id=6247>.

Canadian Independent Film Caucus. *A Level Playing Field for the Documentary.* <http://www.cab-acr.ca/english/research/1998.shtm>.
"Companies Plan History Networks." *American History Illustrated* 28:4 (September/October 1993): 15.
Decision CRTC 99-106. <http://www.crtc.gc.ca/archive/eng/ Decisions/1999/DB99-106.htm>.
Flynn, John. "It's All History Now." *Adweek* 46:18 (29 April 1996): 6
Granatstein, J. L. *Who Killed Canadian History?* Toronto: Harper Collins, 1998.
"*History Channel* Dumps Corporate Profile Series." *Advertising Age* 67:24 (10 June 1996): 2.
"*History Channel* to Debut." *History Today* 29:6 (February 1995): 12.
"History Plan Rewritten." *Advertising Age* (7 June 1996).
Hoffman, Tod. "Making History." *McGill News Alumni Quarterly* (Fall 2001).
Investors' Overview. <http://www.allianceatlantis.com/corporate/ inv_relations>.
McKay, John. "Four New Cable Outlets Getting Ready to Launch," *Canadian Press* (11 May 1997).
McKillop, A. B. "Who Killed Canadian History? A View from the Trenches," *Canadian Historical Review* 80:2 (1999): 269–99.
Moore, Christopher. "*History Television*: Stay Tuned." *Beaver* 78:1 (February/March 1998): 50–51.
Osborne, Ken. "Review of Granatstein, *Who Killed Canadian History?*" *Canadian Historical Review* 80: (March 1999): 114–18.
Palmer, Bryan D. "Of Silences and Trenches: A Dissident View of Granatstein's Meaning." *Canadian Historical Review* 80:4 (1999): 676–86.
Saul, John Ralston. *Reflections of a Siamese Twin: Canada at the End of the Twentieth Century.* Toronto: Penguin, 1998.
St. Germain, Pat, and Bill Brioux. "Sex Charge Kills Pioneer Dream." *Sun Media*, 7 June 2000.
Suissa, Sydney. Interview by author, June 2000.
Transcript of Proceedings for the Canadian Radio-Television and Telecommunications Commission Canadian Television Policy Review 14:9. <http://www.crtc.gc.ca/eng/transcripts/1998/tb1014.htm>.
Vittert, Mark. "Thankful for History." *Triangle Business Journal* 13:13 (28 November 1997): 39. <http://triangle.bizjournals.com/triangle/stories/1997/12/01/editorial3.html>.
Williams, Robert. "Pioneers Press On." *Winnipeg Sun*, 27 June 2000.
Wright, Robert. "Historical Underdosing: Pop Demography and the Crisis in Canadian History." *Canadian Historical Review* 81:4 (December 2000): 646–67.
———. *Virtual Sovereignty: Nationalism and the Making of Modern Canada.* Toronto: Canadian Scholars' Press, 2004.

2

Teaching History:
The Future of the Past

LEO GROARKE

Why study history? Because "it's there"?

It may be "there" in a different sense than a mountain, but it is still there in a way that can capture our imaginations. And especially the imaginations of those of us who make history our vocation. Whatever others may think, historians will appreciate why someone might tackle the considerable challenges involved in an attempt to establish the cost of olive oil in classical Athens, the extent to which David Hume read French philosophy, or the strategic errors that undermined the German offensive during the Battle of Britain.

The claim that we study history "because it's there" is attractive precisely because it refuses to justify history in terms of something else. Like mountain climbing, history is not, it boldly asserts, justified because it can help the economy, create more patriotic citizens, or function as a means to some social good. History is valuable in and of itself.

It is easy to see why historians like such sentiments. It is more difficult to see how they can convince politicians, educators, or the general public that history should play a central role in primary, secondary, or post-secondary education. For this is an audience which is much more sceptical of history. Some of its members – including some of those in positions of power and influence – believe that the study of history, and especially the study of it in any depth, is irrelevant or, worse, an impediment to a useful life today.

The need to justify history's role in education in a way that makes sense to the non-historian is pressing in an era in which education depends upon the support of a public which eyes the traditional liberal arts with suspicion; which understands itself in terms of new realities such as a global economy and new forms of communication technology; and which often confuses education with technical and vocational training. In such a climate, one cannot defend history by appealing to the sentiments of those who are already committed to it. Such appeals only raise the question of why these individuals should determine the shape of public education. And this invites a chain of reasoning which threatens to consign history, like mountain climbing, to the realm of private recreation.

In other eras, the study of history could be justified by appealing to world views which were committed to some kind of historical consciousness. This is difficult in post-modern times, for post-modernism rejects the historical awareness that characterized the modern outlooks which preceded it. As Gerald Press writes, "The idea of history that has informed the distinctively modern social theories, philosophies, and theologies is that history is telic, or goal-directed: there is an end or goal – a *telos* – toward which history is moving, which may be known either by rational inquiry into the facts or by revelation, and in relation to which all prior actions and events have both their meaning and their value."[1] This view of history guarantees its importance, for it imbues all events with a significance which is determined by establishing their place in a grand historical narrative. Everything that happens is therefore understood by calibrating its place in a historical cycle that culminates in Christianity's second coming, Marxism's triumph of the proletariat, or some other end. An ahistorical consciousness is more in keeping with post-modernism, which rejects attempts to interpret the world in terms of a grand design or telos. Even Fukuyama, who is committed to a historical *telos*, undermines its significance by arguing that the "end of history" has arrived with the full realization of the principles of liberal democracy.[2]

In lieu of a grand historical narrative which makes history matter, we need to ask how historians can convincingly maintain that history should occupy a central place in public education. This will require something more than an appeal to our own fascination with historical questions. The basis of this appeal could be broadened by enlisting the public's historical curiosity, but the extent and depth of this curiosity is debatable[3] and this justifies history by making it a popular diversion, not an essential discipline within contemporary education.

A more robust defence of history's place in education must, I think, be founded on an account of it which ties it more directly to the issues of today. I propose a defence that argues that history is an invaluable resource which we must use if we wish to deal effectively with the intellectual, political, social, and practical issues of today. If this is true, then history is more than a diversion. It is rightly seen as one of the core disciplines in the education system, for every educated person must wrestle with such issues – even if they do not share the historical curiosity which may motivate a professional or an amateur historian.

One might illustrate this point of view with the political cartoon I have reproduced below. It is a comment on our former prime minister that I concocted to make a point about visual persuasion.[4] One might call it "The Jean Chrétien Weathervane" or "How Jean Chrétien Makes the Decisions that Matter to Canadians."

It presents the prime minister as a politician who is governed, not by his own convictions, but by the winds of public opinion. This is a charge which has been made on a number of occasions. It was levelled during the Canadian election in 2000, when Chrétien was criticized for going to the polls early, in order to benefit from the outpouring of sentiment precipitated by the death of Pierre Trudeau.

Putting aside the political issues it raises, the Chrétien cartoon demonstrates the notion that history is a resource, for it borrows an idea found in an American cartoon which Mischa Richter published in the *New York Times* thirty years ago.[5] The Richter cartoon is also a weathervane, though one which features, not Chrétien, but an obese American Senator. This version of the weather vane insinuates that Senators are

Leo Groarke 61

Figure 2.1
The Jean Chrétien Weathervane

the fickle followers of public opinion. Thirty years later, the same iconography – substituting Chrétien for the Senator – makes an analogous comment on a Canadian prime minister. Other instances of the same iconography could easily be catalogued.[6]

The relationship between the Chrétien and Richter cartoons underscores the fundamental point that circumstances and ideas today have significant affinities to circumstances and ideas of the past. In this modest sense, history does repeat itself. This explains the utility of historical reflection, for it explains why the circumstances and ideas of the past can illuminate the circumstances and ideas of today. In the case of the Chrétien cartoon, one could trace the sceptical attitude to democratic politicians it expresses all the way to ancient times, to Plato's criticisms of democracy in the *Republic*, where he argues that elected leaders are not real leaders, for they succeed by pandering to the desires and sentiments of the general public.

Looked at from the point of view of illustration, the Chrétien cartoon shows how the history of cartooning can inform incisive comments on the politics of today. On the basis of many similar examples, one might easily argue that the whole history of illustration demonstrates the relevance of history, for it is a history of images and themes that can be recycled to create images which are appropriate to today. It is in view of this that contemporary cartoonists like Draper Hill engage the history of their craft in a practical way, borrowing from historical precedents which they adapt to contemporary subject matter.[7]

Much the same can be said of other kinds of history. In a discipline like philosophy, one might ask, not how we can learn from the history of ideas, but how we can fail to do so. How can we doubt that we can learn something important about the meaning of life, the constraints of human nature, the value of society, the good life, the dictates of justice, the limits and extent of knowledge, etc. by studying the works of thinkers like Plato, Aristotle, Descartes, Hobbes, Gandhi, Nietzsche, Wittgenstein, Russell, Arendt and de Beauvoir?

As in the case of illustration, the history of philosophy is in part significant because modern and contemporary ideas have significant historical antecedents – much more than we usually imagine. It is, for example, commonly said that Descartes is the father of modern philosophy and even modern thought. Many locate the origins of modernity in the famous argument which begins his *Meditations*. According to this view, the "hyperbolical" doubts that he indulges are a radically new argument for scepticism which sets the stage for his and other modern attempts to build a foundation for a universal knowledge. Three hundred years later, it is the unravelling of the attempt that signals the arrival of post-modernism.

While there is much that might be said in favour of this account of modern and contemporary philosophy, the cycle that it identifies does not originate with Descartes, for the argument which is the basis of the scepticism that motivates his philosophy can be traced to ancient times. A version of it, which may be the basis of his first meditation, is found in Cicero's account of Academic skepticism in his *Academica*. Later versions are featured in the philosophy of the eleventh century Islamic philosopher, al-Ghazali, and in the *Universal Treatise* of Nicholas of Autrecourt, whose works were burned during the fourteenth century.[8] The extent to which these historical precedents anticipate Descartes is especially clear in the case of al-Ghazali; Henry Lewes remarked that everyone would "have cried out against the plagiarism"[9] if a translation of Ghazali had existed when Descartes wrote. M. M. Sharif has gone further, arguing that the similarities between al-Ghazali and Descartes' *Discours de La Méthode* are so great that Descartes must have borrowed from his Islamic predecessor.[10]

In the present context, it suffices to say that such similarities illustrate the point that we might study an eleventh century Islamic thinker, not because we are curious about eleventh century Islam or the civilization that produced it, but in order to shed light on one of the fundamental arguments that defines the modern era. Insofar as post-modernism is a perspective that concludes that the argument cannot be refuted – a conclusion it shares with Academic skepticism, al-Ghazali and Nicholas of Autrecourt – the works of such thinkers are particularly pertinent to contemporary philosophical concerns. They are more, not less, intriguing because they propound conclusions at variance with those that Descartes suggests.

It is easy to find similar examples in the philosophy of Hume and other moderns.[11] They show that the sceptical crisis which precipitates modernity[12] – and ultimately gives rise to contemporary positions like pragmatism and post-modernism – is not unique, but has earlier precedents in the history of scepticism.[13] The richness of the history this implies is evident in Benson Mates' recent study of Sextus Empiricus and ancient Pyrrhonism, the ancient outlook which is usually described as the original scepticism. According to Mates, the ancient Pyrrhonians pushed doubt much further than modern or contemporary thinkers do, engaging a more radical sceptical experiment than we have hitherto imagined.[14] Mates is not sympathetic to this experiment, but it is of great interest in sceptical times, and might easily be mined for perspectives, ideas and conclusions that can illuminate our own sceptical crisis.

Some may argue that these examples are too abstruse to demonstrate the relevance of history to general education, for they are of interest only to the intellectual or the philosopher. One might reply that intellectual endeavours of this sort have a place in general education, though a defence of history need not depend on this reply. For it can equally be said that the value of historical reflection is not limited to such endeavours. Most significantly, it must play a role in the formation of thoughtful social and political policy, for the examination of earlier antecedents is an important way to empirically study the issues raised by particular policies. In cases which require that we think critically about new policy initiatives, a reflection on related experiments or precedents in the past may be our only recourse, precisely because we have no other basis from which we can extrapolate conclusions.

An example that may illustrate this point is Ian Clark's study of the doctrine of limited nuclear war and military policies that assume it.[15] Because there have been no limited nuclear wars of the sort that this implies, this is not a matter which can be easily examined. In the absence of actual instances of such war, much policy is founded on little more than speculation. Clark establishes a better basis for reflection by studying the history of ancient, medieval and modern attempts to limit war. On the basis of this historical reflection, he is able to establish plausible conditions which are a prerequisite for success. He then considers these conditions in the circumstances that are likely to characterize the conduct of nuclear war, concluding that the notion of limited nuclear war does not withstand close scrutiny. The result is a careful, thorough look at an issue which could put all our lives at stake. Historical reflection is one of the key ingredients that makes the discussion possible.

The relevance of history to the nuclear debate is demonstrated in a different way in the critique of the nuclear industry which has been developed by Stephen Hilgartner, Richard Bell and Rory O'Connor.[16] The crux of their analysis is a history of the industry's attempt to define the language used in debates about nuclear power in a way that makes it difficult to criticize the industry. They coin the term "nukespeak" for the vernacular that results. Their analysis demonstrates both the power of historical inquiry and also the significance of the ideas of the past, for their account is inspired by the ideas in George Orwell's 1946 essay "Politics and the English Language,"[17] and his novel, *Nineteen Eighty-Four*. One might summarize their conclusion as the claim that the nukespeak of the nuclear industry is reminiscent of the "newspeak" used to stifle dissent and promote "doublethink" in Orwell's world of Big Brother.

The extent to which issues of language, communication and persuasion can be illuminated by theories and ideas from the past is more generally evident in the discipline of rhetoric, which is constantly informed by a historical consciousness that applies the history of rhetoric to the issues of today. Aristotle could not have imagined the forms of communication that technology has made possible, but the theory of persuasion he develops in his *Rhetoric* is still used to assess the strength and force of the arguments they communicate. It is in view of this that Aristotle's theory remains a standard way to teach the principles of rhetoric and argument assessment.[18] When Kathleen Welch argues that we need a new "electric" rhetoric, she still maintains its ties to ancient rhetoric, invoking an Isocratean perspective which she adapts to fit contemporary needs.[19] Looked at from the point of view of its subject matter, it is not surprising that rhetoric constantly engages its history. The attempt to communicate effectively and to persuade others which motivated ancient rhetoric is still a valued goal and will continue to remain important.

Constancy of this sort often makes the ideas of the past relevant to our own concerns, though history's value does not depend entirely on it. In many cases, historical reflection is valuable because it forces us to look at things in ways that challenge our assumptions. The very differentness of history can open up new vistas and new ways to conceive of ourselves and our lives. This aspect of historical inquiry is well illustrated in John McLaren's contribution to the present volume, which investigates the history of attitudes to law and property, demonstrating "[t]he cultural contingency of viewing and constructing landscapes, and thus land management."[20] In such a context, the different attitudes to land and property which history can unearth allow a more critical approach to our own view of them, and can inspire new ways of dealing with the issues of property, land and rights, especially in the context of aboriginal land claims and cross-cultural differences.

Even arcane views from the history of physics, human physiology, astronomy or chemistry – views we no longer take seriously – can be important because they can inform a history of science which demonstrates how it evolves, along with its relationship to social, economic and cultural endeavours. The study of the history of science therefore plays a central role in attempts to understand the nature of science. Good examples of this can be found in Kuhn's and Feyerabend's rejection of the naive view of the scientific method and scientific inquiry that often characterizes the texts used in educating scientists.[21] In a scientific age like our own – an age in which science is one of the fundamental forces that shapes our world – this suggests that the study of the history of science is one important way to understand our own world. As such an understanding must be the basis of responsible science policy, the history of science has another crucial role to play in the social and political arena.

The study of outdated theories and ideas can also be important because it unearths theories and ideas which merit reconsideration. An example that illustrates how this may happen is John Chamberlin's recent study of Langland's poetics, the medieval arts, and the view of language they embrace. According to Chamberlin, such study can reveal a view of language which is a serious alternative to the view which characterizes contemporary figures like Saussure, Derrida, and Rorty.[22] Whether Chamberlin is right or not, his discussion illustrates how serious historical inquiry can force us to reconsider theories and ideas which are potential alternatives to those our time assumes. Discussion of this sort is fertile ground for the ideas and theories which can act as catalysts for further inquiry and ultimately expand our knowledge.

One might easily enumerate other examples to illustrate the point that history, even history which is regarded as arcane or obsolete, is a crucial resource which can help us more productively engage the issues of today.[23] This is a powerful way to justify the claim that history should play a central role in contemporary education, but it raises the question whether the history that this justifies is the history that we teach. Within the university, one might easily argue that it is not, for this is an arena in which history has, like other contemporary disciplines, become a specialized pursuit. This has allowed the development of specialized expertise, but it has also separated the study of history from the study of the present. In the process, historians have become specialists who study and preserve primary historical documents, and the reflection on their relevance to today has been relegated to the fringes of historical inquiry, where it is not regarded as an essential aspect of historical research.

The result of such developments is a cadre of historians who have impressive abilities in narrow fields, but little ability to reflect on the broader significance of their research. In such an era, professional prestige is attached to publications in professional journals which are of interest only to the specialist – journals which discuss the arcana of historical data with impressive rigour, but have little to say to the non-specialist, who regards the articles they publish as dull and unimportant. As one reads in the guidelines for submission published by a journal on ancient times which has tried to break this paradigm and speak to a broader audience, "If you propose submitting a paper that has been rejected by one of the professional journals, we urge you to rewrite it. The fact that it wasn't quite dull enough to be accepted there doesn't mean that it is lively enough for *Arion*."[24]

Against this background we can better understand the anomalies that characterize the state of history today. On the one hand, we live in a time in which historical scholarship has been carried to lengths which would have been difficult to imagine in earlier times and places. The detailed study of the minutiae of historical documents which characterizes doctoral dissertations and other forms of historical research would probably astound earlier figures known for their interest in history – even intellectual giants like Aristotle, Hume, Montaigne and Bayle. Despite these historical riches, we live at a time when historical reflection plays a very minor role in public discourse and debate. No one doubts the need to understand the issues that we face from a scientific, an economic, or a social scientific point of view. In contrast, historical inquiry is not treated as an essential part of such deliberation.

An approach to history that puts greater emphasis on its ability to shed light on contemporary issues does imply that we should pay serious attention to primary historical research. For there is a sense in which it provides a basis for all historical reflection. But the proposed approach to history suggests that this is only the beginning of historical inquiry, which should be motivated by an attempt to assess the significance of history and uncover aspects of it which are relevant to our own situation. Looked at from this point of view, the preparation and study of primary historical documents is an important prolegomenon to the crux of historical inquiry, but no more. In an academic and intellectual world which has divided the different facets of knowledge into separate fiefdoms, the prolegomenon has instead become an end in itself. Because it does not incorporate the attempt to establish the significance of historical findings, it is not surprising that this is something which is not readily apparent to the public which is asked to support historical endeavours.

One might justify the specialization that now characterizes the discipline of history by arguing that the ability to master the minutiae of historical data is the best preparation for the attempt to understand and assess its relevance to contemporary concerns. This view contains a grain of truth – for a command of primary documents is an important prerequisite for careful comment on their relationship to the issues of today – but there is little reason to believe that the training that makes a specialist adept at considering some small corner of the past provides the knowledge and abilities needed to understand how history relates to the issues of today. Understanding the microscopic details of history requires a vast knowledge of the past, a fine attention to detail and technical expertise. Understanding their significance in the broader scheme of things requires a significant knowledge of the past, but it must be combined with an in depth knowledge of the issues of today and the ability to place details in context and recognize their broader significance.

If one wishes to assess Plato, not as an antiquarian figure, but as a philosopher who has something to say to those interested in philosophy today, then one needs an in-depth knowledge of philosophy today. One needs, above all else, the skills that make someone a good philosopher – the ability to follow the nuances of philosophical arguments, the ability to see the big picture, the ability to holistically assess philosophies and their consequences, the ability to distinguish what is and is not philosophically significant, and so on. The notion that this is something that can be developed by training someone in the specialized treatment of historical data is a curious one which inconsistently appreciates the complexities of the problems of the past but not the complexities of the problems of today.

It is especially difficult to see how the specialization which characterizes history as a discipline can be employed as a methodology which can inform a broad discussion of periods of the past that may shed light on our lives today. For such specialization implies a process of reduction and compartmentalization which proceeds by reducing broader questions to narrower ones which are said to be more tractable. This is a process which has been spectacularly successful in the realm of science, but it is much less clear that it can build a basis for a broad understanding of history. Thus the reductionism it implies can in principle be carried on indefinitely, leaving the history of an epoch in so many pieces that it is difficult to put it back together. Instead of building a solid basis for a broader understanding, a reductionist approach to history may in this way promote interminable debates over historical irrelevancies.[25] The attempt to understand the broad significance of a time by settling the issues that arise about its details can in this way undermine the very goal that motivates the process.

One approach to history which might serve as an alternative to the one that now characterizes history departments can be built upon a vision of history that sees it as an interdisciplinary endeavour emphasizing history's links to the present by underlining its links to other contemporary disciplines. To some extent, history is already carried on in this way in subdisciplines like the history of philosophy, the history of art, the history of psychology and the history of ideas, which are often practised outside of "History" departments. Indeed, most contemporary disciplines incorporate a subdiscipline labelled "the history of x." While subdisciplines of this sort have their pitfalls – most notably, a tendency to consider developments in a particular discipline apart from broader historical currents that affect them[26] – their proximity to contemporary disciplines often means that they teach and study history in a way that more clearly places historical reflection within the context of contemporary concerns. To this extent, the historical reflection they promote is particularly amenable to the defence of history I propose.

One might contrast the approach to history I have elaborated with that assumed by Robert Wright in his contribution to this volume. The focus of his discussion is television history, which he portrays as a form of "infotainment" which debases its supposed subject matter. Putting aside some peculiar features of his complaints,[27] the perspective I suggest is much more sympathetic to the suggestion that non-historians should wrest history from the hands of specialists who have failed to "provide the social, cultural, economic and political architecture within which Canadians contextualize their lived experience."[28] Until historians themselves better recognize that they have a responsibility to preserve and discuss not only history, but also its importance and relevance to contemporary lives, there is a case to be made for the suggestion that we must depend on journalists and other academics to do so. The professional discipline "History" will have to earn a more central role in such discussion by demonstrating a greater commitment to teaching and studying history in ways that better integrate it with contemporary issues and concerns.

Historical education of this sort will have to balance the study of the details of history and the study of the issues of today. This requires a general education and an interest in interdisciplinarity which fosters an in depth understanding of contemporary issues and concerns. In the process we must develop a fundamentally different approach to history than the one that dominates the discipline today. It is this generalism and interdisciplinarity which imply a different approach to history than the one that now characterizes specialized history departments. In the process, historians should not hand history over to journalists, other academics and television producers, but they should be willing to work with them, and they must recognize that professionals of this sort have a unique understanding of the contemporary *zeitgeist* and the issues and cultural nuances it makes pertinent. Clearly, this can be an invaluable asset in the attempt to create a history which is both credible and relevant to today.

"Why teach history?" Not, I propose, because it's there. Rather, we should teach history because it is a resource that can shed light on the lives we live today. We can learn from history because earlier times and thinkers were confronted with problems, ideas and circumstances which have affinities to those that confront us today. We can learn from them both when past ages are committed to concepts and views similar to our own, and when they have views that are notable for their differences. Only a fool would ignore his past experience when confronted with a new situation. It would be equally foolish to ignore our collective history. This is why history should occupy a central place not only in the liberal arts curriculum, but in primary, secondary and post secondary education.

One might go even further. For it might easily be argued that we need history, that it is only by historical reflection that we can deal adequately with the personal and societal issues that we confront. If this is true, then it follows that historians have a moral responsibility to ensure that this reflection is properly conducted, not merely through a responsible dealing with the historical data which must be the foundation of historical research, but with a responsible understanding of the ways in which it can be applied to contemporary issues. And society and the public have a responsibility to support this endeavour.

Not surprisingly perhaps, this defence of history has its own historical precedents. One of the most vehement is found in Nietzsche, whose work is guided by a profound commitment to historical reflection, but a reflection which is hostile to history as a discipline pursued as an intellectual recreation divorced from the concerns of the day. As he writes in the first paragraph of "The Use and Abuse of History for Life":

> To be sure, we need history. But we need it in a manner different from the way in which the spoilt idler in the garden of knowledge uses it, no matter how elegantly he may look down on our coarse and graceless needs and distresses. We need it for life and action, not for a comfortable turning away from life and action.... We wish to use history only insofar as it serves living. But there is a degree of doing history and a valuing of it through which life atrophies and degenerates. To bring this phenomenon to light as a remarkable symptom of our time is every bit as necessary as it may be painful.[29]

Endnotes

1. Gerald Press, *The Development of the Idea of History in Antiquity* (Montreal: McGill-Queen's University Press, 1982), 4.
2. Francis Fukuyama, *The End of History and the Last Man* (Hamondsworth: Penguin, 1992).
3. Robert Wright, elsewhere in this volume, states that he sees "evidence of a far deeper, essentially *cultural* dislocation in public life." (Robert Wright, "The Way We Were? History as Infotainment in the Age of *History Television*," 52).
4. Drawn by Stephen Guenther. © Leo Groarke 1998.
5. The cartoon is reproduced as the frontispiece in Charles Press, *The Political Cartoon* (Rutherford: Fairleigh Dickinson University Press, 1981). See his comment on page 338.
6. As I write, I have happened across a verbal equivalent in *The Peninsula*, a Bay Area California newspaper which includes, in the midst of the 2004 presidential campaign, an op-ed essay entitled "Kerry is just a political weather vane" (14 July 2004, on page 11B). A very early instance of the weather vane iconography is found atop the famous gothic town hall in Oudenaarde Belgium, which dates from the thirteenth century. In this case, the point is not that "Hans the Warrior," a famous protector of the town, is fickle but (apparently) that he is steadfast and protects the town no matter how "the wind blows."
7. For some good examples of this process, see the Art Gallery of Windsor, *Draper Hill: Political Asylum: Editorial Cartoons by Draper Hill* (Windsor: Art Gallery of Windsor, 1985), especially, 8–9, 16–17, 64 and 66.
8. For an account of Descartes' argument and its relationship to earlier versions of the same argument, see Leo Groarke, "Descartes' First Meditation: Something Old, Something New, Something Borrowed," *Journal of the History of Philosophy* 22:3 (July 1984): 281–301.
9. Henry G. Lewes, *The Biographical History of Philosophy*, vol. 2. (London: C. Knight, 1846), 50.

10 M. M. Sharif, ed., *A History of Muslin Philosophy* (Wiesbaden: Pakistan Philosophical Congress, 1963).

11 Another pivotal argument in modern philosophy is Hume's famous critique of cause, which is in many ways the centre point of his philosophy. But it is not an argument which is new with Hume. Rather, it has a long history which can be traced to Hellenistic philosophy – to the critique of "signs" that Sextus Empiricus elaborates in his works. For an account of Hume's argument and its antecedents, see Leo Groarke and Graham Solomon, "Some Sources for Hume's Account of Cause," *Journal of the History of Ideas* 52:4 (October – December 1991): 645–63. Julius Weinberg has made the case that Nicholas of Autrecourt's version of the argument is the basis of a philosophy which is in many ways like Hume's, dubbing Nicholas "the medieval Hume." (See Julius Weinberg, *Nicolaus of Autrecourt: A Study in 14th Century Thought*. New York: Greenwood Press: 1948, 1969). Still, it is not clear whether Hume had any knowledge of Nicholas' or Sextus' version of the argument, though he could have easily read the latter in Thomas Stanley's popular seventeenth century *History of Philosophy: Containing the Lives, Opinions, Actions and Discourses of the Philosophers of Every Sect. Illustrated With the Effigies of Divers of Them the History of the Chaldaick Philosophy* (London: T. Basset, 1687).

12 See, for example, the account in Richard Popkin, *The History of Scepticism from Erasmus to Spinoza* (Berkeley: University of California Press, 1979).

13 For one attempt to recognize these precedents, see Leo Groarke, *Ancient Skepticism: Anti-Realist Trends in Ancient Thought* (Montreal: McGill-Queen's University Press, 1990).

14 See Benson Mates, *The Skeptic Way: Sextus Empricus's Outlines of Pyrrhonism* (New York: Oxford University Press, 1996).

15 Ian Clark, *Limited Nuclear War: Political Theory and War Conventions* (Princeton, NJ: Princeton University Press, c1982).

16 Stephen Hilgartner, Richard C. Bell, Rory O'Connor. *Nukespeak* (Harmondsworth: Penguin, 1982).

17 George Orwell, "Politics and the English Language," *A Collection of Essays* (Garden City, NY: Doubleday, 1954).

18 As in Edward P.J. Corbett and Robert J. Connors' popular text, *Classical Rhetoric for the Modern Student* (New York: Oxford University Press, 1999).

19 Kathleen Welch, *Electric Rhetoric: Classical Rhetoric, Oralism, and a New Literacy* (Cambridge, MA: MIT Press, 1999).

20 John McLaren, "The Memory of Property: The Challenge of Using the Past to Enlighten the Lawyers of the Future," in this volume (81).

21 Thomas Kuhn, *The Structure of Scientific Revolutions*, 2nd ed. (Chicago: University of Chicago Press, 1970). Paul Feyerabend, *Against Method: Outline of an Anarchistic Theory of Knowledge* (London: Verso, 1976).

22 See the "Conclusion" of John Chamberlin, *Medieval Arts Doctrines on Ambiguity and Their Place in Langland's Poetics* (Montreal: McGill-Queen's University Press, 2000).

23 For one final example from political theory, see Renato Cristi, *El pensamiento político de Jaime Guzmán: Autoridad y libertad* (Santiago: Ediciones LOM, 2000). Cristi's book is a historical study of the thought of Jaime Guzman in the context of his work establishing the Chilean constitution. It is not pure history but an attempt to shed light on Guzman's political philosophy and, in the process, shed light on the issues of authority and freedom which face us all in our liberal times.

24 "Advice to Prospective Contributors," *Arion: A Journal of Humanities and the Classics*; <http://www.bu.edu/arion/submit.htm> (15 June 2004).

25 One might compare the issues raised in Zeno's paradoxes of motion, which suggest that motion is impossible because it can be divided into an endless series of parts which can never be completed. According to the Dichotomy one can never cross any distance d because this distance can be divided ad infinitum, making the attempt to cross it an attempt to cross an infinite series of distances (½ d, 1/4 d, 1/8 d, …). One might compare this situation to the attempt to understand a field by compartmentalization and specialization, for one can always divide the different parts of it into more and more subparts, creating an endless series of subfields which can never be traversed.

26 Of course, the same criticism could be made of much of the history that takes place within "History" itself.

27 He takes *History Television* to task because it "employs no historians" but his own account suggests that it uses historians extensively (see Wright, "The Way We Were?", 49). But why should it be assumed that its administrators, who have professional qualifications in journalism (and in one of two cases, a BA in history), are on these grounds deficient (more fundamentally, why should historical credentials be the principal qualifications used in judging whether they are appropriate administrators).

28 Wright, "The Way We Were?", 52.

29 Friedrich Nietzsche, "On the Use and Abuse of History for Life" (1873), trans. by Ian C. Johnston; <http://www.mala.bc.ca/~johnstoi/Nietzsche/history.htm> (15 June 2004).

Bibliography

"Advice to Prospective Contributors." *Arion: A Journal of Humanities and the Classics.* <http://www.bu.edu/arion/submit.htm>.

Art Gallery of Windsor. *Draper Hill: Political Asylum: Editorial Cartoons by Draper Hill.* Windsor: Art Gallery of Windsor, 1985.

Chamberlin, John. *Medieval Arts Doctrines on Ambiguity and their Place in Langland's Poetics.* Montreal: McGill-Queen's University Press, 2000.

Clark, Ian. *Limited nuclear war: political theory and war conventions.* Princeton, NJ: Princeton University Press, c1982.

Corbett, Edward P.J., and Robert J. Connors. *Classical rhetoric for the modern student.* New York: Oxford University Press, 1999.

Cristi, Renato. *El pensamiento político de Jaime Guzmán: Autoridad y libertad.* Santiago: Ediciones LOM, 2000.

Feyerabend, Paul. *Against method: outline of an anarchistic theory of knowledge.* London: Verso, 1976.

Fukuyama, Francis. *The End of History and the Last Man.* Harmondsworth: Penguin, 1992.

Groarke, Leo. "Descartes' First Meditation: Something Old, Something New, Something Borrowed." *Journal of the History of Philosophy* 22:3 (July 1984): 281–301.

———. *Ancient Skepticism: Anti-Realist Trends in Ancient Thought*. Montreal: McGill-Queen's University Press, 1990.

Groarke, Leo, and Graham Solomon. "Some Sources for Hume's Account of Cause." *Journal of the History of Ideas* 52:4 (October – December 1991): 645–63.

Hilgartner, Stephen, Richard C. Bell, and Rory O'Connor. *Nukespeak*. Harmondsworth: Penguin, 1982.

Kuhn, Thomas. *The Structure of Scientific Revolutions*. 2nd ed. Chicago: University of Chicago Press, 1970.

Lewes, Henry G. *The Biographical History of Philosophy*, vol. 2. London: C. Knight, 1846.

Mates, Benson. *The Skeptic Way: Sextus Empricus's Outlines of Pyrrhonism*. New York: Oxford University Press, 1996.

Nietzsche, Friedrich. "On the Use and Abuse of History for Life." Trans. Ian C. Johnston. <http://www.mala.bc.ca/~johnstoi/Nietzsche/history.htm>.

Orwell, George. "Politics and the English Language." In *A Collection of Essays*. Garden City, NY: Doubleday, 1954.

Popkin, Richard. *The History of Scepticism from Erasmus to Spinoza*. Berkeley: University of California Press, 1979.

Press, Charles. *The Political Cartoon*. Rutherford: Fairleigh Dickinson University Press, 1981.

Press, Gerald. *The Development of the Idea of History in Antiquity*. Montreal: McGill-Queen's University Press, 1982.

Sharif, M. M., ed. *A History of Muslin Philosophy*. Wiesbaden: Pakistan Philosophical Congress, 1963.

Stanley, Thomas. *History of Philosophy: Containing the Lives, Opinions, Actions and Discourses of the Philosophers of Every Sect. Illustrated With the Effigies of Divers of Them the History of the Chaldaick Philosophy*. London: T. Basset, 1687.

Weinberg, Julius. *Nicolaus of Autrecourt: A Study in 14th Century Thought*. New York: Greenwood Press: 1948, 1969.

Welch, Kathleen. *Electric Rhetoric: Classical Rhetoric, Oralism, and a New Literacy*. Cambridge: MIT Press, 1999.

II

"Sharper Than Any Two-Edged Sword": History, Colonialism and Land

Those of us who at certain times look to grasp something beyond history must search for it as the remembering of a negated tradition.
– George Grant

History, for its part, has been described as a document-bound discipline. If something was not written, preferably in an official document, it was not historical. Thus were pre-literate societies excluded from history and labelled prehistoric, or perhaps proto-historic. The best they could hope for was to become historic by extension, when they came into contact with literate societies.
– Olive Patricia Dickason

3

The Memory of Property: The Challenge of Using the Past to Enlighten the Lawyers of the Future

JOHN MCLAREN

¶ Introduction

This chapter describes an experiment in teaching legal history that links three law schools on two continents. The program known as OZCAN has three objectives.

First of all it seeks to expose students to the legal cultures of two groups of British colonies in Australia and Canada in order to illustrate: a) comparisons and contrasts between the legal evolution of these jurisdictions; b) the contingent and contextual factors that explain discrete legal developments in the constituent colonies; c) the relative influence within particular colonies of the law and legal culture of the colonizing power, of that locally produced in response to domestic conditions and, of that borrowed from other colonies faced with similar problems.

Secondly, the program facilitates teaching and learning through a web-site-based set of materials that emphasizes common themes and relative experiences within settler colonies; the importance of lateral as well as linear thinking in constructing and interpreting the historical record; and, the importance of historical documents, biographical information and a rich vein of interpretative and contextual material, including critical commentary, artistic works, photographs, maps, literature, poetry, ballads, video material and linked web sites to understanding and connecting colonial legal cultures.

Thirdly, OZCAN encourages and promotes dialogue and discussion on comparative issues in colonial history between the students and faculty at the three participating schools, as well as external mentors, through the use of an interactive discussion program – Web Board.

The course itself is divided into two sets of complementary modules:

> contextual modules which are designed to provide students with a common base of knowledge about the development of colonial legal cultures in the two countries and,

> interactive modules that are designed to encourage collective reflection and discussion of more specific issues, namely, crime and morality; Aboriginal-settler relations; immigration and citizenship; labour and class; and, the cultures of the legal profession.

The University of Victoria undertook the academic design for the contextual modules and the University of British Columbia (UBC) the design of the interactive modules. The Learning Technologies Group, Division of Continuing Studies at the University of Victoria has provided technical design work and support throughout the four years the program has been running. Australian National University (ANU) has taken responsibility for providing historiographic input from Australia and for video conferencing.[1]

¶ The Significance of Property and Property Rights

A primary feature of the course is the assertion of the centrality of issues of property, property rights and property law to an understanding of colonialism, colonial settlement and colonial legal culture. In the

British imperial system settler colonies were established for settlement by European migrants who expected to secure land as well as a socio-economic future based upon it by appealing to English law and the rights of ownership and possession within that system. Both imperial and colonial politicians and officials and members of the judiciary in large part supported this objective.[2]

Where tension developed between the administrators and judges, on the one hand, and settlers, on the other, was in dealing with Aboriginal peoples. The latter had very different notions of land use and management based on communal understandings and principles, and felt a strong spiritual connection to the land they inhabited. While settlers were intent on being granted or taking land for themselves with the greatest degree of legal security – even if it meant dispossession of the indigenous inhabitants of the area – some imperial and colonial officials and judges endeavoured to provide a degree of protection for Aboriginal people, their culture, law and land base. Sadly, in the end, it was all too often the priorities of the settlers and their political representatives that won out, with land grabbing and forcible exclusion, whether illegal or clothed with the pretence of legality, prevailing.[3]

The designers and teachers of OZCAN also want the message to be clear that there is in both countries a direct relationship between the historical hold of property rights on the colonial imagination and contemporary disputes over territory and property between Aboriginal people and the successors to earlier generations of European settlers. This point is made by a process of relating contemporary interpretations and historical material through functional, relational or situational themes. To illustrate this approach to teaching the focus in this chapter is the substance and methodology of the first nine pages of materials in the first contextual module which is entitled "Constructing, Law, Space and their Subjects: Landscape, Topography and Culture."

The cultural contingency of viewing and constructing landscapes, and thus land management, is illustrated up front by demonstrating in the web materials the diversity of contemporary understandings within European political and legal culture about Aboriginal land use. This is done at the outset by juxtaposing in a provocative way two recent observations of the significance of "emptiness" in representations of colonial landscapes. In the first a Canadian judge puts his cultural mark on an assessment of land use by two First Nations in northern British Columbia:

> I visited many parts of the territory which is the principal subject of this case during a 3-day helicopter and highway "view" in June 1988 which is described in Schedule 1 to this judgement. I also took many automobile trips into the territory during many of the evenings of the nearly 50 days I sat in Smithers. These explorations were for the purpose of familiarizing myself, as best I could, with this beautiful, vast and *almost empty* part of the province.[4]

Here we have explained in writing the idealized European pictorial representation of the wilderness or frontier. Set against what might at first blush seem like a neutral description of an "almost empty" landscape is the critical comment of an Australian cultural historian who introduces the reader to the colonialist cultural baggage which is often shrouded by but underlies such statements as that of the judge:

> The imperial endeavour encourages construction of space as a universal, measurable and divisible entity, for this is a self-legitimizing view of the world. If it were admitted that different cultures produced different spaces, then negotiating these would be difficult, if not impossible. Constructing a monolithic space, on the other hand, allows imperialism to hierarchize the use of space to its own advantage. *In imperial ideology the Aborigines do not have a different space to that of the explorers; rather they underutilize the space imperialism understands as absolute.* The construction of a universal space also allows a homogeneous mapping practice to be applied to all parts of the world: maps become an imperial technology to facilitate and celebrate the further advances of explorers, and display worldwide imperial possessions.[5]

In this passage Simon Ryan explains the instrumental intellectual exercise in which colonizers both old and new have engaged when they wish to emphasize particular physical attributes of the land in order to justify the denial of serious Aboriginal use of a particular geographic area, and thus promote the superior claim of any actual or prospective use by the settler community.

Reflection by students on the claim often made by lawyers and some judges that recognition of property rights and law involve an objective, value-neutral process of analysis, is encouraged further by introducing them to the views of critical geographers who have investigated the deployment of law as well as culture in the construction of space. This work provides a critical matrix for assessing the claims of law to being unbiased and rational and for emphasizing the reification of the concepts of property and possession in the European systems of law. Moreover, it alerts students to the reality of what is going on behind the scenes, since

> ... within legal thought and practice are a number of representations – or "geographies" – of the spaces of political, social, and economic life. In much the same way that law relies in various ways on claims concerning history, so it both defines and draws upon a complex range of geographies and spatial understandings. While struggling to make sense of the ambiguity and complexity of social life, agents – whether judges, legal theorists, administrative officers, or ordinary people – represent and evaluate space in different ways.... The legal representation of space must be seen as constituted by – and, in turn, constitutive of – complex, normatively charged and often competing visions of social and political life under law.[6]

One powerful way in which geography and law come together to construct "reality" in the way suggested by the critical geographers is in the process of mapping. Here is a particularly graphic form in which the link between culture and the use and management of land can be visualized. Mapping may represent the physical markers of the land and their significance to its use and occupation in both a material and spiritual sense, as it does for Aboriginal peoples, or it may reflect both its physical features, as well as the potential for surveying and controlling its natural features, and the radical reformation of the landscape and use of the land and its resources, that is either explicit or implicit in much European mapping of territory.

Map 3.1 of the Red River settlement provides an interesting layered and competing cultural understanding of landscape. It embodies the physical features and topography of the area as a First Nations person might have understood them. Superimposed on those physical features are the bold strips of development along the banks of the Red and Assiniboia Rivers representing the long, narrow Metis river lots, based on the Quebec seigneurial system of land holding. Finally, beginning

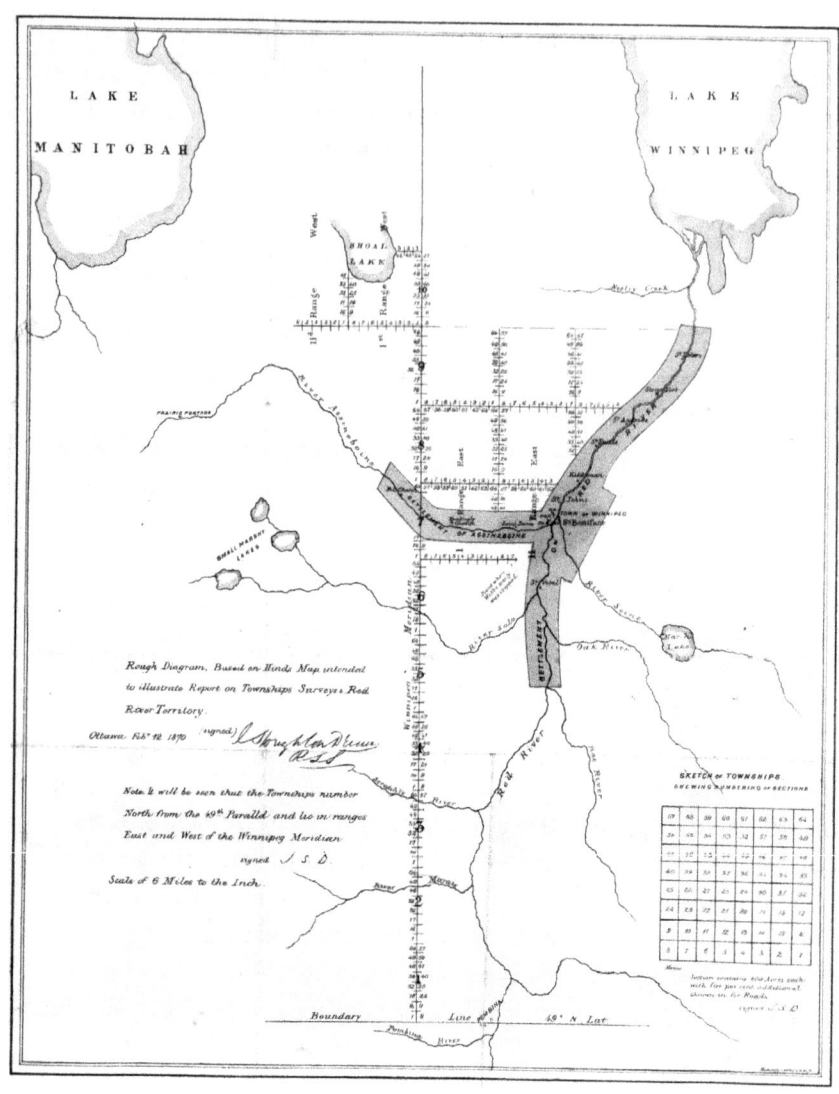

Map 3.1   Map of the Red River Settlement, 1872.[7]

to impinge on both these visions is the division of the land according to the Dominion homestead system, evident in the standardized system of square blocks of land designed for agricultural use by European settlers.[8]

In stressing the pivotal role of the organization and control of property, especially land, in colonial settler societies, it is also important to understand that within the colonizing culture there may be a diversity of interests and motives at play both in envisioning the landscape and carrying out the settlement process. Distinctions sometimes need to be drawn between the objectives and feelings of imperial bureaucrats, colonial officials, land barons and plain ordinary settlers looking for a new start. As formal legal documents and texts rarely point to these distinctions, this is one point at which an appeal to contemporary literature seems appropriate to explain the attitudes of the tens and then hundreds of thousands of colonial settlers who, in migrating, had in view no more than the modest hope of owning their own plot of land:

> In all of their lives till they came here, they had never ventured, most of them, out of sight or earshot of a village steeple that, as they stooped to carry stooks and lean them one against the other, was always there when they looked up, breaking the horizon beyond the crest of a rise or across open fields.
>
> Out here the very ground under their feet was strange. It had never been ploughed. You had to learn all over again how to deal with weather: drenching downpours when in moments all the topsoil you had exposed went liquid and all the dry little creek-beds in the vicinity ran wild; cyclones that could wrench whole trees up by their roots and send a shed too lightly anchored sailing clear through the air with all its corrugated iron sheets collapsing inward and slicing and singing in the wind. And all around, before and behind, worse than weather and the deepest night, natives, tribes of wandering myalls who, in their traipsing this way and that all over the map, were forever encroaching on boundaries that could be insisted on by daylight but in the dark hours, when you no longer stood there as a living marker with all the glow of the white man's authority about you, reverted to being a creek-bed or ridge of granite like any other, and gave no indication that six hundred miles away, in the Lands Office in Brisbane, this bit of country had a name set against it on a numbered document, and a line drawn that was empowered with all the authority of the Law.[9]

Here, in this concise but evocative passage, David Malouf summons up the remembered experience of the settlers of their place of origin, the alien nature and inhabitants of the often stark terrain they had come to, and the colonists' urge to convert the latter into some replica of the former by taming it, something the formal law could not do for them.[10]

The point already made about the cultural contingency of landscapes and land use, regulation and management, especially as it relates to Aboriginal-settler relations, is also open to illustration and enrichment by appeal to other non-legal sources. Contemporary Aboriginal art sometimes articulates in a vivid fashion the very different mindsets of colonial settlers and Aboriginals about the significance of the land and its use to them:

Figure 3.1, an evocative painting by Australian Aboriginal artist Sally Morgan, shows the white farmer as "Lord of All He Beholds," hungry for individual dominion over the land in order to exploit it for economic and social purposes, while ignoring the spiritual significance of the land to its Aboriginal owners. The accompanying text explains the Aboriginal relationship to land and the historical significance of the painting:

> This painting is about the conflict between Aboriginal people and pastoralists in their attitudes to the land. There are stations all over my grandmother's tribal land, and that is one way of seeing that particular environment. The Aboriginal people have always had deep spiritual and emotional ties to the land, which is thought of as the mother. The mother is afforded respect and love and dignity. Rather than belonging to anyone, we belong to her. She is the one who nurtures us and keeps us well. This contrasts with the idea of reaping great material benefits from land ownership.
>
> The painting is also historically based. The top half of the painting dominates the bottom – or, at least, is trying to. This relates to the repression, dispossession and destruction of Aboriginal culture and land. The pastoralist is to be pitied if he cannot see the richness he is trampling on.

Of central importance is the black bird, which is a dual symbol of spirituality and death.[12]

The observations of the more astute explorers and of anthropologists are also instructive in providing insights into the very different ways in which Aboriginal peoples and Europeans constructed and mapped out in

Figure 3.1   Painting by Sally Morgan, *My Grandmother's Country*.[11]

their minds the landscape which they competed for in colonial territories. Paul Carter has succinctly captured the value of this evidence contrasting the linear conceptions of place in the Australian Aboriginal mind with the boundaries of enclosure erected by Europeans in constructing property regimes in the following passages.[13] Eyre writes:

> … the very regions, which, in the eyes of the European, are most barren and worthless, are to the native the most valuable and productive…. For the Alyawarra, boundary sites lie at the center of things, not at their periphery. The idea of the boundary area as 'points capable of confirmation by means of a visual survey from a single position on the ground' is, Moyle says, 'foreign to Alyawarra thinking.'… Aboriginal ways of thinking about the world they inhabit, their historical space, have been increasingly clarified by recent anthropologists. Tindale might have felt a methodological need to plot aboriginal 'boundaries' on the unhistoried space of the white map, but as he himself notes elsewhere, when he questioned Aborigines about their territories, they tended to describe them as a succession of camp-sites. As they spoke, they might draw a line, a way, rather than a circled territory. The last and the first camp-site might be the same place, but they were represented at opposite ends of the line.

Increasingly with the recording of evidence of indigenous peoples themselves about the use of land by and its significance to them there is access to the most reliable accounts of the place of land, its resources and creatures in Aboriginal cultures.

One sympathetic Australian non-Aboriginal observer who has captured the detail and power of stories of Aboriginal people sharing their understanding of their indissoluble connections with the land, its inhabitants and topography is Deborah Bird Rose. In *Nourishing Terrains* she quotes Paddy Fordham Wainburranga, a Rembarrnga man of Arnhem Land, who spoke of these matters in a story he told about his country:

That's what this part of Arnhem Land is like. Other places are all right but here in the middle you've got to talk to the country. You can't just travel quiet, no! Otherwise you might get lost, or have to travel much further. That's law for the center of Arnhem Land. For Rembarrnga people.

My father used to do it. We used to get up early in the morning and he'd sing out and talk. Sometimes he didn't talk early in the morning, only when traveling and we used to stop and he'd talk then in language.

It would make you look carefully at the country, so you could see the signs, so you could see which way to go.... The law about singing out was made like that to make you notice that all the trees here are your countrymen, your relations. All the trees and the birds are your relations.

There are different kinds of birds here. They can't talk to you straight up. You've got to sing out to them so they can know you.[14]

This simple story provides eloquent testimony to the ability of Aboriginal Australians to communicate with their surroundings and work with the land and its creatures to traverse it efficiently and safely and to make the best use of the resources that are needed to sustain human life and welfare. Similar examples can be found in the accounts by Canadian indigenous people of their uncanny ability to read the land and to track and find its bounty. The ability of the Inuit inhabitants of Arctic Canada to assess snow and ice conditions, and reflection of that skill in their many forms of wording to describe those elements is but one example of this phenomenon.[15]

It is not only in artistic material, whether pictorial or written, that the divergence between European and Aboriginal understanding of space and its value can be illustrated. The general significance of mapping or cartography has already been noted. The juxtaposition of Aboriginal and European maps helps to underline this point. In the OZCAN materials are two distinctive examples of maps from Aboriginal and settler society, drawn from Canadian sources, which show a decidedly different set of markers and contours, separating a hunter-gatherer from a settled, agricultural and commercial society. These are the sort of maps which could well have legal as well as explanatory significance in demonstrating distinctive patterns of land use and the conflicts to which they may give rise when they come into contact.

In Map 3.2, drawn by Hugh Brody during his long sojourn with the Beaver people in northeastern British Columbia, there is superimposed on an ordinance survey map of Dawson Creek and Fort St. John, with its precise grid system, the winding hunting trails in the West Moberly

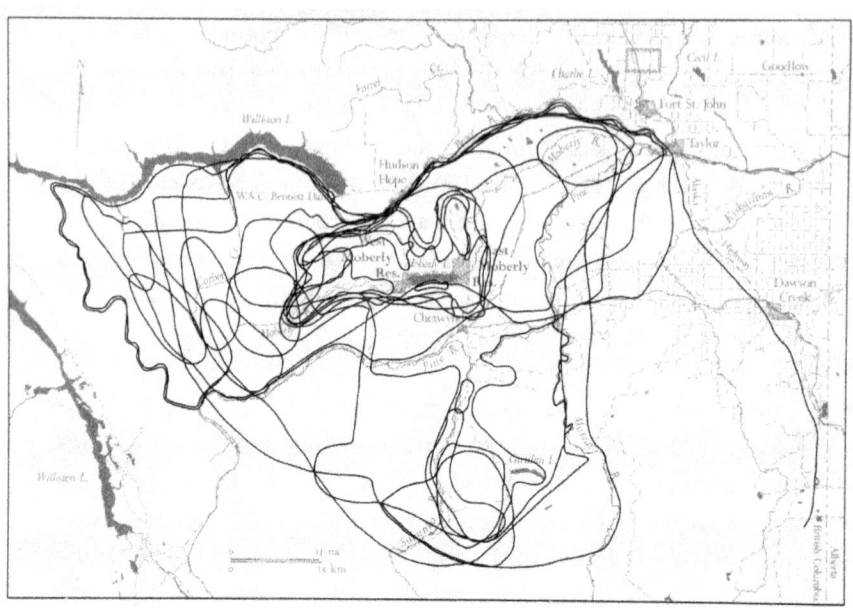

Map 3.2 Map of the hunting grounds of the Beaver people of northeastern British Columbia.[16]

Lake Reserve. This form of mapping is now much in use by archaeologists working for First Nations in British Columbia as they develop land-use profiles for land claims and treaty negotiations.

By contrast with Brody's map, the following representation (Map 3.3) of a rural Albertan landscape by Dominion land surveyors intent on reducing the area to the homesteading grid demonstrates how geometric and unyielding this view of land and its use was. Set boundaries and closely ordered regulation of land holding and use are shown as central to this system of reconstructing what had been, it was thought, empty space for purposes of productive, agricultural development.[17]

The continuing relevance in terms of public and legal policy of divergent conceptions of landscape and its cultural significance can also be represented by visual material that combines the cartographic and artistic. A particularly good example is provided from an Australian source. In two photographs that appeared in a leading Australian newspaper,

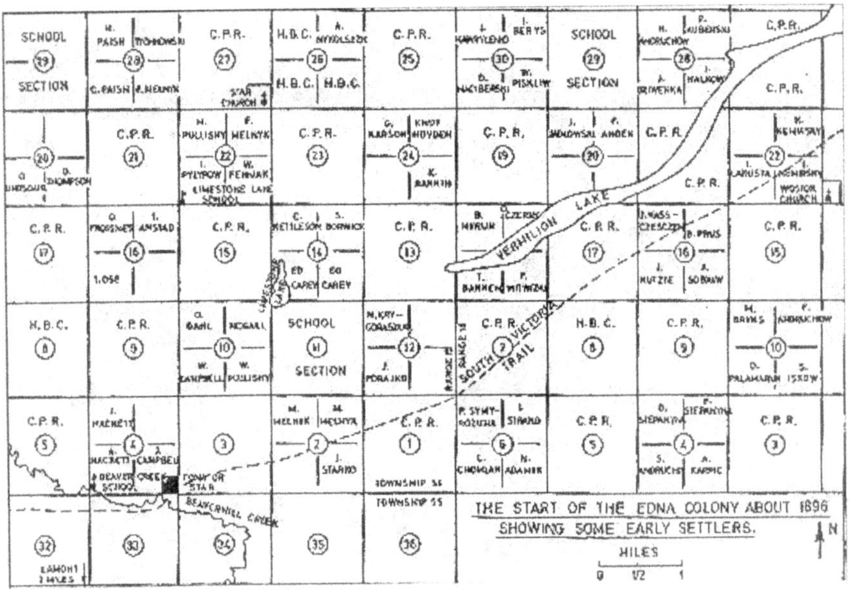

Map 3.3   A grid map of homestead divisions in Edna, NWT, now Alberta.[18]

Western Australian Aboriginal peoples from the Kimberly Ranges are pictured painting their understanding of their territory on a giant canvas (Figure 3.2).

This canvas was designed as both a work of art and as a land-claims artifact. The painters, men and women from the Walmatjarri, Wangkajungka, Mangala and Juwaliny language groups, were mapping the claims of their people to land in the Great Sandy Desert. The canvas was being produced in part as evidence to submit to the Native Title Tribunal and its Commissioner, Fred Chaney. As one Aboriginal leader, Tommy May, in explaining the project wryly put it: "If [non-Aboriginals] can't understand our word they can see our painting. It says the same thing."

In order to demonstrate that tensions relating to the cultural significance of land were not invariably confined to relations between Aboriginal and European communities, the Canadian experience with pacifist

John McLaren   91

Figure 3.2: Photograph of Western Australian Aboriginals painting their traditional territory.[19]

religious communalists, such as the Russian-speaking Doukhobors, who desired to live on and work communally the land they were allocated or secured is also considered in this module. Here tension existed between two European traditions of land holding and working. Despite concessions which had been made by amendments to the Dominion Lands Act to communal religious groups and to co-operative farming operations settling in the Prairies,[20] there was disagreement between the Doukhobors and the Dominion authorities over the import of these concessions between 1899 and 1907. The conflict related to the conditions the settlers had to satisfy to be eligible for homestead, registration of homestead allocation and the steps required to patent homesteads. As the Dominion lands bureaucrats became frustrated at dealing with the Doukhobors over issues of landholding and husbandry, and the political will to preserve concessions to communal farmers among federal politicians

Figure 3.3: A photograph of Doukhobor women engaged in communal farming near Yorkton, Saskatchewan, 1899.[21]

faded in the face of pressure for land from other settlers, Ottawa resiled from its earlier undertakings and sold off much land reserved for this communalist group to non-Doukhobors.[22]

This story of increasing tension is illustrated nicely by reference to a series of photographs and maps.

In Figure 3.3 Doukhobors, primarily women, are depicted working together in common fields around their village. This was the agricultural tradition brought with them from Russia. It did not fit well with a system of individualized agricultural settlement represented by the homesteading regime in the Prairies, which required farm families to live on and work discrete half sections of land. Although the Dominion government conceded that the Doukhobors were entitled to settle and farm communally in this way according to the amendments to the Dominion Lands Act, the fact that Doukhohobor families concentrated

John McLaren 93

Figure 3.4: A photograph of the Doukhobor village of Voskrisennie, near Kamsack, Saskatchewan, c. 1900.[23]

on communal agriculture and so seemingly left large areas assigned to them untilled worked against them as pressure grew for the release of land to non-Doukhobors.

The next two representations, Figure 3.4, a photograph of the neat, geometric Doukhobor village settlement based on the Mennonite *strassendorf* plan, and Map 3.4, a surveyor's map of a Doukhobor settlement set against the homestead grid, demonstrates how two different conceptions of ordered development might clash. The Doukhobors stressed order in the layout of their settlements, but it was order according to their localized assessment of the relationship between community, topography and access to resources, such as water. As the map shows with the village plan lying askew the survey grid, this view could be at odds with the Dominion land surveyors' view of landscape with its emphasis on a much more systematic and all embracing cadastral plan that stressed

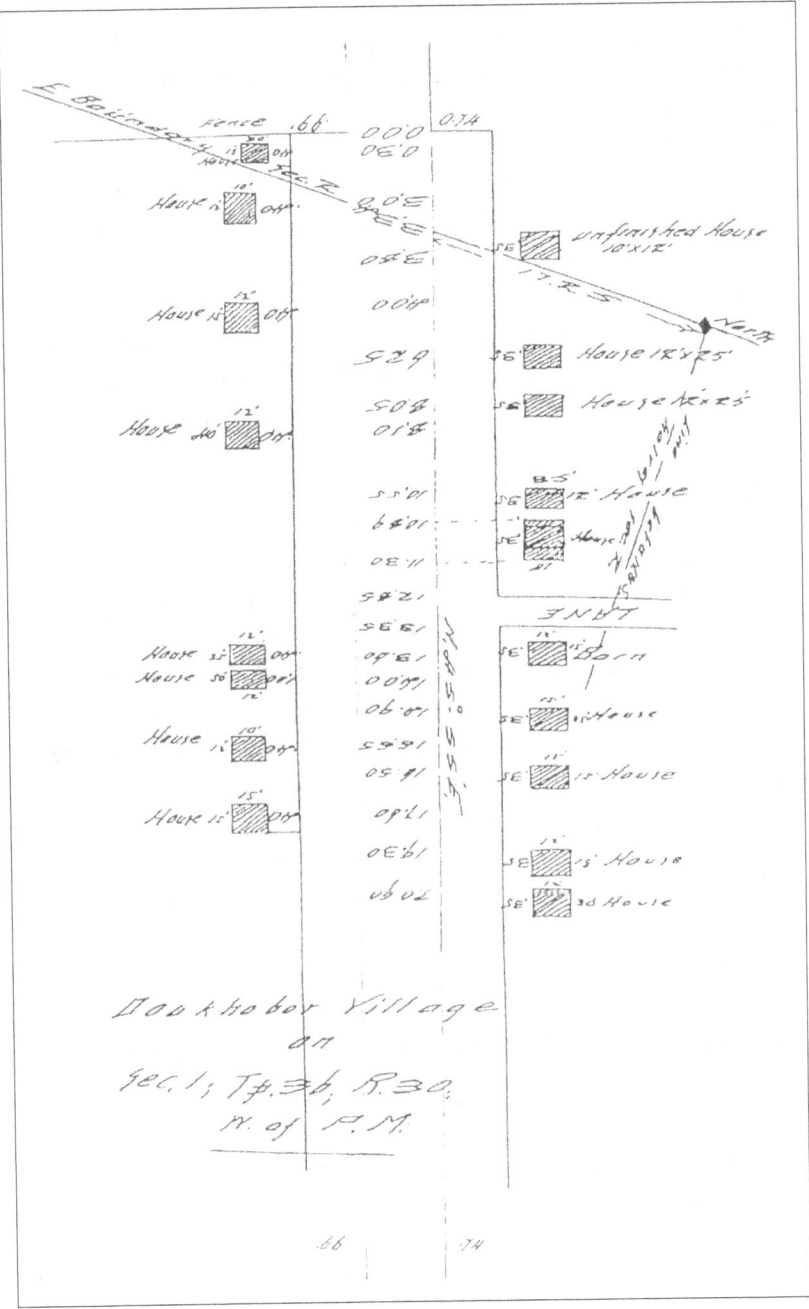

Map 3.4: A Dominion land surveyor's map of the village of Troitzkoe, North Colony, Saskatchewan, 1900.[24]

unrelenting uniformity across vast regions. The independence shown by Doukhobors in planning their villages was a matter of considerable frustration to those surveyors.

To emphasize again that this story is not merely of historical interest, the attention of students is drawn to the ongoing conflict between the remaining rump of the Sons of Freedom and the government of British Columbia over whether New Settlement might be run communally. Some of the families in this small community who adhere to the Sons of Freedom position that they are called to lead the simple, traditional life of the Doukhobors in Russia, insulated from malign external influences, believe that their faith requires them to foreswear the ownership of land and directs them to work and live communally as stewards for the real owner, God. This view and the theological justification for it is encapsulated in a sign erected at the entrance to the community by this group in 1995 which declared: "This land is the mother of us all and like the air we breath is a gift of God for all inhabitants. It should not be bought or sold, or be bartered with. Placing boundaries and stakes upon Mother Earth is exploiting it. All mankind are children of God, free to enjoy the land through love and harmony with all creation."[25]

The construction of space in cultural and legal terms is not limited to land mass, but extends to the oceans as well. This reality is illustrated in the module by directing the students to a video of a lecture given by legal historian Brian Simpson. "Eating People is Wrong" is based in part on the English law criminal case of *Regina v. Dudley and Stephens*.[26] In that case two members of a yacht's crew who were implicated in the killing and eating of the ship's boy after the vessel foundered and sank were convicted for murder. The crew had survived for over three weeks at sea with their minimal food supplies exhausted. When all hope of immediate rescue seemed lost, and in the absence of any consensus on drawing lots, the youngest member of the crew who had least dependents was selected and killed by the master with the approval of the first mate. In the case, Simpson argues, one sees a conflict between the custom of the sea accepted by mariners which permitted such conduct *in extremis* and Victorian legal thought that stressed the need to "keep the upper lip stiff" and avoid "barbarity" at all costs. In the former construction the high seas were sometimes wild and unforgiving, a place in which departures from the normal rules governing human conduct were necessary and therefore permissible if greater disaster was to be avoided. By contrast in the latter construction the high seas, whatever their condition, were subject to the same regime of legal order that obtained on British soil and brooked no departure from the rules of "civilized" conduct.[27]

The issue of how the use and management of land is socially constructed in colonial settler societies is not exhausted at the end of the materials already described. The material and insights provided by the first nine pages of Contexual Module #1 are connected to issues raised for discussion in later contextual modules. For example, a segment of Contextual Module #2 which deals with "Patterns of Colonial Governance and Law" explores the extent to which tensions of the sort set out above are evident in the law of the colonizing power itself – a part of its legal heritage, as it were. Despite the historical amnesia which often existed in the colonies and indeed in Britain itself, there are parallels and connections between the dispossession of Aboriginal peoples from their land and the "rationalization" of land holding and enclosure of common land and waste in the colonizing power itself. Therefore, in the second module the work of Janet Neeson[28] and E. P. Thompson[29] on enclosure is highlighted along with visuals relating to the process and effects of enclosure in Britain.[30] Thompson's work is then analyzed to understand how this mindset, which viewed land both as the *locus* of exclusive ownership and as a commodity, was transferred to the colonies, especially those in India and North America.[31]

Students are shown that contestation within European ranks in Australia and Canada was widespread on a number of issues. These included the status of Aboriginal connection with the land and Aboriginal title and settlers' rights. There was tension between settlers and their political representatives on the one hand, and imperial and colonial politicians and officials committed to a degree of protection for indigenous peoples on the other, as well as the almost inevitable dispossession of Aboriginal peoples from their land or its substantial diminution. All of these phenomena are also underlined in later contextual modules. In tracing these stories the work of writers such as Robert A. Williams Jr., Garth Nettheim and colleagues, Hamar Foster, Richard White, Bruce Kercher, Alex Castles and Michael Harris are used. Official documents, case law, legislation, representations from popular culture and and documentaries like Henry Reynold's *Frontier* are also deployed.[32]

Finally, the point is made in later modules that the fissures over land holding within the European colonial community committed to individualized ownership or possession, were predicated upon differences of opinion about the material and legal significance of particular forms of land use and on class division. Here the particular focus is the story of Australian pastoral squatters and their disputes with colonial governments and officials, and between them and "selectors," immigrants granted land from which to make a modest but adequate living. The pioneer work of Andrew Buck on the law and politics of land settlement in New South Wales is particularly helpful, as one is able to see how pressure from the several interests was reflected in legislation which sought to balance received and locally generated law to produce results satisfactory to colonial conditions and the different conceptions of land use at stake.[33]

¶ Conclusion

The overall purposes of this course are to challenge law students to relate what they learn about the law and its contemporary significance and application to history and culture, and to do that in a way which is more reflective and critical than has often been the norm in traditional courses on the history of the Common Law. Emphasis is also placed on demonstrating the differences between the ahistorical vision of "history" that lawyers and judges often possess – with its emphasis on forensic persuasion – and history as practised by historians, which roams far and wide seeking to understand the political, social, economic and intellectual impulses to and contexts of events.

Students are required to apply the insights they develop both in website-based discussion with other students and with faculty, including outside experts, and in a major research paper or project in which they must use primary materials and relate their topics to broader political, social, economic and/or intellectual impulses and contexts, as the case may be.

In the end, it is hoped that through this course students will recognize: 1) the importance of an understanding of legal culture; 2) the connections between contemporary legal issues and the historical record; 3) the value of an understanding of history and historical method in working in the future with live legal issues.

As the historian David Lowenthal has reminded us, the past is a foreign country.[34] Our perception of it is largely formed by history, which is affected, not only by constantly evolving evidence, but by ever shifting contemporary concerns that colour the work of the historian. Members of the legal profession would do well to reflect on the similarities between the practice of history and the practice of law. The point here is not to suggest that the "lessons of history" can assist us with models for what we do now and in the future. Rather it is to assert that, without a clear idea of where we have been in the past, we cannot begin to understand the present or how we might negotiate the future. Nowhere is that negotiation more fraught with complexities than in the realm of colonialism and its impact on perceptions of land.[35]

Endnotes

1. The visitor's web site is <http://web2.uvcs.uvic.ca/courses/law.demo>.
2. See A. R. Buck, John McLaren and Nancy E. Wright, *Land and Freedom: Law, Property Rights and the British Diaspora* (Aldershot: Ashgate, 2001).
3. Sidney Harring, *White Man's Law: Native People in Nineteenth-Century Canadian Jurisprudence* (Toronto: Osgoode Society, 1998); Roger Milliss, *Waterloo Creek: The Australia Day Massacre of 1838, Governor George Gipps and the British Conquest of New South Wales* (Sydney: UNSW Press, 1994).
4. McEachern C. J. in *Delgamuukw v. British Columbia* [1991] B.C.J. No. 525 (QL), at 35; Contextual Module #1, 1 (author's emphasis). The trial decision was varied by the BC Court of Appeal (1993), 104 D.L.R. 4th 470, and reversed in part by the Supreme Court of Canada [1997] 3 S.C.R. 1010.
5. Simon Ryan, *The Cartographic Eye: How Explorers Saw Australia* (Cambridge: Cambridge University Press, 1996), 4–5; Contextual Module #1, 1. Emphasis added.
6. Nicholas Blomley, *Law, Space and Geographies of Power* (New York: Guildford Press, 1994), xi; Contextual Module #1, 1.
7. National Archives of Canada (NAC), National Map Collection, H12/720/Red River; Contextual Module #1, 2.
8. For an extensive historical account of the Dominion lands system, see Chester Martin, "Dominion Lands Policy" in W. A. MacKintosh and W.L.G. Joerg, eds., *Canadian Frontiers of Settlement*, Vol. II (Toronto: MacMillan of Canada, 1938), 195–545.
9. David Malouf, *Remembering Babylon* (New York: Pantheon Books, 1993), 9–10.
10. The power of literature, as a vessel for remembered experience is underlined by Carol Duncan in her essay on *travessao* consciousness, a unique way of viewing the

world in which the borders between past, present and future are less rigidly defined (see "*Travessao*: African Diasporic Migratory Subjectivity and the Making of History," in this volume. Also, in this section, Nancy Wright develops a local reading of the dominant discourses around land appropriation and aboriginal property rights using popular literature as one important source (see "Reading the Past: The Dispossession of the Poor and the Aborigines in Colonial New South Wales," especially 104–5).

11 *Contemporary Aboriginal Art from the Robert Holmes Court Collection* (Perth, WA, Heytesbury Holdings, 1990), plate 75, 97; Contextual Module #1, 2.
12 *Contemporary Aboriginal Art*, 122.
13 Paul Carter, *The Road to Botany Bay: An Exploration of Landscape and History* (New York: Alfred Knopf, 1988), 344–45; Contextual Module #1, 3.
14 Deborah Rose Bird, *Nourishing Terrains: Australian Aboriginal Views of Landscape and Wilderness* (Canberra: Australian Heritage Commission, 1996) Contextual Module #1, 4. In this book Aboriginal people explain in prose and poetry the significance of their land to them, their culture and relationships, more specifically of the Dreamtime and its permanent imprint on the landscape and in the law and culture of the people.
15 See Hugh Brody, *The Other Side of Eden: Hunters, Farmers and the Shaping of the World* (Vancouver: Douglas & McIntyre, 2000), 48–53.
16 Map by Karen Ewing taken from Hugh Brody, *Maps and Dreams* (Vancouver: Douglas & McIntyre, 1988), 165 (reprinted by permission of the publisher); Contextual Module # 1, 6. This map is the perfect visual representation of Carol Duncan's *travessao* consciousness. In this conception of reality, time is not a straight line. This notion is rich with potential for those seeking to understand how the past has an impact on both the present and future.
17 Supra, note 8.
18 Author's private copy; Contextual Module 31, 6.
19 *Weekend Australian Magazine*, 28–29 June 1997; Contextual Module #1, 4. The location of this remarkable exercise in communal art was Pimini on the northern fringes of the Great Sandy Desert.
20 Dominion Lands Act, Stat. Can, 1886 c. 54, s. 37, as amended Stat. Can. 1898, c. 31, s.3.
21 British Columbia Archives and Records Service (BCARS), Doukobor Photograph Collection, E-07238, Contextual Module #1, 7.
22 For a detailed study of these events, see Carl J. Tracie, *"Toil and Peaceful Life": Doukhobor Village Settlement in Saskatchewan 1899–1918* (Regina: Canadian Plains Research Centre, 1996).
23 Saskatchewan Archives Board (SAB), Doukhobor Photograph Collection, B2111, Contexutal Module #1, 7.
24 C. F. Aylesworth, Jr., D.L.S. Field Book, #7397, Contextual Module #1, 7.
25 Sign at the entrance to New Settlement in 1995, noted by the author in November of that year, Contextual Module #1, 8.
26 (1884) 14 Q.B.D. 273.
27 See Brian Simpson, *Cannibalism and the Common Law: The Story of the Tragic Last Voyage of the Mignonette and the Strange Legal Proceedings to Which it Gave Rise* (Chicago: University of Chicago Press, 1984).
28 Janice Neeson, *Commoners, Common Rights, Enclosure and Social Change in England 1700–1820* (Cambridge: Cambridge University Press, 1992).

29 E. P. Thompson, *Whigs and Hunters: The Origin of the Black Act* (New York: Pantheon, 1975).
30 Module #2, 12–14.
31 E. P. Thompson, *Customs in Common* (New York: New Press, 1991), 159–75.
32 See Robert A. Williams Jr., *The American Indian in Western Legal Thought* (New York: Oxford University Press, 1990); Heather McRae, Garth Nettheim and Laura Beacroft, *Indigenous Legal Issues: Commentary and Materials*, 2nd ed. (North Ryde, NSW: LBC, 1997); Hamar Foster, "Indigenous People and the Law: The Colonial Legacy in Australia, Canada, New Zealand and the United States," in Douglas Johnston and Gerry Ferguson eds., *Asia Pacific Legal Development* (Vancouver: UBC Press, 1998), 466–90; Richard White, *The Middle Ground: Indians, Empires and Republics in the Great Lakes Region 1650–1815* (Cambridge: Cambridge University Press, 1991); Bruce Kercher, *An Unruly Child: A History of Law in Australia* (Sydney: Allen & Unwin, 1995), 3–20; Alex C. Castles and Michael C. Harris, *Law Makers and Wayward Whigs: Government and Law in South Australia* (Adelaide: Wakefield Press, 1987). See also Module #3, 1–2, 22; Module #4, 9, 16; Module #5, 7, 13, 17.
33 See, e.g., Andrew Buck, "Property Law and the Origins of Australian Egalitarianism," *Australian Journal of Legal History* 1 (1995): 145. See Module #2, 21.
34 David Lowenthal, *The Past Is a Foreign Country* (Cambridge: Cambridge University Press, 1988).
35 Diane Kirby and Catherine Colborne, eds., *Law, History, Colonialism: the Reach of Empire* (New York: Palgrave, 2001).

Bibliography

Blomley, Nicholas. *Law, Space and Geographies of Power*. New York: Guildford Press, 1994.
Brody, Hugh. *Maps and Dreams*. Vancouver: Douglas & McIntyre, 1988.
———. *The Other Side of Eden: Hunters, Farmers and the Shaping of the World*. Vancouver: Douglas & McIntyre, 2000.
Buck, A. R., John McLaren, and Nancy E. Wright. *Land and Freedom: Law, Property Rights and the British Diaspora*. Aldershot: Ashgate, 2001.
Carter, Paul. *The Road to Botany Bay: An Exploration of Landscape and History*. New York: Alfred Knopf, 1988.
Castles, Alex C., and Michael C. Harris, *Law Makers and Wayward Whigs: Government and Law in South Australia*. Adelaide: Wakefield Press, 1987.
Contemporary Aboriginal Art from the Robert Holmes Court Collection. Perth, WA: Heytesbury Holdings, 1990.
Dominion Lands Act, Stat. Can. 1886, c. 54, s. 37, as amended Stat. Can. 1898, c. 31, s.3.
Foster, Hamar. "Indigenous People and the Law: The Colonial Legacy in Australia, Canada, New Zealand and the United States." In *Asia Pacific Legal Development*, edited by Douglas Johnston and Gerry Ferguson, 466–90. Vancouver: UBC Press, 1998.
Harring, Sidney. *White Man's Law: Native People in Nineteenth-Century Canadian Jurisprudence*. Toronto: Osgoode Society, 1998.

Kercher, Bruce. *An Unruly Child: A History of Law in Australia.* Sydney: Allen & Unwin, 1995.

Kirby, Diane, and Catherine Colborne, eds. *Law, History, Colonialism: the Reach of Empire.* New York: Palgrave, 2001.

Lowenthal, David. *The Past Is a Foreign Country.* Cambridge: Cambridge University Press, 1988.

Malouf, David. *Remembering Babylon.* New York: Pantheon Books, 1993.

Martin, Chester. "Dominion Lands Policy." In *Canadian Frontiers of Settlement, Vol. II,* edited by W.A. MacKintosh and W.L.G. Joerg, 195–545. Toronto: MacMillan of Canada, 1938.

McEachern C. J. In *Delgamuukw v. British Columbia,* [1991] B.C. J. No. 525.

McRae, Heather, Garth Nettheim, and Laura Beacroft. *Indigenous Legal Issues: Commentary and Materials.* 2nd ed. North Ryde, NSW: LBC, 1997.

Milliss, Roger. *Waterloo Creek: The Australia Day Massacre of 1838, Governor George Gipps and the British conquest of New South Wales.* Sydney: UNSW Press, 1994.

Neeson, Janice. *Commoners, Common Rights, Enclosure and Social Change in England 1700–1820.* Cambridge: Cambridge University Press, 1992.

Rose, Deborah Bird. *Nourishing Terrains: Australian Aboriginal Views of Landscape and Wilderness.* Canberra: Australian Heritage Commission, 1996.

Ryan, Simon. *The Cartographic Eye: How Explorers Saw Australia.* Cambridge: Cambridge University Press, 1996.

Simpson, Brian. *Cannibalism and the Common Law: The Story of the Tragic Last Voyage of the Mignonette and the Strange Legal Proceedings to Which it Gave Rise.* Chicago: University of Chicago Press, 1984.

Thompson, E. P. *Whigs and Hunters: The Origin of the Black Act.* New York: Pantheon, 1975.

———. *Customs in Common.* New York: New Press, 1991.

Tracie, Carl J. *"Toil and Peaceful Life": Doukhobor Village Settlement in Saskatchewan 1899–1918.* Regina: Canadian Plains Research Centre, 1996.

White, Richard. *The Middle Ground: Indians, Empires and Republics in the Great Lakes Region 1650–1815.* Cambridge: Cambridge University Press, 1991.

Williams Jr., Robert A. *The American Indian in Western Legal Thought.* New York: Oxford University Press, 1990.

4

Reading the Past: The Dispossession of the Poor and the Aborigines in Colonial New South Wales

NANCY E. WRIGHT

The "land question" – the question of who should have access to the land – has long been a feature of political and social life in Australia. One illustration of conflicting and competing narratives about property is the Federal Court decision handed down in 1998 by Justice Olney, who rejected the Yorta Yorta community's claim to native title. What makes the decision in *The Members of the Yorta Yorta Aboriginal Community v The State of Victoria and Others* relevant to the concept of "the lessons of history" is Justice Olney's treatment of historical evidence.[1] He dismissed as unreliable and contradictory the extensive evidence provided by expert witnesses and by Yorta Yorta elders who recounted their people's oral histories. In contrast, he accepted as credible and weighty one documentary source, the book *Recollections of Squatting in Victoria* by Edward Curr, a colonial settler whose veracity was not only questioned by expert witnesses during the trial but also by government officials in Curr's own lifetime.

Curr, Diane Barwick has documented, was criticized for his "ignorance of Aborigines ... in a series of official investigations ... culminating in an 1881 Parliamentary inquiry."[2] Justice Olney, as Roderic Pitty has shown, ignored basic methodological issues in evaluating historical evidence when accepting Curr's book as credible, documentary evidence.[3] The assessment of historical narratives as evidence in native title cases, in particular, directs our attention to the important role of historians as individuals able to provide guidance about the assessment of historical evidence, including oral and written narratives.[4] Equally importantly, the decision by Justice Olney illustrates the problem of interpreting different competing narratives of property.

The debate surrounding the decision in *Yorta Yorta v Victoria* recalls earlier manifestations of the land question in New South Wales in the mid-nineteenth century. The questions of who should own or occupy land and whether it should be the rich man or the poor man who has access to it, in the late twentieth century as in the nineteenth century, have been answered in New South Wales by disregarding the history of the land's continuous occupation by aboriginal people. "The land question" in the nineteenth century produced, not only political and social debate but also multiple and conflicting narratives about property and land ownership. What sources might reveal to us the lessons of this topic in its particular historical settings? How can we locate the variety of texts used in different historical periods in order that we might "read" the land question in the context of the culture in which it was articulated?

This chapter will develop a "local reading" of the sources of political debate in colonial New South Wales in order to avoid simplified or totalising narratives about land ownership. One method of "local reading" is that used by anthropologist Clifford Geertz to assemble a "thick description" of a culture by compiling detailed information from its different institutions and practices.[5] By identifying the recurrent patterns, Geertz assembles from his research local knowledge of a culture. Historiography, I argue, can practice a similar methodology by assembling texts drawn from different institutions of nineteenth-century colonial culture. Newspapers are one invaluable source for such information because they record not only parliamentary debates and law reports of the decisions in the colony's superior courts but also political commentary and popular fiction. To produce a "local reading," however, we cannot simply use newspapers to document what was said by members of Parliament or judges about the land question. Instead, we must assemble a reading of colonial culture by identifying recurrent discourses used by a variety of institutions. Indeed, a question that must be addressed when assembling "local knowledge" from such information is whether the discourses of politicians and judges was distributed to, and received by, the general public. In order to provide an example of an interdisciplinary method that produces a "local reading" of colonial culture, this article identifies discourses that recur in a variety of texts circulated by newspapers, including Parliamentary debates, political commentary and popular fiction. These are the social discourses that circulated among various social institutions, not only the government and the law, but also popular culture.

My analysis will focus on discourses shared by texts, including polemics by social reformers and politicians as well as a serialized novel, *The Poor Man*. This novel was published in the *Sydney Mail*, the weekly magazine of the *Sydney Morning Herald*, from 12 March to 17 September 1864. *The Poor Man*, according to its anonymous author, presented to its readers answers that the lessons of recent history provided to "the land question." The serial purported to reveal to readers the harm caused to working class people by the Robertson Land Acts. A liberal government had implemented this legislation in 1861 in order to foster egalitarian distribution of land and land ownership. According to the narrative of *The Poor Man*, in the three years following the passing of this legislation honest families of the working class were impoverished rather than enriched by land ownership. This narrative about property, written in the 1860s, as I will show, participated in discourses not only about property law but also about social class, gender, civility and cultivation that circulated among social institutions, such as the government and the law, as well as popular culture. More importantly, as I will explain subsequently, these discourses had been used previously in the 1830s to justify the dispossession of Aborigines of their land in New South Wales.

In mid-nineteenth century New South Wales, arguments for free selection of agricultural holdings, one reform of the land law advocated by liberals, aimed to remedy the discrepancies between the wealthy class of squatters and the poorer classes.[6] By enabling any person to enter the Crown Land squatting runs of a pastoralist and "select" an area in order to establish a farm and buy land in freehold from the Crown, liberals hoped a poor man could better provide for his wife and children. Liberals advocating land law reform included "middle-class pamphleteers and journalists" who, as Christina Twomey documents, "infused their calls for free selection with claims about its encouragement to respectability and domesticity among working-class men and its ability to improve the lives of women and children."[7]

The growth of urban poverty in Sydney during the 1850s drew attention to the destitution and neglect of children who, John Ramsland notes, were viewed "by newspapers as a threat to law and order and to public respectability which the growing middle class was attempting to foster. Concern was expressed about the exploitation and corruption of the street children themselves – especially the girls."[8] References to children left unprotected in urban working-class neighbourhoods, while the male head of household searched for work or gold, recurred in liberals' arguments that it was necessary to "unlock the lands."[9] Social reformer Caroline Chisholm, for example, argued that the "longing for land" among the poorer classes arose, not from a desire for wealth, but from a desire to secure the well-being of children endangered by life in the city. "A rural life," Chisholm believed, "sanctifies childhood, gives an industrious stimulus to the young – a certainty of home for the aged. What parent of thought can look on our crowded streets and witness the little children in bye-ways without feeling a desire to give them a healthier home, and one away from town danger?"[10]

When advocating change on behalf of the poorer classes, liberal politicians echoed Chisholm's agrarian discourse that opposed the benefits of rural life to the dangers of urban dwelling.[11] Daniel Deniehy, among other liberals, argued that reform of the land law would benefit the poor. When debating the consequences of allowing squatters to monopolize the land, Deniehy, like Chisholm, appealed to sentiment. He described to parliament the benefits that would arise from distributing the land among rich and poor alike. He urged that preference be given to small-scale agriculture, "which mainly gave a love of country and home, and promoted industry and happiness throughout a community."[12] Inspired by ideals such as love of one's homeland and desire for a secure home life, Deniehy and others advocated that the poorer classes be given access to the land. In a similar vein, John Robertson asserted that land ownership was a means to remedy the ills of the poor man, such as drunken, violent and disorderly behaviour, which conservatives argued made the poor ill-suited to own property.[13]

The poor man who lived on his own property, liberals posited, would raise his own and his children's standard of living. Liberals argued that "the poor man," a rhetorical figure for the unemployed and propertyless, was denied access to the land as a consequence of the imperial Waste Lands Occupation Act of 1846. That statute, liberals believed, had "locked up" the land on behalf of wealthy pastoral interests by endowing the pastoral lessees – the squatters – with pre-emptive rights of purchase. The result, argued the liberal John Dunmore Lang in October 1860, was that "a great change came over the spirit of our colonial dream. Instead of the systematic encouragement which the Government had given to the occupation of the land for the purpose of cultivation, every difficulty imaginable was from that period thrown in the way of the cultivator."[14]

Following the defeat of the conservative and pastoral interests in the election of 1860, a liberal ministry under the premiership of Charles Cowper passed the Robertson Land Acts of 1861, which introduced the principle of "free selection before survey," to allow "the poor man" to possess and cultivate land. This legislation, which allowed any person to enter the Crown land squatting runs of a pastoralist and "select" an area, prior to survey, in order to establish a farm and buy land in freehold from the Crown, was bitterly opposed by conservative pastoral interests.[15] In the mid-1860s, immediately following the implementation of the Robertson Land Acts, conservatives, in parliamentary debates and in newspapers, problematized the liberals' sympathetic representation of the poor – their class position, needs and agency. It is from these texts, including the serialized novel *The Poor Man*, that this chapter constructs a local reading of the meanings of competing narratives about property that used the discourses of social class, gender, civility and cultivation.

The narrator of *The Poor Man*, Mr. Pepper, is a wealthy property owner who sympathizes with the poor man's desire to own land. He journeys from his home in Sydney to free selectors' cottages, where he meets families of free selectors, the Jacksons and the McCabes. The trope of the journey in the serial establishes for a reader what Peter Hulme has called "the boundaries of civility."[16] For many conservatives in mid-nineteenth century New South Wales, civility implied ideals such as reason, stability and order, this last meaning the social order of "British civilization" or the class system.[17] "For colonial reformers like Wakefield," Paula Hamilton explains:

> the principle aim of colonisation was to re-create British civilization in the colonies. Wakefield's theory outlined the form of that civilization as well as the means for bringing it about. He argued that access to land should be restricted. A high or "sufficient" price ensured a proper balance between capital and labour and therefore the reproduction of a British society "purged of its grosser economic and civil restrictions but with its clearly defined hierarchy of classes carefully preserved."[18]

When poor, labouring men possessed land, as happened in New South Wales during the 1860s, the traditional class system was inverted. *The Poor Man* uses the discourses of gender and childhood to argue that, in order to protect civility, it is necessary to restore class boundaries disordered by land law reform enacted in New South Wales. The novel juxtaposes tender sentiments raised by the harsh lives of motherless girls with the humour of grotesque masculine and androgynous characters in order to convince readers that free selection has only harmed the poor. Because of the crossing of class boundaries facilitated by the Robertson Land Acts, the countryside of New South Wales is inhabited with children who are grotesques, hybrids created by the confusion of classes that results when members of the "poor" working class become free selectors, that is, property owners living on the land. As Mr. Pepper traverses the properties owned by the Jacksons and the McCabes, he moves further into the bush and from the city, the latter being the topographical boundary of civility. In this manner the satire inverts the dichotomy of the city and the country that was prevalent in the liberals' agrarian discourse praising the benefits of rural life.

In the family of Peter Jackson, the surviving male child, Tom, has prematurely crossed a boundary not only into adulthood but into a geriatric state because of his harsh life on the land. Mr. Pepper interprets "the peculiar nature" of the Jackson boy's clothes as signs that indicate a confusion of child and adult. Rather than simply and appropriately noticing the poverty signified by the boy's costume, Mr. Pepper notices that other than a blue shirt "his only article of dress was a pair of trousers, which had evidently been made in the first instance for a full-grown man. They had now, with a surprising ingenuity, been made to serve without the slightest assistance from needle and thread, as trousers, coat, and waistcoat, all in one. The waistband was brought up over the shoulders and buttoned round the neck."[19]

The comical appearance of the boy counteracts the reader's response to the fact that his oversized, used clothing indicates that he performs the tasks of an adult worker. When regarding the hand-me-down clothes of the Jacksons' son, Mr. Pepper's attention focuses on other meanings; it distresses him that the boy's costume does not typify clothes worn by the poor members of the working class in the city but instead parodies the "trousers, coat, and waistcoat" worn by middle-class gentlemen.[20] Mr. Pepper's attention is not held long by these signs of the confusion of classes. His thoughts return quickly to the boy's age, a concern revealed by Mr. Pepper's reference to legends about old men and children's stories: "As I looked at him and marked the wizened countenance, I could not help thinking of the old German legends of the little old men that haunted the Hartz Mountains or the Black Forest, and played such tricks with travellers; or rather of the old English nursery yarn of Tom Noddy, who was all head and no body."[21] Pepper's allusions transform the boy's appearance from a comically and raggedly dressed child into a physical grotesque. These perceptions, conflating the extremes of old age and youth in the Jacksons' son, perplex Mr. Pepper when he attempts to determine the age of the "man boy": "It was utterly impossible to say how old he was, though at a first glance ... when I got nearer and studied his countenance, and saw there the traces that nothing but the cares and troubles of life could have left, I set him down progressively as I got nearer to him, heard his speech, and noted his remarks, at twenty, thirty, forty, fifty."[22] The absurdity of the ideas provoked by his appearance, clothes and voice only exaggerates the comic tone of the satirical portrait of the young "poor man."

The satire modulates from comedy to sentiment when Mr. Pepper notices that experiences and responsibilities that prematurely age the young are evident not only in Tom but in the family graveyard where three of the Jacksons' children are buried. The graveyard becomes a symbol of the effect of free selection on the family. In Mr. Pepper's eyes, their surviving daughter, Mary Jane, "a pretty blue-eyed child, certainly not more than nine years of age"[23] deserves the reader's sympathy. Upon the young girl falls the responsibility of the domestic economy of the family because her mother, Lizzy, is bedridden and dying. Like her brother, Mary Jane is denied experiences considered customary for children; indeed, for her childlike behaviour is a punishable offence. She is subjected to the brutality of her brother who "disciplines" his sister if she attempts to play rather than attend to household chores. The fact that two children are the principals in a scene of domestic violence in no way lessens the sentiments of pity and fear it evokes in a reader. It undermines the arguments of social reformers who believed that a rural environment would improve domestic life and prevent violence within the home.[24]

In the Jackson family, domestic violence arises because Mary Jane's behaviour conforms with what Mr. Pepper considers to be norms of childhood; that is, she plays games. Tom destroys his sister's homely toys, sticks with which she plays a game imitating work in the stockyards. When Mr. Pepper observes the sticks that Mary Jane values as toys, he sympathizes with what he describes as a child's need for play:

And this, thought I to myself, as I regarded the poor little thing, who, whilst yet an infant, was not only deprived of every infantile amusement ... is juvenile Australia thrown upon its own resources for playthings in the bush. The child will have toys of some kind, and if it has not the halfpence to buy for itself, it will make or invent for itself. The ... bush child has her stockyard with which she imitates from her own inventions the scenes that come oftenest to her eyes, and have the most interest for her.[25]

Mr. Pepper's sentimental observations on Mary Jane's game highlight the significance of gender to his understanding of the deleterious effects of free selection on social norms. When discussing "children" generally, Pepper uses neuter pronouns. When discussing "the bush child" as a species of "child," he shifts to the feminine gender. In fact just as "the poor man" served in political discourse as a synecdoche of the poorer classes of labourers, Mr. Pepper uses female children as rhetorical figures for "juvenile Australia ... in the bush." He fashions from Mary Jane the type of "the poor little thing," a figure for whom sentiment and sympathy are appropriate. It is because he believes that the boundary demarcating masculine and feminine genders is confused for bush children that Mr. Pepper regards Mary Jane with special concern. Mary Jane, who lacks a doll to cultivate the proper maternal conduct, devises a game that imitates the work of her father and brother. The interest that the stockyard creates in Mary Jane seems to Pepper perverse, if not grotesque, because it hybridizes labour that is conventionally divided between men and women. The suppression of her playfulness, a quality that defines the experience of childhood for Mr. Pepper, signifies the erosion of civility fostered among the working class by life in the bush.

Mr. Pepper attributes the transgression of gender and age boundaries not to the agency of the poor free selectors but instead to the free selector's land. Rather than assuming that the poor free selectors have chosen to alter the constructs of childhood and feminine gender by requiring the young girl to perform what are conventionally an adult woman's responsibilities, Mr. Pepper assumes that, as a result of their distance from the civilising effects of the city, Peter Jackson's family is subject to a deforming and debilitating power of the land. This assumption about the consequences of living outside the boundary of civility is evident when Mr. Pepper looks at Mary Jane and observes: "she was tall for her age, pale and thin, as though the dank moisture of the bush in which she lived was forcing her, like the vegetation around, into an unnatural and sickly growth.... [S]he was a perfect model of fairness, with the beautifully liquid blue eyes, and the bright flaxen locks that are so frequently found amongst Australian maidens."[26] The unchildlike and "unfeminine" height of Mary Jane recalls the disproportionate height of the trees that grow wildly near the clearing where she lives. It is not simply norms of feminine conduct but also the health and beauty of female children that are threatened by life on the land in Mr. Pepper's view. Boundaries such as youth and age, masculine and feminine, nature and civility dissolve, leaving only grotesques in the bush.

The harsh life to which Mary Jane is subjected due to her father's determination to own property seems sheltered when compared to the experiences of the two daughters of Sandy McCabe, who owns a nearby property. Their only shelter is a makeshift tent where the two motherless girls care for themselves while their father is at the pub. For the McCabes, the ideal of domestic family life, described by Caroline Chisholm, is not secured but instead destroyed by owning land in the bush. The representation of the McCabe family inverts the agrarian paradigm of a bucolic rural life safe from a fetid urban environment. The wife of Sandy McCabe was not deserted by him in the city, a fate social reformers and philanthropists portrayed as a particular evil. Instead, she accompanied him to the country where, a reader is led to suspect, she sickened and died because medical care was unavailable.

As a consequence of their mother's death, McCabe's two daughters remain neglected and virtually abandoned in the bush. While ten-year-old Betsy hunts a possum for dinner, her younger sister waits abjectly alone in the tent. Upon first sight of the younger sister, Mr. Pepper believes he is looking at a "heap of rags"; he admits because the rags were "huddled together in so extraordinary a manner ... I never for a moment dreamt that they clothed a human being, until I observed the long flaxen locks that hung down tangled and straggling, and formed the apex of the heap.... The heap at the fire showed no signs of vitality."[27] The unkempt, ragged adult clothes worn by the Jacksons' son indicated his dislocation from the norms of childhood. In contrast the reification of the younger daughter of Sandy McCabe as a heap of rags dissociates her from humanity and life. Her fair hair, a conventional sign of the femininity of 'Australian maidens,' according to Mr. Pepper, resembles rags more than a human characteristic. Her lack of vitality is attributed to her family's impoverished life on their free selection, a parcel of land that is merely uncleared bush.

The destitution of these young girls is attributed to their father's neglect of the land. Their lives reflect the fact that their father has owned the property for ten months without cultivating it. McCabe scorns such labour as unprofitable. His capital outlay after purchasing his free selection, which includes the only water source in the area, is merely the price of a shepherd's outfit. He makes a living from extorting provisions from an adjacent station owner by threatening to fence in the water.[28] McCabe's livelihood is a kind of land speculation, which, as Pepper notes, contradicts the purpose of the Robertson Land Acts. According to liberals, these were intended not only to make the poor man "the equal of those by whom he had been so long down trodden," the pastoralists, but more importantly to make the poor man independent through "the cultivation of the soil."[29] McCabe insists, "it's the way ... that the freens o' the people intended. They wanted him to mak a spoil o' the spoiler, and to feed upon his lawful and legitimate enemy, the rich man. An after a' the years they've had at us, it's no too much to gie us a bit o' a turn."[30] The "spoils" taken by McCabe imply a battle between social classes in which the victor overpowers his oppressor thanks to free selection.

Sandy McCabe is called "the Stringy Barker" by the narrator, who defines the epithet to mean "everything that's regular out and out mean and dirty."[31] Whereas it was conventional to use the adjective "stringy bark" in a laudatory sense to describe people and a life belonging to the uncultivated bush,[32] the epithet "stringy Barker" is much more derogatory in *The Poor Man*. McCabe's characterization as a drunken trickster plays upon popular prejudice and the ethnic stereotype of the Irish immigrant.[33] Class and ethnic prejudices that conflated the idea of reprehensible working class behaviour with Irish immigrants are harnessed by *The Poor Man* to compare two free selectors who fail to successfully cultivate their land. Unlike Peter Jackson, who is a model of an industrious, honest and sober Anglo-Australian worker, Sandy McCabe is uncouth, lazy and dishonest. With the character of McCabe, in particular, the dissociation of the free selectors, both adults and children, from civility involves a dissociation from the law. McCabe's means of earning a livelihood without cultivating his property makes him a boundary creature, a grotesque hybrid of the bushranger and pastoralist.

The land law, the satire implies, is a regulatory discourse that orders civil society. Changes in the land law that dissolve class boundaries disorder society. Because the Robertson Land Acts deregulated social boundaries, according to Mr. Pepper, a different application of criminal law to juveniles impoverished by free selection was made necessary. The displacement of bush children, particularly young girls, from civility brings before Mr. Pepper's eyes:

pictures of children I had seen elsewhere, who, for food's sake, had pilfered, stolen, had done many a thing that they ought to have left undone, and I traced these poor offending little ones, in my fancy, back to their homes – homes such as the Stringy Barker gave to his children, with hunger, destitution, drunkenness, and ill-usage – the only gods that sat around the hearth; and I wondered how, from such causes, any other result could be expected.[34]

Where else might Mr. Pepper have seen such children, in his own words, such "poor offending little ones"? Certainly the plight of the poor and poor children in particular had been popularized in fiction and political tracts after the social unrest of the 1840s in England by the writings of Dickens and Mayhew.[35] But Mr. Pepper leaves unspecified where he had encountered such children previously. To specify where he had seen them would be to remove the boundary of the city and the bush that he uses to differentiate civility from barbarity.

The social ideas and political discourse of *The Poor Man* serial in fact recall nineteenth-century evangelical children's literature more than Dickens's writings. This is established by the narrator's advice to the reader about attitudes to poor children; he does not refer to juvenile poverty or deprivation but instead to "Juvenile Depravity." His theological terminology conflates the Christian doctrine of the moral corruption and innate sinfulness of the human soul with the working class and the poor. Civility, including a social order that could administer discipline, morality and the law to shape a child's soul, are as implicit to the discourse of the satire as to evangelical children's literature. According to Humphrey Carpenter, evangelical children's literature "preached not the relief of social misery through practical, earthly reforms, but taught that the poor should tolerate their lot in this world in the secure knowledge that there were better things to come hereafter."[36]

Rather than advocating social change, like that implemented by the Robertson Land Acts, evangelical children's literature and *The Poor Man* serial proposed that each person accept her lot, particularly her social class. An example of a "reward" book, distributed by churches in Australia during the nineteenth century, illustrates these ideas. *The Dairyman's Daughter*, an evangelical tract by the Rev. Legh Richmond, articulated a conservative political discourse directed to a working class audience: "My *poor* reader," advised the narrator, "the Dairyman's Daughter was a *poor* girl, and the child of a *poor* man. Herein thou resemblest her; but dost thou resemble her, as she resembled Christ? Art thou made *rich* by faith?"[37] Evangelicals, such as Richmond, according to Elisabeth Jay, "had never been tempted to elevate poverty as a virtue, but held in curious tension the ideas of a station in life appointed by God and the Puritan work ethic, which encouraged men to see in secular success, a sign of God's favour, and, in misery or squalor, a sign of punishment."[38]

A comparison of evangelicals' attitudes to emancipationists and the working class highlights ideas about social position. For evangelicals, according to Stuart Piggin:

> To be transported was, in the majority of cases, not a life sentence. To be working class was. Convictism was a phase which the evangelicals, along with others, did their best to ameliorate and then abolish. The evangelicals understood that their attitude to the convict system was to be like their attitude to slavery. That was easy. What their attitude should be to the working class has always been more problematical.[39]

Convictism, a social position resulting from the application of law to crime and poverty, should, evangelicals believed, be disregarded after a sentence was served. Using the law, including land law reform, to alter the class position of poor workers was, on the contrary, suspect to evangelicals and conservatives, who shared the idea that the class system was a basis for establishing "British civilization" in the colony.

Evangelical zeal to reform the poorer classes, particularly when organizing institutions and programs to aid destitute children, John Ramsland explains, was guided by "high conservative lines, which reinforced the prevailing British class structure in the colony. The encouragement of upward social mobility and self-improvement through education were not important considerations."[40] Organizations and institutions established within Sydney to aid poor children, in Ramsland's words, aimed to produce "an industrious, respectable, religious, highly moral and loyal labouring class content with their station in life and unquestioningly obedient."[41]

The Poor Man voices the conservative social idea that one must accept one's lot, or class position. Mr. Pepper's thoughts on the need to temper law by recognizing the circumstances that cause juvenile crime imply that the friends of the poor were mistaken in assuming that property ownership, facilitated by the Robertson Land Acts and free selection, necessarily would improve the circumstances of poor working class children. What the satire ultimately proposes is that repossession of their property would be an act of charity beneficial to poor free selectors. They had been dislocated from a stable class structure that offered the benefits of a life of subjection to, and dependence upon, a paternal and rightful propertied class of pastoralists and squatters. Mr. Pepper, who freely advises, comforts and attends free selectors and their children throughout the satire, exemplifies the paternalism of the propertied class towards the poorer classes. According to the serial, the confusion of working and propertied classes caused by the Robertson Land Acts, initiated a wide-ranging transgression of boundaries that customarily differentiated masculine and feminine genders, child and adult, and lawful and criminal behaviour in New South Wales. The satire leaves unstated the boundary most pressing to the conservative interest, that is, a boundary that differentiated a propertied class from dispossessed persons. The latter would constitute a dependent working class only if the Robertson Land Acts were dismantled.

By claiming to reflect sympathetically the life of "the poor man" three years after he had the opportunity to become a free selector, *The Poor Man* purported to prove that the poor worker had not benefitted from his life on the land as a small-scale agriculturalist. In the political satire, cultivation serves as a metaphor to explain what the free selectors lack, that is, culture and a productive life within a social structure. During parliamentary debates conservatives proposed other ways of situating the working classes on the land based on the assumption that the poor man must be located within a well-defined class system. For example, when debating the Crown Lands Alienation Bill, Mr. Moriarty advised that mechanics of the working class could be best situated under the guidance of a class of gentlemen land owners; he explained that:

He had seen a little of the squatting districts of this country within the last twelve months, and he had seen what he believed to be, under some circumstances, a very happy state of things. He had seen a gentleman occupy a small area of land, managing personally all his concerns, and showing an example of industry and sobriety to all the men employed under him. These men were, he thought as happily circumstanced as any poor labouring man could be, comfortably housed, rations *ad libitum*, and a farm at their disposal to cultivate when they wished to supply themselves with superfluities.[42]

Rather than owning property, the poor man, Moriarty argued, would be happiest living and working on a gentleman's land. In such circumstances, he maintained, the gentleman would cultivate the poor man's character while the latter cultivated the gentleman's land. Similarly, the satire argued that by nature and by experience the poor man was unable to cultivate his land and thereby forfeited any "right" to own land. Thus, the poor man would not be impoverished but protected by dispossession.

What is the origin of the satire's usage of "cultivation," particularly in relation to its narratives about property and land tenure? Cultivation of the bush, in liberal political discourse, was the means to transform the poorer classes of workers into prosperous members of the propertied class. In the satire, Mr. Pepper voices the ideas and idioms that liberal political discourse associated with "cultivation." He reminds Sandy McCabe that the Honourable John Robertson:

… expressly instituted free selection for the purpose of encouraging *cultivation*, and so making smiling fields where once were *desert* places and happy homes where once were only haunts of the kangaroo and wallabi…. It was entirely and solely for the poor man – to give him the equal of those by whom he had been so long down trodden – to put him in possession of his birthright – the land – which was his property by right, as much as it was that of the wealthiest.[43]

The conjunction of the idioms "cultivation," "desert," "the land" and "birthright" alludes pointedly to debates about the land law in the 1830s. Many jurists in the 1830s attempted to justify the English claim to possession of every inch of Australia by citing William Blackstone, who in his *Commentaries on the Laws of England* differentiated colonies won by conquest and treaty from others where "lands are claimed by right of occupancy only, by finding them *desert* and *uncultivated*, and peopling them from the mother countries."[44]

Henry Reynolds has explained that because Australia was not "desert" but inhabited by Aborigines, it is questionable to assert, following Blackstone, that in that colony "English law was 'immediately there in force' on the assumption that no prior legal code and no land tenure had ever existed."[45] Yet this is an assumption shared by liberals and conservatives who debated the land question in the late 1850s and early 1860s. Moreover, it is accepted by Mr. Pepper who imagines that the poor man, by cultivating the land, could transform "desert places," as he describes them, inhabited previously only by kangaroos and wallabi. The land, to his mind, was an unpeopled desert until squatters and pastoralists arrived on it. In the 1830s, parliamentary and popular political narratives about property spoke in similar terms, with some participants contending that the Aborigines did not have a claim to the land because it belonged to those who first cultivated it.

The fact that the Aborigines did not base their existence upon cultivation, some argued, provided a means to apply Blackstone's assertion to Australia. Cultivation as the means to prove possession was used to evade other accepted legal and political theories of sovereignty and land tenure that acknowledged the Aborigines' possession of the land. For example, the Sydney barrister Richard Windeyer argued on 26 October 1838 that the Aborigines "had no right to the land" because it rightfully "belonged to him who should first cultivate it."[46] In the *Sydney Morning Herald* on 7 November 1838 an anonymous column, titled "Crown Lands," made a similar assertion. The article justified the appropriation of the land without determining land tenure by means of treaty by contrasting the examples of the indigenous people of America and Australia. There was, according to the article, no

analogy between the two cases. The American Indians were divided into nations, having fixed localities – they cultivated the ground, and understood the right of property. Not so, however, with the natives of New Holland. This vast country was to *them* a common – they bestowed no labor upon the land – their ownership, their right, was nothing more than that of the Emu or the Kangaroo. They bestowed no labor upon the land and that – and that *only* – it is which gives a right of property in it.

As Henry Reynolds has explained, this popular argument that cultivation proved occupancy of land provided no basis in English or international law to dispossess occupants, such as the Aborigines. Indeed, the argument failed to explain the claim to possess land made by Australian pastoralists, most of whom did not actually cultivate their land. It was a deeply flawed argument that, in Reynolds's words, failed to account for many facts, including the fact that "there was no legal obligation to cultivate freehold land. The proprietor did not "lose his title by his voluntary throwing his land out of cultivation and permitting it to become a waste producing nothing but thistles and weeds."[47]

In parliamentary debates about the land law from 1857 to 1861 liberals ignored this fact. In order to establish the poor man's claim to possess land, the liberals noted that the pastoralists and squatters, who merely grazed animals on the land, did not fulfil the colonial dream of improving the land by putting it under crop. It was the poor man's role as a cultivator that in liberal political discourse identified an improvement that he could bring to the colony by becoming a free selector. When refuting this liberal argument, the narrator in *The Poor Man* tacitly refers to the fact that the free selectors had not successfully cultivated the land and therefore had no basis for their possession of it. Like the liberals in parliamentary debate, the conservative satire used the narrative connecting cultivation and land tenure without specific allusion to its use to dispossess the Aborigines.

What do we learn from engaging in a "local reading" of colonial narratives, like *The Poor Man*? Examination of the different discourses constructing the narrative reveals how they function, in this instance, to evade addressing the vested interests of squatters when justifying their arguments about class and the land law. The discourse of social class calls upon sentiment to justify the different social positions of rich and poor. Paternalism towards social inferiors was the responsibility imposed by custom upon the wealthy, landed classes. Instead of a rational legal code defining the obligations of the aristocracy and gentry towards the poorer classes of workers, the social system endorsed for Australia, not only by Wakefield but also by conservatives, depended upon the exercising of sentimental bonds of paternalism and charity.

The Poor Man establishes a dichotomy between the legal rights rationally but mistakenly defined by the Robertson Land Acts and the sentimental bonds established by the traditions of the British class system. It also satirizes liberal politicians as irrationally self-interested and their legislation as erroneous. This satire undermines the liberals' social ideal of egalitarianism by representing it as the cause of suffering in sentimental scenes that recommend to readers the "benefits" of a conservative social order. The novel uses the discourses of feminine gender and childhood in order to construct the poor as ineffectual individuals who, because they lack agency, require the paternalistic guidance of a wealthy propertied class, represented by Mr. Pepper. Opposing repossession of free selections purchased by the poor, the serial advises, will only lead to harsher legal measures. Mr. Pepper can only admonish others to respond paternalistically when he thinks of the future of female children of poor free selectors; he advises, "Let stern Morality visit some of these homes and see for himself what Juvenile Depravity has to bear withal, and he will deal more gently with *her* when the policeman Law brings *her* before him."[48]

Mr. Pepper implies that liberal social reforms will only subject the childlike poorer classes to the judgment of sterner authorities: the Law and Morality. The reference to juvenile depravity – caused rather than remedied by the rural life of free selectors – echoes ironically the wording of *The Report of the Select Committee on the Condition of the Working Classes of the Metropolis*. That report, published in 1860 in order to promote arguments for reform of the land law, stated, "The streets of Sydney are infested by a large number of vagrant children, or children entirely neglected by their parents; and some of the revelations of juvenile depravity are appalling and almost incredible."[49]

According to *The Poor Man*, nothing had changed since the poor left the city after 1861 and became free selectors. Consequently, in 1864 this serial novel argued it was best to dispossess free selectors who remained on their land. This argument exploited the sentiments raised by representations of wives and children who served in tracts of liberal social reformers, in Christina Twomey's words, as "legitimating figures" to promote reform of the land law.[50] *The Poor Man* also uses the discourse of cultivation – which in preceding decades had validated colonists' appropriation of the land from the Aborigines – to justify the dispossession of another subordinated social group, the poor. A "local reading" reveals how recurrent discourses circulating in colonial New South Wales constructed one widely-accepted narrative about property and land ownership that contradicted another fundamental text of their society: the biblical tenet that the poor should inherit the earth.

Endnotes

1. *The Members of the Yorta Yorta Aboriginal Community v The State of Victoria and Others* (1998) 1606 Federal Court of Australia (18 December 1998).
2. Diane E. Barwick, "Mapping the Past: an Atlas of Victorian Clans, 1834–1904," *Aboriginal History* 8:1/2 (July 1984): 103.
3. Roderic Pitty, "A Poverty of Evidence: Abusing Law and History in Yorta Yorta v Victoria (1998)," *The Australian Journal of Legal History* 6:1 (2000): 1–21.
4. See David Ritter, "Whither the Historians? The Case for Historians in the Native Title Process," and Christine Choo and Shawn Hollbach, "The Role of the Historian in Native Title Legislation," *Indigenous Law Bulletin* 4:17 (December 1998 / January 1999): 4–8.
5. Clifford Geertz, *Local Knowledge: Further Essays in Interpretive Anthropology* (New York: Fontana Press, 1993).
6. A. R. Buck, "'The Poor Man': Rhetoric and Political Culture in Mid-Nineteenth Century New South Wales," *Australian Journal of Politics and History* 42:2 (1996): 203–19.
7. Christina Twomey, "Without Natural Protectors: Responses to Wife Desertion in Gold-Rush Victoria," *Australian Historical Studies* 28:108 (1997): 22–23.
8. John Ramsland, *Children of the Back Lanes: Destitute and Neglected Children in Colonial New South Wales* (Sydney: New South Wales University Press, 1986), 226.
9. Anne O'Brien explains that female and juvenile dependents were the concern of earlier legislation in New South Wales, such as the *Deserted Wives and Children's Act 1840*, in *Poverty's Prison: The Poor in New South Wales, 1880–1918* (Melbourne: Melbourne University Press, 1988), 89–92.
10. *Age*, 6 December 1854.
11. Twomey, "Without Natural Protectors," 26.
12. *Sydney Morning Herald* (hereafter cited as *SMH*), 27 November 1857.
13. In response to G. Madeary's question of whether poor men would "be more temperate if they possessed land?", John Robertson responded, "Yes" [see "Colonial Parliament of New South Wales," *SMH*, 20 November 1857].
14. *SMH*, 10 October 1860.
15. Buck, "The Poor Man," 216–17.
16. Peter Hulme, "Polytropic Man: Tropes of Sexuality and Mobility in Early Modern Discourse," *Europe and its Others*, ed. Francis Baker et al., 2 vols. (Colchester: University of Essex, 1985), 2: 26.
17. Greg Melleuish, *The Sydney Intellectual Milieu, c.1850–c.1865* (MA Dissertation, University of Sydney, 1980), 115–20.
18. Paula Hamilton, "'Tipperarifying the moral atmosphere': Irish Catholic immigration and the state 1840–1860," *What Rough Beast? The State and the Social Order in Australian History*, ed. Sydney Labour History Group (Sydney: George Allen & Unwin, 1982), 15.
19. "The Poor Man," *Sydney Mail* (hereafter cited as *SM*), 7 May 1864.
20. Marion Fletcher, *Costume in Australia 1788 to 1901* (Melbourne: Oxford University Press, 1984), 95–96.
21. *SM*, 7 May 1864.
22. Ibid.
23. Ibid.

24 On domestic violence in colonial Australia see Anne O'Brien, *Deserted Wives and Children's Act 1840* and Kay Saunders, "Domestic Violence in Colonial Queensland: Sources and Problems," *Historical Studies* 21:82 (1984), 68–84.
25 *SM*, 7 May 1864.
26 Ibid.
27 *SM*, 18 June 1864.
28 McCabe is accused of 'dummying' the property of the squatter; however, not only free selectors but also squatters, or pastoral lessees, were participating in 'dummying' in order to purchase land inexpensively. See C. J. King, *An Outline of Closer Settlement in New South Wales* (Sydney: Government Printer, 1957), 84.
29 *SM*, 25 June 1864.
30 Ibid.
31 *SM*, 4 June 1864.
32 Rolf Boldrewood, *The Colonial Reformer* (London: Macmillan, 1890).
33 Hamilton, "'Tipperarifying the moral atmosphere'," 18–19.
34 *SM* 2 July 1864.
35 Gertrude Himmelfarb, *The Idea of Poverty: England in the Early Industrial Age* (London: Faber and Faber, 1984), 312–70.
36 Humphrey Carpenter, *Secret Gardens: The Golden Age of Children's Literature* (Boston: Houghton Mifflin, 1985), 6.
37 Cited in Elizabeth Jay, *The Religion of the Heart: Anglican Evangelicanism and the Nineteenth-Century Novel* (Oxford: Clarendon Press, 1979), 179. J. S. Brattan, *The Impact of Children's Fiction* (Totowa, NJ: Barnes & Noble Books, 1981), 36 explains that, after its first publication in the evangelical newspaper *The Christian Guardian*, Richmond's tract was subsequently printed in a collection of his writings titled *The Annals of the Poor*. See M. J. Quinlan, *Victorian Prelude: A History of English Manners, 1700–1830* (New York: Columbia University Press, 1941), 124 on the circulation of 1,354,000 copies of Richmond's tract.
38 Jay, *The Religion of the Heart*, 179.
39 Stuart Piggin, *Evangelical Christianity in Australia: Spirit, Word and World* (Melbourne: Oxford University Press, 1996), 11.
40 Ramsland, *Children of the Back Lanes*, 226.
41 Ibid., 11.
42 *SMH*, 11 October 1860.
43 *SM*, 25 June 1864; emphasis added.
44 William Blackstone, *Commentaries on the Laws of England*, 2 vols. (18th ed. London, 1823), 1: 104 (emphasis added).
45 Henry Reynolds, *The Law of the Land* (Ringwood: Penguin, 1987), 33.
46 *The Colonist*, 27 October 1838. See Roger Milliss, *Waterloo Creek* (Sydney: University of New South Wales, 1994), 463–64 and 494–96.
47 Reynolds, *The Law of the Land*, 75.
48 *SM*, 2 July 1864.
49 *Report from the Select Committee on the Condition of the Working Class of the Metropolis* (Sydney: Government Printer, 1860), 10.
50 Twomey, "Without Natural Protectors," 22.

Bibliography

Barwick, Diane E. "Mapping the Past: an Atlas of Victorian Clans, 1834–1904." *Aboriginal History* 8:1/2 (1984): 100–31.
Blackstone, William. *Commentaries on the Laws of England*. 2 vols. 18th ed. London, 1823.
Boldrewood, Rolf. *The Colonial Reformer*. London: Macmillan, 1890.
Brattan, J. S. *The Impact of Children's Fiction*. Totowa, NJ: Barnes & Noble Books, 1981.
Buck, A. R. "'The Poor Man': Rhetoric and Political Culture in Mid-Nineteenth Century New South Wales." *Australian Journal of Politics and History* 42:2 (1996): 203–19.
Carpenter, Humphrey. *Secret Gardens: The Golden Age of Children's Literature*. Boston: Houghton Mifflin, 1985.
Choo, Christine, and Shawn Hollbach. "The Role of the Historian in Native Title Legislation." *Indigenous Law Bulletin* 4:17 (December 1998/January 1999): 7.
"Colonial Parliament of New South Wales," *Sydney Morning Herald*, 20 November 1857.
The Colonist, 27 October 1838.
Fletcher, Marion. *Costume in Australia 1788 to 1901*. Melbourne: Oxford University Press, 1984.
Geertz, Clifford. *Local Knowledge: Further Essays in Interpretive Anthropology*. New York: Fontana Press, 1993.
Hamilton, Paula. "'Tipperarifying the moral atmosphere': Irish Catholic immigration and the state 1840–1860." In *What Rough Beast? The State and the Social Order in Australian History*, edited by Sydney Labour History Group. Sydney: George Allen & Unwin, 1982.
Himmelfarb, Gertrude. *The Idea of Poverty: England in the Early Industrial Age*. London: Faber and Faber, 1984.
Hulme, Peter. "Polytropic Man: Tropes of Sexuality and Mobility in Early Modern Discourse." In *Europe and its Others*, vol. 2, edited by Francis Baker et al., 17–32. Colchester: University of Essex, 1985.
Jay, Elizabeth. *The Religion of the Heart: Anglican Evangelicalism and the Nineteenth-Century Novel*. Oxford: Clarendon Press, 1979.
Melleuish, Greg. *The Sydney Intellectual Milieu c.1850–c.1865*. M.A. dissertation, University of Sydney, 1980.
Members of the Yorta Yorta Aboriginal Community v State of Victoria and Others. 1606 Federal Court of Australia.
Milliss, Roger. *Waterloo Creek*. Sydney: University of New South Wales, 1994.
O'Brien, Anne. *Poverty's Prison: The Poor in New South Wales, 1880–1918*. Melbourne: Melbourne University Press, 1988.
Piggin, Stuart. *Evangelical Christianity in Australia: Spirit, word and world*. Melbourne: Oxford University Press, 1996.
Pitty, Roderic. "A Poverty of Evidence: Abusing Law and History in *Yorta Yorta v Victoria*," *Australian Journal of Legal History* 6:1 (2000): 1–21.
"The Poor Man," *Sydney Mail*, 12 March to 17 September 1864.
Quinlan, M. J. *Victorian Prelude, a History of English Manners, 1700–1830*. New York: Columbia University Press, 1941.
Ramsland, John. *Children of the Back Lanes: Destitute and Neglected Children in Colonial New South Wales*. Sydney: New South Wales University Press, 1986.
Report from the Select Committee on the Condition of the Working Class of the Metropolis. Sydney: Government Printer, 1860.

Reynolds, Henry. *The Law of the Land*. Ringwood: Penguin Books, 1987.
Richmond, Revd. Legh. *The Annals of the Poor*. London: T. Nelson, 1860.
Ritter, David. "Whither the Historians? The Case for Historians in the Native Title Process," *Indigenous Law Bulletin* 4:17 (December 1998/January 1999): 4.
Saunders, Kay. "Domestic Violence in Colonial Queensland: Sources and Problems," *Historical Studies* 21:82 (1984): 68–84.
Twomey, Christina. "Without Natural Protectors: Responses to Wife Desertion in Gold-Rush Victoria." *Australian Historical Studies* 28:108 (1997): 22–46.

5

Understanding Property in Australian History

A. R. BUCK

¶ Introduction

"There is nothing which so generally strikes the imagination and engages the affections of mankind as the right of property, and yet there are very few who give themselves the trouble to consider the origin and foundation of that right." So wrote "An Australian" in a letter to the editor of the *Sydney Morning Herald* of 29 March 1856 on the topic of land reform, which so animated colonial society. However, "An Australian" had plagiarized his words from Sir William Blackstone.[1] The incident throws into sharp relief the twin themes of both this chapter and the conference at which these issues were first presented: the sometimes questionable appropriation of historical sources for contemporary political purposes on the one hand, and inability to understand the politics of contemporary issues without reference to the legacy of the past, on the other.

In contemporary Australia the topic of land ownership remains a topic of heated debate. In that debate, history itself has become a battleground.[2]

On the one side, some academic historians have highlighted past injustices towards the indigenous population, who were dispossessed of their land.[3] On the other, conservatives, such as Prime Minister John Howard, have condemned historians for writing what he calls "black armband" history.[4] Rather than acknowledge and apologize for the dispossession of a people and the destruction of a culture, he has argued that it is the ordinary suburban Australians who are made to suffer and feel guilt for crimes they did not commit, and it is they, not the indigenous population, who deserve compassion. This chapter represents part of that ongoing battle over the interpretation of the past.

¶ Bitter Springs

In 1950 an Ealing studios film about the relationship between white settlers and the indigenous population on the nineteenth-century Australian frontier, called *Bitter Springs*, was released. In one scene of the film, a settler, by the name of King, moving his flock of sheep, together with his family and employees, across the outback towards the land he plans on taking up, encounters a government trooper by the name of Ransom, with his aboriginal trackers. Relieved to be told he is not far from water, King invites the trooper to a drink over the campfire. The following discussion takes place:

Trooper: Where are you making for?
Settler: Back of the Truscott Ranges. You know the country?
Trooper: Yes, I know it. The government haven't leased you land there, have they?
Settler: Yeah, I got a map here. Here we are, the shaded block. See …
Trooper: And all for eighty pounds a year …
Settler: That's right. There's nothing wrong with it, is there?
Trooper: No, nothing wrong. *Karagani* the natives call that water-hole – means 'Bitter Springs.' Water's got a sharp taste they tell me. It's good water though. Call the natives that live there the *Karagani* – spring's been their tribal home for a thousand years. Two perhaps. Since the time we were savages, anyway. [He pauses] A thousand

years. One day a bloke walks into the government land office in Adelaide – 800 miles away – bangs down eighty quid – they hand him a piece of stamped paper – the *Karangai* haven't got a tribal home anymore; it's a sheep property. Ah, it's happening all over the place, and we're left to clean up the trouble.

Settler: What trouble?

Trooper: Their hunting disturbs your stock; your stock disturbs their game.

Settler: [becoming belligerent] Well, if they don't like it, they can get themselves some other water.

Trooper: No, that's just what they can't do. You see, there's a tribe on every water-hole in that country. Two tribes can't survive on one water-hole; wouldn't be enough game to go around. Besides, the land's sort of sacred to them. They don't budge easy.

Settler: Look, I've come out here to breed sheep and I don't aim to let no mob of stone-age blacks stand in my road!

Trooper: [becoming exasperated] Then show 'em your paper; they'll understand that – those of them that can read.

Settler: They'll have to!

Trooper: That's not exactly a fair way of looking at it Mr. King. The *Karagani* won't see any of your eighty quid. They've never heard of money – wouldn't know what to do with it if you gave it to them. But I'll tell you this; they do know that water-hole is their tribal ground and no bit of paper is going to convince them otherwise.

At this point two of the aboriginal trackers come up and briefly speak to the trooper in their native tongue. The trooper briefly replies in their language. They depart.

Settler: You seem to be on their side. Now look, I've got title to this land, haven't I?

Trooper: Mr. King, when whites take over Abo land there are three ways of dealing with the natives: one, you can shove 'em off; two, you can ease them off; three, you can find some way of taking them in with you. Now you've got to make up your mind what you're going to do. You've both got to use the same water-hole someway. So watch how you go about it, that's all.

The trooper walks sadly away, and the settler looks at him, stubborn, yet uncomprehending.⁵

The scene, and the movie, are surprisingly perceptive for the period and the movie deserves to be better known. But for the purposes of this chapter, the scene transcribed above highlights many of the themes with which I am concerned – completely antagonistic attitudes towards the land, the total inability of the settler to understand the indigenous point of view, the settler's refusal to see that there is even an alternative position on the question that needs to be taken into account, the incompatibility between a concept of ownership based on traditional use and one based on "a piece of paper," the commodification of property, measured in monetary terms and an alternative, aboriginal concept of property in which money and the attendant idea of commodification is irrelevant.

It is impossible to address all these issues in this chapter, so I propose to examine the reasons that made it extremely difficult for the settler mentality to understand or take account of alternative conceptions of property. I will do this by examining the conflict between opposing conceptions of property in settler society, in order to explain why a concept of property that was commodity-oriented came to dominate and replace, in hegemonic terms, a plurality of property concepts. Why was it, for example, that settlers with experience of communal ideas of property in their country of origin, shed those communal ideas and were deaf to the articulation of communal ideas of property among the indigenous populations they encountered? As John McLaren has pointed out, the history of settler societies is also a story of "historical amnesia."⁶ Why was it that settlers with recent experience of customary-based communal land systems, as had existed in the Scottish highlands before and during the clearances, or in the English countryside before and during the parliamentary enclosures of the late eighteenth and early nineteenth centuries, so readily embraced a commodity concept of property in new lands?

The answer, in part, lies in the fact that the expectations upon property in the colonies were significantly different from assumptions underlying the law of property that had been inherited from Britain. This, in turn, led to a tension between rival conceptions of property, a tension which, as shall be explained, was resolved in favour of a commodity-oriented idea of property which was antagonistic to alternative conceptions, whether they be aristocratic, communal or aboriginal conceptions of property. As this is such a vast topic, I propose in this chapter to focus on two important dimensions of that story: the question of the difference between "real" and "personal" property, and the fate of the idea of "the trust" in the law and concept of property. In order to tease out the contours of this transformation, I will begin with the seemingly prosaic laws of mortgagability in mid-nineteenth century New South Wales.

¶ Liens on Wool

On 10 August 1843 William Charles Wentworth introduced a bill into the New South Wales Legislative Council that would have profound implications for the concept of property in Australia.[7] The bill was the Liens on Wool Bill that proposed an innovative method of raising mortgage finance. A severe economic depression affected the economy of New South Wales in the early 1840s; as a result the price of wool and stock fell dramatically.[8] Many pastoralists, who had over-extended themselves in the late 1830s, faced bankruptcy and ruin. Part of their problem was that they leased, rather than owned, land in freehold and with the collapse of wool and stock prices they lacked the collateral to raise the finance necessary to trade their way out of their new circumstances.[9]

In 1842 the Constitution Act had established a partially elective parliament, based on restricted property qualifications, with legislative capacity.[10] The New South Wales parliament now represented a body of pastoralists – or as they were known, "squatters," after their practice of "squatting" the stock on Crown land – who found themselves in severe financial distress. Accordingly, Wentworth proposed a method of securing credit when the value of existing forms of collateral had collapsed. Wentworth's object, he claimed, in bringing forward the bill, "was to give relief to a class of persons, whose property was comparatively valueless; in the present state of things parties were unable to obtain advances either upon their land or wool." The core element of the proposed legislation was, in Wentworth's words:

... to give validity to the mortgage of stock, which stock was to be limited to sheep, cattle and horses. This clause would virtually repeal the clause in the Insolvent Law, by which all the effects of an insolvent were unreservedly distributed among creditors. The creditors, however, would suffer no hardship inasmuch as the registry would enable persons to see, upon the payment of a small fee, whether the property was mortgaged or not, and if they did not take that trouble, it would be their own laches if they did not know whether the property were encumbered.[11]

In fact, the bill was proposing that pastoralists, who lacked the one type of property the banks would lend money on – freehold land – be allowed to raise mortgage finance on a type of property that was somewhat intangible: the wool clip, or, more to the point, the projected value of the wool clip as it grew on the sheep's back. It was a novel idea, and it should come as no surprise that this measure was voted into law by a legislature with significant investment in the pastoral industry.[12]

But the measure was met with hostility in London, where, in a dispatch on 20 October 1844, the Secretary of State for the Colonies, Lord Stanley, informed Governor Gipps that the Act was repugnant to English law, and would, unless previously repealed, be disallowed before 22 July 1846.[13] Stanley complained to Gipps that this was a measure

so irreconcilably opposed to the principles of legislation immemorially recognized in this country, respecting the alienation or pledging of things moveable, that under any other circumstances than those in which the Colony has unhappily been involved it would not have been in my power to decline the unwelcome duty of advising her Majesty to disallow it. The same circumstances may, perhaps, furnish an apology for an enactment, tending so directly to give unwonted facilities for borrowing money, and increasing the evil of excessive credit, under the penalties of which the Colonists have so long and so severely laboured.... The disasters of New South Wales will ere long have passed away, but there will remain on the Colonial Statute Book, a law expressly authorising transactions which the law of England regards as affording the conclusive indication of fraud. It is a law which will place society at the mercy of any dishonest borrower, and will stimulate the speculative spirit which is so important to discourage.[14]

Needless to say, Stanley's views were not shared in the colony. Defence of the measure, and opposition to the Imperial position represented by Stanley, was voiced in detail in the evidence given before the Select Committee appointed to inquire into the working of the Act, in 1845.[15] Indeed, the measure actually united pro- and anti-squatting forces in colonial politics. An anti-squatting journal such as *The Weekly Register* approved of the principle, arguing that it would "permit the capitalist to lend money on any security that he may deem sufficient."[16] Why did the law relating to mortgage finance raise such feeling, and what were the implications of that law?

On the one hand, liens on wool undermined certain fundamental characteristics of property in English law. English land law, as adopted into New South Wales, was peculiar in two important respects. First, the law possessed a political logic, because it was a mechanism to maintain a land-title nexus vital to the perpetuation of aristocratic power in England.[17] Second, "property" was divided quite distinctly under English law into real and personal property. As one contemporary English commentator argued, "The distinction between real and personal property, which pervades the law of England, is very suggestive. It recalls to mind a time when the possession of land was the only source of wealth, and the only source of distinction."[18]

On the other hand, liens on wool threw into sharp relief the disparity between assumptions regarding the concept of property embedded in English law, and the expectations upon property in a colonial context. In particular, liens on wool highlighted the irrelevance of the distinction between "real" and "personal" property in Australia. As Leslie Duguid, Managing Director of the Commercial Bank, said of pastoral livestock: "They form, in my opinion, the 'real property' of this country."[19] This was a view strongly held in the colony. As one writer in *The Atlas* claimed:

The distinction between real and personal property – unknown to the civil law, and springing out of a state of feudal tenure, almost every vestige of which has long since passed away – is one of the most objectionable parts of English law, seeming to be framed with the object of enabling a man to retain, for the purpose of ostentation and political corruption, the dominion over land, the beneficial ownership of which has long departed never to return, and by indulging the most fantastic and unreasonable caprices in the disposition of land, to bequeath to an unfortunate family the miseries of endless litigation.[20]

The meaning of property that was emerging in New South Wales was both the cause and the consequence of legal innovation. One important related legal innovation was the Crown Leasehold.

¶ Crown Leaseholds

In 1846 the British government passed the Crown Land Sales Act[21] to legalize the hitherto unauthorized occupation of Crown land in New South Wales by the creation of a new form of tenure: the Crown leasehold.[22] The passage of that Act and its accompanying colonial implementing regulations of 9 March 1847 legitimized the system of "squatting" on Crown land. The Act of 1846 also validated a new concept of property in that property in land was seen as a mere object, the ownership, or occupation of which, bestowed rights of exploitation without the corresponding obligation of trust. When property was perceived as an inheritance, it implied an attendant duty of trust, as did an inheritance.

The consequences of these developments were obvious to contemporaries. Nor were they accepted without some disquiet. A writer in *The Guardian* in 1844 wrote:

> The inducement to industry, to the cultivation and improvement of the land, is entirely distinct, where the land is only held from another, and where it is the *bona fide* property of the occupier. In the former case the smallest obstacle is sufficient to induce a wish to change his position. A latent jealousy and ill-feeling at the thought that the best fruits of skill and industry will ultimately revert to the proprietor, is another objection to this system of leasehold in comparison with freehold. In the latter case the possessor is bound to the spot for better or worse; he must subdue it by labour and culture, for it is his own: it is the inheritance of his children.[23]

Similarly, the moral dimensions of the idea of land as a trust were captured well in the pages of the *Colonial Magazine* in 1842:

> England, in addition to that common law which renders every man responsible for the prosperity of his own house, has a duty of trust to fulfil in respect of colonial occupancy; those immense tracts being committed upon moral

conditions not less binding than the Eden covenant, to the keeping of this great country; and it cannot be denied, in looking round upon all sides of this question, that the moral covenant has been forfeited. Everyone knows, that if a man hold house or land upon certain agreements, the stipulations therein must be fulfilled, or forfeiture ensues. If Alpha take a farm of Omega, the land must not be impoverished; or if premises, upon a repairing lease, the stipulation must be maintained. Upon such moral obligations the colonies are held, if such conditions are not maintained, they become worse than useless, in ministering to national pride and idleness, with a long reckoning for dilapidation incurred, and all through calling them by our name, without appropriating them to proper use – the maintenance and happiness of British subjects.[24]

But such sentiments only had relevance in an agricultural, rather than a pastoral economy. The imperial legislation of 1846, however, recognized the supremacy of pastoral pursuits in New South Wales.

The impact of this decision on the role of property in the nineteenth century was enormous. In England, since the Statute of Tenures in 1660 there has been but one type of estate in land as of the Crown – that of free and common socage. Indeed, by that statute the legal foundations of feudalism were swept away in England. Since 1847 in New South Wales, however, there have been two types of estate in land as of the Crown: estate in free and common socage and estates for years. But not only were there two types of estates in land co-existent in nineteenth century New South Wales, but those estates were reflective of competing concepts of property. "That a system so iniquitous," pronounced *The Citizen* on 9 January 1847,

should exist in any country protected by British laws, is alike disgraceful to the Home and Colonial government – a system the offspring of avarice, and fostered by misrepresentation and injustice – a system utterly at variance with the political truism, *"that the land of the colony is held in trust by the monarch for the Nation at large,"* and therefore we consider the Land Regulations, as already existing, to be utterly unconstitutional.[25]

Yet by 1847 support had been voiced for a concept of property wherein the relationship between the occupier and the lord was not one of trustee, but one of protection by law of the occupier's rights over the land occupied and exploited. "The first principle of squatting," noted Gideon Scott Lang in 1845, is "that the Squatter shall have full power to settle without restrictions whatsoever he can find unoccupied pasture, and to take possession of as much land as his stock can occupy."[26] The land, in a very stark way, is seen merely as a means of production, an object to depasture stock on, for wealth under squatting comes from the stock, not the land. When property becomes the means to acquire wealth rather than the measure of wealth, the notion of what property is has begun to slide.

¶ The Trust Concept

For a colonial conservative such as Sir Alfred Stephen, property was: "A test of the possession of other attributes, intellectual or moral, or both; essential to the due exercise of the franchise – which was itself a trust, for the use and benefit of the community. And the possession of property afforded a guarantee, that its owner would be likely to discharge that trust faithfully."[27] The concept of the trust was imbricated deeply within the conservative relationship between property and politics. As property was held in trust for the future, both within the family, and within the landed interest as the collective expression of those families, so was possession of the franchise seen as a trust imposing high moral standards on its discharge. Thus, for the conservative, the possession of landed property was not valued as an end in itself – as an object or a commodity. Rather, it was regarded as a trust, imposing certain conditions to be fulfilled by the trustee, principally not to damage or destroy it for personal gain, but to protect it and improve it for the owner's heirs and the heirs of his heirs. Over and above this, the franchise was not to be exploited for individual or class gain, but to be exercised on behalf of the nation as a whole.

Of course, that was merely the self-image. In the view of their radical opponents, the interests of the nation as a whole too often were simply equated with the interests of the ruling propertied class. Interestingly, the notion of the trust was less relevant to property in a democracy. A large part of the rationale for acquiring and holding property in an aristocratic society, such as eighteenth century England, was that property gave one access to power when that access was restricted. In a democracy, however, property is removed from its direct access to political power and as such, is reduced rapidly to the level of a commodity – an object to be owned, exploited, even abused and destroyed, depending on the whim of the owner. There was no point in regarding it as a trust. The very logic of property in an emergent democracy such as mid nineteenth century New South Wales was fundamentally different from the logic of property in an aristocratic society such as eighteenth century England.[28]

The laws of real property in Australia during the nineteenth century still expressed a concept of property that was part English, yet increasingly at odds with the social, economic and political conditions of the colonial context. "On the subject of landed property," commented an editorial in the *Empire*,

> such is the force which sound views of political economy have attained that a distinguished member of the English aristocracy, the late Secretary of State for the colonies, Lord STANLEY, publicly avowed his conviction that the owners of land, are trustees of their estate for the public weal and, as such, instead of "doing as they will with their own," are bound to use and enjoy their property in such a manner as to render it a source of good to others as well as to themselves.[29]

What the *Empire* recognized was that the central element of the existing concept of property was the notion that tenure implied obligation. To whom was that obligation due, and what was its nature? As the ownership of property on an individual scale was held to be the relationship of a trustee to an inheritance, so was property perceived on a social scale. "The ownership of land, then," noted the *Sydney Morning Herald* on 15 April 1859, "is in the nation. It belongs to the British crown as trustees for the nation." The question that then arose, however, was who exactly constituted "the nation"?

For *The Citizen*, on 9 January 1847, it was "the hardworking labourer ... the industrious operative," and in particular, "the small capitalist, who, accustomed to agricultural pursuits, has visited this colony in the hope of procuring for himself, a portion of the soil which is the *property of the British nation*."[30] Compare this to the reflections of Robert Lowe, writing to Thomas Mitchell in April 1851, thanking him for: "Two letters on the subject of the land question which certainly show in a very forcible light the injustice which is likely to be committed under the squatter's pre-emptive rights. I regret, however, that I cannot agree with you in a wish to see the land retained under imperial control. I admit the soundness of your theory, but the trustee is too ignorant and too negligent to perform his trust."[31] The implication in Lowe's argument is that the squatters comprise the nation, and they, rather than the Crown, should be allowed to administer their own patrimony. The divergence of opinion over the relevance of the trust concept of property is illustrated by the statements of Governor Gipps and W. C. Wentworth during the 1840s. As Gipps saw it: "The lands are the unquestionable property of the Crown, and they are held in trust by the Government for the benefit of the people of the whole British Empire. The Crown has not simply the right of a landlord over them, but it exercises that right under the obligations of a Trustee."[32] Gipps was affirming the inherited logic of property – as an idea and as expressed in law. That logic embodied such principles as the belief that the land was held in trust, that the "owner" was merely a tenant, and that the ultimate owner was the Crown. In comparison, Wentworth felt that, like chattel property, the land should be "owned" by its occupier. He was arguing, in effect, that colonial conditions were not in accord with English law. "It was true, no doubt," he stated,

> in point of law, that these spacious domains, which formed the squatting stations of the country, did vest in the Crown by virtue of its prerogatives; but the Crown was but the trustee for the public. It was evident that all the value of this country, whether of the city, or of its remotest acres, has been imparted to it by its population, and consequently the country itself is our rightful and first inheritance ... these wilds belong to us and not to the British Government.[33]

¶ Property and Democracy

With the establishment of manhood suffrage in New South Wales in 1858, the questions of who constituted the nation, and for whom the land was held in trust, were further complicated. The *Sydney Morning Herald* on 15 April 1859, although admitting that the land did "belong to the British Crown as trustee for the nation," was concerned that among "the less informed" there was a general notion of "an abstract right to the possession of the soil," whereby access to land was seen to be the right of "every man ... who drives a cart in the street; every man who stands behind a counter; and every man who plies his boat upon the harbour." This, needless to say, was offensive to the conservative *Sydney Morning Herald*. It opined that "When the people are told that the land is theirs ... when it is attempted to suggest the idea that ownership is vested in individual electors, and as giving them personal rights to go up and possess the country," this "simply rob[bed] one class of people for the doubtful benefit of another." For the *Sydney Morning Herald*, the land was not "the property of every Englishman" and tenure of that land should only reside with he "who can reap the advantages of the fertility of the soil.... His ownership was essential to his industry, and the consequence of that industry is the supply of the wants of many." In this way the labour theory of property of John Locke informed the editorial writer of the *Sydney Morning Herald*.[34]

The notion of rights to property articulated by the *Sydney Morning Herald* in the late 1850s recalls the arguments of squatters, such as Wentworth, in the 1840s; that is, that tenure implies, not the obligation of a trust, but protection to exploit the land, and the right to such tenure derives from the ability to so exploit. The *Sydney Morning Herald*, on more than one occasion, sought to repudiate specifically:

The doctrine that "the people" so-called, have a right to the whole territory of New South Wales – that any man among them is entitled to say "these lands are mine" – to talk of possession as if they were born into the world with the right to an appropriation ... that each one is entitled to make himself a DUKE OF ARGYLE or BUCCLEUGH – at least in the range of his territory. It is thus that the democrat and the aristocrat under different guises display the same spirit.[35]

What the *Sydney Morning Herald* accurately recognized was that the notion of property as an inheritance to be held in trust excluded the colonial squatter and capitalist, whose claim to property depended on his exploitation of it.

Because the principal form of estate in land in England was a freehold of inheritance, freehold there was taken to be synonymous with property. For freehold after all, was *real* property; leasehold was not real property, but instead *personal* property. When questioned about the feelings of familial attachments that may have been associated with squatting runs, Chief Justice Sir Alfred Stephen, replied to the Select Committee on Intestacy on 23 July 1858 that it was "scarcely possible for me to answer any question about squattages; because I do not certainly know what kind of property it is; whether it be anything or nothing."[36] Of the relationship between a freehold of inheritance and tenure in the definition of property, Stephen was, however, quite specific. It was his opinion that change to the law of inheritance which would put realty on the same footing as personalty would effect, he claimed, " a complete revolution in all that affects real property."[37]

If the law were thus changed, Stephen argued, no man could henceforth take land by inheritance: "the existing tenure of land will be destroyed because the tenure is to a man and his heirs." Freehold – real property – was such precisely because it was a tenure of inheritance; that was the crux of the tenure. "Any radical change," Stephen pointed out, "in the law of inheritance, necessarily involves, as I apprehend, a radical change in the tenure of property." Stephen's confusion as to whether squattages were "anything or nothing" with respect to property, was not the result of ignorance on his part, but the consequence of a strict reading of English law. In English law he found a concept of property at variance with the existence of squatting runs and their attendant concept of property, which implied rights without duties. For Stephen, on the contrary, "Property entails duties, quite as much as it confers rights."[38] His was a concept of property in accord with the existing English law of real property but increasingly at variance with the realities of the colonial situation.

Now compare Stephen's reflections with those of the correspondent "Brutus" in the *Sydney Morning Herald*:

A man's property is as sacredly his as divine and human laws can make it; and I hold, that no man, or body of men, has, or can have, the slightest pretense for dictating how, or in what manner, or for what remuneration, that property shall be employed … If a man be possessed of property there should be no earthly power to control its enjoyment – it is his own to all intents and purposes, and if it pleases him, he has a just and indisputable right to cast it into the sea.[39]

From such a vantage point, the concept of property as a trust was irrelevant. But for a conservative such as Stephen, who harked back to an essentially eighteenth-century vision of English society, the relationship between property and politics was rooted in the notion of a fixed and stable society in which landed property itself was fixed and stable. It was for this reason that men like Stephen favoured freehold as a tenure, for a freehold of inheritance encouraged permanence and improvement of the soil. "No man," noted John Fletcher Hargraves to the Select Committee on Intestacy in July 1858, "will ever build on a leasehold tenure if he can obtain a freehold of inheritance, and the shorter the lease the less substantial the building or other improvement."[40]

For similar reasons men like Edward Deas Thomson desired "to see the land in the hands of permanent holders," as he noted to the Select Committee on the Present State of the Colony in 1865: "You attach people to the country forever if they become permanent possessors of the land; as I have before said, they leave it as an inheritance for their children; while, if they have no permanent tenure, after they have acquired wealth they withdraw their capital and retire to the mother country."[41] Clearly, conservatives such as Deas Thomson were not concerned with the common people but with the patriarchal landowner as they saw him; a representative of the men who would govern in the place of democracy. Terence Murray was very specific on this point when he addressed the Select Committee on the Present State of the Colony in 1865:

There is nothing, in my opinion, so injurious as to the tendency of things in the present system to throw the whole freehold property of the country in the hands of very small proprietors ... to my mind that is a pernicious policy which would exclude from our rural districts the higher type of English country gentleman, with capital, his social influence and his fine example ... and I say that with a keen perception of what the democratic tendencies of the country must be.[42]

Hence, in the conservative mentality, not just property, but freehold property – and that on a substantial scale – was to be encouraged because it was the tenurial basis of "the higher type of English country gentleman."

However, in the Australian colonies land did not have the same social and political implications, buttressed by tradition, as it did in England.

Land was more of a commodity in Australia. "Land is always bought," noted the English *Solicitor's Journal*:

> either with a view to its resale at a profit, like any other article of commerce, or to be retained by the proprietor for his own use, or for the benefit of his family. In Australia, and in all other new colonies, if the system of conveyancing there suits the requirements of trade the most necessary object is accomplished.... However, while land with us is not much used in commerce, it is the great basis on which family settlements are constructed.[43]

This was precisely why the laws designed to achieve that end, the laws of entail and primogeniture, were fiercely protected from reform in nineteenth century England. But as the Chief Justice of New South Wales, Sir Alfred Stephen, acknowledged in 1857: "Land here is not like land in England, there it remained in the same family for years and years, here it passed rapidly from hand to hand; was as much an article of trade as a bale of commerce."[44] To properly appreciate the consequences of this, we must keep in mind that land was an article of commerce precisely because of the egalitarian nature of land ownership in colonial Australian society.

Land reformers in mid-nineteenth-century New South Wales were fond of invoking John Stuart Mill in aid of their cause. The reasons are obvious. As Mill had argued in *The Principles of Political Economy*, first published in 1848: "It is not the subversion of the system of individual property which should be aimed at; but the improvement of it, and the participation of every member of the community in its benefits."[45] The reform of the inherited laws of real property in nineteenth century New South Wales was not designed to liberate "the poor man" from the institution of private property, but to incorporate him into the regime of private property.[46] But it was a regime, as we have seen, that had little appreciation of the notion of the trust concept. Indeed, some commentators recognized that the commodification of property, in a context of egalitarian land ownership, led to crass materialism, most notably evidenced by the practice of speculation. As the *Empire* commented: "In a colony where the population is rapidly increasing by immigration, there is a mode of getting rich at the expense of other people, which could not be carried on to the same extent in a long settled country, namely by purchasing land and leaving it unoccupied, unimproved, until the labours of others in the neighbourhood have enhanced the value of the property."[47] Materialism and egalitarianism together would inform the concept of property that was to emerge triumphant during the course of the nineteenth century in the Australian colonies. It rejected the idea of the trust, just as it refused to accept alternative, aboriginal and communal notions of property. The price that was paid for its triumph was, some would argue, rather high.

¶ Conclusion

At the beginning of this chapter I quoted a scene from the 1950 film *Bitter Springs*. In this chapter I have tried to explain why the settler in the movie, like actual settlers in colonial Australia, and even many contemporary Australians, find it difficult to accept or even understand alternative conceptions of property to the one that they hold. At the end of the film, after the settler, determined to take control of "his" land, has antagonized the *Karagani* people, provoking a violent response, the trooper returns to drive the *Karagani* off their/the settler's land. The trooper, bitter at what he has been ordered to do, confronts the settler:

Trooper: Well, you've got everything your own way, Mr. King. You wanted the blacks off your land and you've forced the government to do the job for you. Well, that's my order – out they go, the lot of them. Where they go, I don't know; I guess nobody cares.

But the movie baulks at such a bleak ending. The trooper moves towards the settler, who sits tending his wounded son.

Trooper: Well, Mr. King?
Settler: Fighting don't get you nowhere, Mr. Ransom. [He looks down at his son.] I found that out. What was it you said to me once about dealing with the natives?
Trooper: I said you could shove 'em out; you could ease them out …

Settler: No, I tried that.
Trooper: Or you could take them in with you. Do you want to try that too?
Settler: Could I ever make them understand?
Trooper: Maybe ... the point is you understand, that's the big thing. It's a start.

It would be comforting to imagine that, armed with an understanding of history, we did not repeat its mistakes, that, like the settler in the movie, we could say, as a society, that we too understand. In this chapter I have tried to contribute to that understanding through a brief history of the concept of property in Australian history. But as a society we, in Australia, continue to be denied those comforts. More importantly, however, the dispossessed continue to bear the burden of their dispossession.[48]

Consequently, we are left with the question of why we should examine the history of property rights as we have done here. The answer is simple. Property rights are not simply topics of academic enquiry, they are what they are: rights. And those rights are disputed, fought over, lost and, hopefully, restored. For this reason I conclude with a statement that many of us are familiar with, but which is too often forgotten in academic scholarship: "The philosophers have only *interpreted* the world in various ways; the point is to *change* it."[49]

Endnotes

1. Sir William Blackstone, *Commentaries on the Laws of England*, [1766] vol. 2, facsimile edition (Chicago: University of Chicago Press, 1979), 2.
2. Stuart Macintyre and Anna Clark, *The History Wars* (Melbourne: Melbourne University Press, 2003).
3. For a good introduction to a vast literature, see Henry Reynolds, *The Law of the Land* (Ringwood: Penguin Books Australia, 1987).
4. Mark McKenna, "Metaphors of Light and Darkness: The Politics of 'Black Armband' History," *Melbourne Journal of Politics*, 25 (1998), 67–84. For a conservative alternative to so-called "black armband" history, see Keith Windschuttle, *The Fabrication of Aboriginal History* (Sydney: Macleay Press, 2002), and for a rebuttal of Windschuttle see Robert Manne, ed., *Whitewash: On Keith Windschuttle's Fabrication of Aboriginal History* (Melbourne: Black Inc., 2003). Conservative attitudes to colonial history in Australia echo the sentiments of Conservatives like J. L.

Granatstein and the Dominion Institute in Canada (see Peter Farrugia, "Navigating the River of History," 9–10, and Robert Wright, "The Way We Were?: History as 'Infotainment' in the Age of *History Television*," 36, both in this volume).

5   *Bitter Springs* (Ealing Studios 1950).
6   John McLaren, "The Canadian Doukhobors and the Land Question: Religious Communalists in a Fee-Simple World," in A. R. Buck, John McLaren and Nancy E. Wright, eds., *Land and Freedom: Law, Property Rights and the British Diaspora* (Aldershot: Ashgate, 2001), 135.
7   See also A. R. Buck, "*Attorney General v. Brown* and the Development of Property Law in Australia," *Australian Property Law Journal*, 2:2 (1994): 128–38.
8   On the crash of the early forties, see Philip McMichael, *Settlers and the Agrarian Question: Foundations of Capitalism in Colonial Australia* (Cambridge: Cambridge University Press, 1984), 167–90. See also Barrie Dyster, "The 1840s Depression Revisited," *Australian Historical Studies*, 25:101 (1993): 589–607; David S. Macmillan, *The Debtor's War: Scottish Capitalists and the Economic Crisis in Australia 1841–1846* (Melbourne: Melbourne University Press, 1960), 1–12; Brian Fitzpatrick, *The British Empire in Australia, 1834–1939*, 2nd ed. (Melbourne: Melbourne University Press, 1949), 71–79.
9   See the minutes of evidence taken before the "Select Committee on Monetary Confusion," *Votes and Proceedings of the New South Wales Legislative Council* 1 (1843), 613–77.
10 A.C.V. Melbourne, *Early Constitutional Development in Australia*, 2nd ed. (St. Lucia: University of Queensland Press, 1963), 269–89. See also David Neal, *The Rule of Law in a Penal Colony: Law and Power in Early New South Wales* (Cambridge: Cambridge University Press, 1991).
11 *Sydney Morning Herald*, 11 August 1843.
12 See Alfred MacHugh, *A Treatise on the Law relating to Bills of Sale, Liens on Crops, Liens on Wool and Stock Mortgages* (Melbourne: 1895), 85–89; R. Else Mitchell, "Liens on Crops and Wool – A Critical Review of the Legislation," *The Australian Law Journal*, 13 (1939): 270–73.
13 *Historical Records of Australia*, first series 24: 57–58.
14 "Select Committee on the Preferable Lien on Wool Act," *Votes and Proceedings of the New South Wales Legislative Council* (1845), 729–30.
15 Ibid., 729.
16 *The Weekly Register*, 9 August 1845.
17 A. R. Buck, "Property, Aristocracy and the Reform of the Land Law in early nineteenth century England," *Journal of Legal History* 16 (1995): 63–93.
18 Richard Denny Urlin, "Are the Laws of Real Property in the Three Parts of the United Kingdom respectively, in their Substance and Tendency, suited to the Present condition of Society? and if not, How should they be Improved?", *Transactions of the National Association for the Promotion of Social Science* (1864), 143.
19 "Select Committee on the Liens on Wool Act," *Votes and Proceedings of the New South Wales Legislative Council* 1 (1845), in evidence 22 August 1845.
20 *The Atlas*, 22 March 1845.
21 9 & 10 Vic., c. 104.
22 For the politics of this Act, see Ken Buckley, "Gipps and the Graziers of New South Wales, 1841–46," in J. J. Eastwood and F. B. Smith, eds., *Historical Studies: Selected Articles* (First Series) (Melbourne: Melbourne University Press, 1967).

23 "The Small Allotment System," *The Guardian: A Weekly Journal of Politics, Commerce, Agriculture, Literature, Science and Arts, for the Middle and Working Classes of New South Wales*, 1 (1844), 162.
24 "Appropriation of Crown Lands: Recommended in connection with a system of parochial colonisation," *Colonial Magazine* 1 (1842), 472.
25 *The Citizen*, 9 January 1847.
26 Gideon Scott Lang, *Land and Labour in Australia* (Melbourne, 1845), 14. Quoted in Michael Roe, *Quest for Authority in Eastern Australia 1835–1851* (Melbourne: Melbourne University Press, 1965), 61.
27 Sir Alfred Stephen, *Speech on the Second Reading of the Bill to Amend the Electoral Law* (Sydney, 1858), 21.
28 Our success in addressing environmental issues might suggest otherwise; see Stephen Haller, "Predictions of Global Catastrophe: Just Another Chicken Little?" in this volume.
29 *Empire*, 11 January 1860.
30 Italics in original.
31 "Robert Lowe to Thomas Mitchell, 1 April 1851," *Sir Thomas Mitchell Papers*, vol. 5, 1850–57, Mitchell Library A294.
32 *Historical Records of Australia*, series 1, XXII, 667.
33 Quoted in C. J. King, *An Outline of Closer Settlement in New South Wales* (Sydney: Government Printer, n.d), 59.
34 See further, Nancy E. Wright and A. R. Buck, "Property Rights and the Discourse of Improvement in Colonial New South Wales" in Buck, McLaren and Wright, eds., *Land and Freedom*, 103–16.
35 *Sydney Morning Herald*, 1 November 1860.
36 "Select Committee on the Landed Property in Cases of Intestacy Bill," *Votes and Proceedings of the New South Wales Legislative Assembly* 1 (1858), 32, in evidence. 23 July 1858.
37 Ibid., vol. 1, 22.
38 Ibid., vol. 1, 33.
39 *Sydney Morning Herald*, 13 September 1843.
40 "Select Committee on the Landed Property in Cases of Intestacy Bill," *Votes and Proceedings of the New South Wales Legislative Assembly* 1 (1858), 42.
41 "Select Committee on the Present State of the Colony," *Votes and Proceedings of the New South Wales Legislative Assembly*, 3 (1865–66), 637.
42 Ibid., vol. 3, 657.
43 *Solicitor's Journal*, 19 January 1861.
44 *Sydney Morning Herald*, 28 August 1857.
45 John Stuart Mill, *The Principles of Political Economy* (Harmondsworth: Penguin, 1985), 367.
46 On "the poor man" as a figure of political rhetoric, see A. R. Buck, "'The Poor Man': Rhetoric and Political Culture in mid-nineteenth century New South Wales," *Australian Journal of Politics and History* 42:2 (1996): 203–19.
47 *Empire*, 11 January 1860.
48 A. R. Buck, "'Strangers in their own land': Capitalism, Dispossession and the Law," in Buck, McLaren and Wright, eds., *Land and Freedom*.
49 Karl Marx, *Theses on Feuerbach* [1845] in Marx and Engels, *Collected Works*, vol. 5 (London: Lawrence & Wishart, 1976), 5.

Bibliography

Blackstone, Sir William. *Commentaries on the Laws of England.* [1766] vol. 2. Facsimile ed. Chicago: University of Chicago Press, 1979.

Buck, A. R. *"Attorney General v. Brown* and the Development of Property Law in Australia." *Australian Property Law Journal* 2:2 (1994): 128–38.

———. "Property, Aristocracy and the Reform of the Land Law in early nineteenth century England." *Journal of Legal History* 16 (1995): 63–93.

———. "'The Poor Man': Rhetoric and Political Culture in mid-nineteenth century New South Wales." *The Australian Journal of Politics and History* 42:2 (1996): 203–19.

Buck, A. R., John McLaren, and Nancy Wright, eds. *Land and Freedom: Law, Property Rights and the British Diaspora.* Aldershot: Ashgate, 2001.

Dyster, Barrie. "The 1840s Depression Revisited." *Australian Historical Studies* 25:101 (1993): 589–607.

Empire, 11 January 1860.

Fitzpatrick, Brian. *The British Empire in Australia, 1834–1939.* 2nd ed. Melbourne: Melbourne University Press, 1949.

Historical Records of Australia, 1st series.

MacHugh, Alfred. *A Treatise on the Law relating to Bills of Sale, Liens on Crops, Liens on Wool and Stock Mortgages.* Melbourne: 1895.

Macintyre, Stuart, and Anna Clark. *The History Wars.* Melbourne: Melbourne University Press, 2003.

Macmillan, David S. *The Debtor's War: Scottish Capitalists and the Economic Crisis in Australia 1841–1846.* Melbourne: Melbourne University Press, 1960.

Manne, Robert, ed. *Whitewash: On Keith Windschuttle's Fabrication of Aboriginal History.* Melbourne: Black Inc., 2003.

Marx, Karl. *Theses on Feuerbach* [1845]. In Marx and Engels, *Collected Works,* vol. 5. London: Lawrence & Wishart, 1976.

McKenna, Mark. "Metaphors of Light and Darkness: The Politics of 'Black Armband' History," *Melbourne Journal of Politics* 25 (1998): 67–84.

McMichael, Philip. *Settlers and the Agrarian Question: Foundations of Capitalism in Colonial Australia.* Cambridge: Cambridge University Press, 1984.

Melbourne, A. C. V. *Early Constitutional Development in Australia.* 2nd ed. St. Lucia: University of Queensland Press, 1963.

Mill, John Stuart. *The Principles of Political Economy.* Harmondsworth: Penguin, 1985.

Mitchell, R. Else. "Liens on Crops and Wool – A Critical Review of the Legislation." *The Australian Law Journal* 13 (1939): 270–73.

Neal, David. *The Rule of Law in a Penal Colony: Law and Power in Early New South Wales.* Cambridge: Cambridge University Press, 1991.

Reynolds, Henry. *The Law of the Land.* Ringwood: Penguin Books Australia, 1987.

"Select Committee on Monetary Confusion." *Votes and Proceedings of the New South Wales Legislative Council* 1.

"Select Committee on the Landed Property in Cases of Intestacy Bill." *Votes and Proceedings of the New South Wales Legislative Assembly* 1.

"Select Committee on the Preferable Lien on Wool Act." *Votes and Proceedings of the New South Wales Legislative Council.*

"Select Committee on the Present State of the Colony." *Votes and Proceedings of the New South Wales Legislative Assembly,* 3.

Solicitor's Journal, 19 January 1861.
Sydney Morning Herald, 11 August 1843, 28 August 1857.
The Weekly Register, 9 August 1845.
Windschuttle, Keith. *The Fabrication of Aboriginal History*. Sydney: Macleay Press, 2002.

III

Past, Present and Future Tense: How Do We Own the Past?

"You must always know the past, for there is no real Was, there is only Is."
– William Faulkner

"History will be kind to me for I intend to write it."
– Sir Winston Churchill

6

Historical Fictions: The Invention of Historical Events for Political Purposes

JOHN S. HILL

¶ Introduction

It can be argued that truth is closely bound up with, rather than clearly separated from, falsehood. Fictions of various sorts play an important role in daily life. Santa Claus, daylight-savings time, art students' copies of originals all offer examples.[1] In contrast to these honest fictions, some fictions are explicitly intended to mislead. Forgeries, frauds, impersonations, and myths involve the creation of artifacts by someone hoping to deceive someone else. Greed in some form provides the most common motive. However, another motive for forgery is the desire to advance a cause or ideology. These politically grounded fictions tend to vary by type with the historical period or subject.

Christianity has been rich in examples. Early Christians produced belated additions to the New Testament and remorseful letters from Pontius Pilate. The medieval Church sought to bolster its position against lay rulers with the Donation of Constantine and the "False Decretals."

Copyist monks in medieval monasteries sometimes took time off from preserving the past to produce it out of whole vellum. More recently, the nineteenth century saw the rise of nationalism, which produced its share of forgeries. Thus, the "Protocols of the Learned Elders of Zion" emerged from the Tsarist secret police in order to justify persecution of the Jews.

Each of these "historical fictions" is an artifact of a particular moment. Careful historical consideration of these fabrications can reveal the preoccupations of those engaged in the deception.[2] The examination of German and American retrospective accounts of how their countries became involved in the First World War clearly provides two of the more fascinating examples of "historical fictions" being created and propagated.

¶ The German Version of the Origins of the First World War: "Patriotic Self-Censorship"

Although the weight of informed historical judgement now finds that Germany did bring on the First World War "through a combination of miscalculation and intent," the inter-war German governments sought to shape historical evidence in order to exculpate Germany and to provide a basis for revision of the Treaty of Versailles in favour of Germany. In the words of one recent student of the German historical enterprise:

> By selectively editing documentary collections, suppressing honest scholarship, subsidizing pseudo-scholarship, underwriting mass propaganda, and overseeing the export of this propaganda especially to Britain, France, and the United States, the patriotic self-censors in Berlin exerted a powerful influence on public and elite opinion in Germany and, to a lesser extent, outside Germany. Their efforts polluted historical understanding both at home and abroad well into the post-1945 period.[3]

From the moment the First World War broke out, observers recognized that responsibility for the war would carry heavy political implications. In Germany, defeat in 1918 proved highly traumatic. Conservative and military leaders refused to accept responsibility for having launched, continued, and lost the war. They determined to throw the blame for defeat on the republicans who were ushered in to clean up the mess at the last moment. The loss of territory, the limitations on political independence, and the high nominal value of the monetary reparations forced on Germany by the peace treaty all compounded the question of primary responsibility for the war. Given the dual hostility to democratic government and the ambition for territorial expansion among the traditional elites in German society, the question of responsibility for the lost war thus had vital importance for domestic politics and international relations.

It should surprise no one that historical evidence became contested. The German left first seized the initiative. On 23 November 1918 the revolutionary government of Bavaria published excerpts from official documents that were intended to demonstrate the guilt of "a small horde of mad Prussian military men," the class enemies of the new regime. On 9 December 1918 the revolutionary government in Berlin assigned Socialist Karl Kautsky to publish a selection of key documents on the July 1914 crisis with much the same purpose in mind.[4]

Conservatives were equally quick to appreciate the importance of the historical record. Although the imperial regime had been displaced by a republic, the old imperial officials remained at their posts. Their initial concern was to place Germany in as advantageous a position as possible in the upcoming peace negotiations with the victorious Allies. To this end, the Foreign Ministry organized an effort to demonstrate that "guilt" for the war had to be shared broadly among the belligerents, rather than assigned narrowly to Germany. At the end of 1918 the Foreign Ministry created an entity which would become the "War Guilt Section" of the Ministry. Its purpose was to coordinate the campaign against the Versailles treaty's historical legitimacy. In January 1919 it was agreed that documentary collections should demonstrate that Germany had merely been responding to the danger of "encirclement" by hostile states. In March 1919 Kautsky's finished report outraged government officials, who blocked further access to the archives and recalled all the secret documents in his possession. Still, they were unable to prevent the publication of his research later in the year.[5]

The Germans were soon disabused of their notion that the Paris peace conference would involve negotiations. On 7 May 1919 the Allied representatives presented a finished draft of the treaty to the German officials for comment, not for negotiation. The German diplomats responded with a "White Book" built around a memorandum exculpating Germany and signed by four eminent scholars, though it was probably written by a Foreign Ministry official.[6] On 28 June 1919 – despite their opposition to the version of events enshrined in the treaty – the Germans were forced to sign. Once the ink was dry on the pact, however, the foremost goal of German diplomacy became its overthrow. The sustained effort to undermine the validity of Article 231, the "war-guilt clause" of the Treaty of Versailles, became a central element in this effort.[7]

To accomplish this goal it became essential to discredit the treaty in the eyes of audiences at home and abroad. Fearing that Kautsky's selection of documents would reveal too much about Germany's responsibility for the war, on 21 July 1919 a more conservative government authorized the creation of another documentary collection by more politically reliable scholars.[8] As German Chancellor Joseph Wirth told a Foreign Ministry official in November 1921, to prepare the ground for criticism of the Versailles Treaty by the "intelligentsia of the enemy countries ... a serious scientifically grounded program of enlightenment as well as objective discussions between German and foreign personalities is to be encouraged in every way, especially through the screening and publication of historical materials and the release of new sources."[9] This collection became the famous forty-volume *Die Grosse Politik der Europaischen Kabinette, 1871–1914*, which was published between 1922 and 1927.[10]

Several post-1945 scholars with access to fuller records have demonstrated that *Die Grosse Politik* was published under abusive conditions.[11] Elements of published documents were falsified or completely ignored; the Kaiser's marginal remarks on documents he read were entirely left out; records of important events were not included and cannot now be found; and the papers of key officials were often returned to the author as "private papers." Once publication of the series had been completed, access to the Foreign Ministry archives was severely restricted. Still, despite its many hidden failings, *Die Grosse Politik* became a gold mine for diplomatic historians of the inter-war period. As the first of the great documentary collections, it "established an early dependence of all students of prewar diplomacy on German materials."[12]

The benefits of this manipulation of historical evidence were soon evident. At its first breath the Treaty of Versailles had failed to satisfy the liberal ambitions of many scholars and they made known their dissatisfaction in print before the treaty had even been signed.¹³ Impressed by the evidence offered by a former Serb diplomat secretly in the pay of the "War Guilt Section" of the German Foreign Ministry, English Radical author E. D. Morel attacked the concept of German war guilt in a series of books published between 1920 and 1922. By 1928 historian G. P. Gooch, one of the editors of the British collection of documents published in response to *Die Grosse Politik*, could maintain that "neither the British nor the German Government or people desired a world war" in 1914.¹⁴ Early on, Gooch had denounced the Versailles Treaty as "essentially a French peace – a Clemenceau peace." In his work, *Recent Revelations of European Diplomacy* he argued that German chancellor Theobald von Bethmann-Hollweg possessed an "unsullied character and love of peace," that the Kaiser had wanted only the "prompt and exemplary punishment of a semi-savage regicide State," that Russian diplomacy had been "crazy," and that the war sprang from the "international anarchy" in which diplomacy had been conducted. Two years later he described the Versailles Treaty as "ruinous" for German democracy and of "crushing severity.¹⁵ "That same year Gooch was one of the signers of a public "Appeal to Conscience" that denounced the "war-guilt clause" in the Versailles Treaty.¹⁶ Thus, in 1925, Gilbert Murray was probably engaging only in the moderate overstatement required by courtesy when he told a German correspondent that "hardly any reasonable person in England continues to talk of Germany as solely responsible for the war."¹⁷

A similarly rapid evolution of opinion took place across the Atlantic. The analogous figure to Gooch in the United States was the diplomatic historian Sidney Bradshaw Fay. Soon after reading Kautsky's selection of documents, Fay announced in the pages of the *American Historical Review* that the documents "clear the German government of the charge that it deliberately plotted or wanted war."¹⁸ Fay then became the *American Historical Review*'s chief reviewer of the collections of European diplomatic documents published after the war. His evaluations demonstrate the powerful hold that *Die Grosse Politik* came to exercise over his thinking.

In his review of the first six volumes of documents, covering the period 1871 to 1890, Fay stated that "Such publication of recent diplomatic secrets which have usually been so jealously guarded in the archives is almost unique in history. It offers a mine of wealth to the historian, and will do much to throw light on dark places and to correct mistaken notions which are current." He noted that the editors "declare that no documents of importance have been concealed. We are inclined to believe, judging by the internal evidence and by what we know already from the works of [other authors], that their declaration is honest and true."[19] A year and a half later, Fay felt equally strongly about the authenticity and completeness of the documents coming from the Caprivi and Hohenloe periods. He believed that the German editors "want to lay bare the whole truth in order to furnish the basis for a correct and just appreciation of Germany's part in European politics, in the hopes that it will have a healing and conciliatory influence in the future."[20] By the time he reviewed the third and fourth batches of documents, Fay no longer felt it necessary to speak of the genuineness of the material, referring simply to "this invaluable collection of documents."[21]

Fay came to regard *Die Grosse Politik* as the documentary gold standard against which other series were measured. His assessment of one collection of British documents was that it "supplements *Die Grosse Politik*, but does not add greatly to what we already know from it, from Tardieu's book and from other sources." He described a subsequent volume as "run[ing] parallel to, and supplement[ing], from the British point of view, material in ... *Die Grosse Politik*." Elsewhere, Fay referred to "the monumental collection of secret archival material recently published in *Die Grosse Politik*" and, commenting this time on a French collection of documents, argued that it "tends to confirm what we already know from the *Livres Jaunes*, the *Livre Noir, Die Grosse Politik* and the first volume of Poincaré's memoirs."[22] In his review of the first volume of British documents he opened with praise for the *Grosse Politik*: "The editors have wisely followed the German example of grouping the documents topically rather than in a strict chronological arrangement." Fay closed the review in the same fashion: "On most questions these British Documents are much less complete and voluminous than the *Grosse Politik*."[23] Summing up after the publication of the final volumes, Fay remarked that *Die Grosse Politik* "is a mine from which students will get the ore from which to fashion golden monographs."[24]

Die Grosse Politik exerted enormous influence over American historians analysing European international relations. As Fay pointed out in 1924:

It was the hope of the editors that it would be used to throw light on the dark diplomatic past. They need have had no fears that it would not be used. Already scores of German magazine articles, monographs, and big books, based on these documents have begun to pour from the press. Even in America they have also been turned to account in a number of excellent studies.

He went on to cite books and articles by William L. Langer, Raymond Sontag and Bernadotte Schmitt among others.[25]

In 1928 came the crowning achievement for Fay when he followed up his earlier analysis with a comprehensive study that relied heavily on the published German documents entitled *The Origins of the World War*. In this massive work Fay handed out responsibility for the war to all of the parties concerned and effectively absolved the Germans of sole guilt. In the opinion of the reviewer in the *American Historical Review*, Fay had demonstrated that "the warlike initiative was Austria's and that Germany's part in their joint policy was always secondary and sometimes reluctant."[26] The American Historical Association appeared to ratify the reviewer's judgement that "No other work has yet appeared in English, French or German which is at once so comprehensive, authoritative, impartial and well proportioned" by awarding the book the George Louis Beer Prize. In 1929 Fay accepted a position in the history department at Harvard University, no doubt at least in part on the basis of the positive critical response to *The Origins of the World War*.

Fay's rapid ascent in the profession owed much to his great ability as a historian, but the availability of the German documents also played an important role. The equivalent British and French collections only began to appear as Fay wound up the research for his study. He admired the "meticulous and impartial editing" work done by G. P. Gooch and Harold Temperley in editing the British documents, which he labelled a "rich mine of diplomatic material."[27] Fay similarly lauded the work of the team led by Pierre Renouvin that was editing the French documents for their "clarity, grasp, and judiciousness."[28] However, the new collections did nothing to shake his confidence in *Die Grosse Politik*.

Indeed, Fay was blind to small signs that cast doubt on the reliability of the German documents. He noted in a 1928 review that the British editors had rejected "the German practice of appending abundant foot-notes which, though very convenient and helpful to the historian, have been regarded as having a propagandist tendency."[29] He does not seem to have taken the possibility of propagandistic editing very seriously, explaining away discrepancies between the two collections. Referring in the same review to a reported offer by Joseph Chamberlain of an Anglo-German defensive treaty, Fay remarks: "This we know from the *Grosse Politik*. But the editors of the British Documents say that they find no references to this Chamberlain offer of 1898.... This extraordinary fact that the British archives contain no mention of this Chamberlain proposal makes it seem likely that it was his own personal venture rather than an official move on the part of the British Cabinet."[30] Similarly, he offhandedly remarks of British Foreign Secretary Lord Grey's actions in one crisis that he "contributed more in this direction than one would gather from the documents in *Die Grosse Politik*."[31]

Fay's indisposition to suspect the editors of *Die Grosse Politik* probably sprang from cultural assumptions rooted in his pre-war upbringing. On the one hand, he believed that a fundamental honesty prevailed among the Western European elites who made national policy. In a 1931 review of two collections of Austrian and Serbian documents Fay revealed his assumptions. The "Balkan mentality and ethical standards were quite different from those obtaining generally in Western Europe – forgeries and political murders were accepted by the Balkan Slavs as more or less legitimate and natural political weapons to which otherwise honourable men might properly resort.... Murders like that of King Alexander in 1903, ... met with no such moral indignation in Belgrade or Sofia as in Berlin, Paris, or London."[32] Deceitful, underhanded behaviour only prevailed outside the core of Western Europe. On the other hand, historians, as the bearers of a particular commitment to truth, formed an elite within an elite. Thus, Fay noted that the "historical specialists are a small minority" on the commission supervising the editing of the French documents, "but it augurs well for the reliability of the work that such a sound scholar as M. Renouvin is taking a leading part in the selection of material."[33] For Fay, the "reputation of the editors [of the Austrian documents] as conscientious scholars is a guarantee, fully justified by an examination of their work, of the honesty and care with which the task of selection and editing has been done."[34]

Only belatedly did Fay recognize the possibility of biased editing and then he did not apply the recognition to either the German documents or the integrity of professional historians. In a 1936 review of one of the French volumes dealing with the 1905 Moroccan crisis he noted that "an official *Livre Jaune* on this subject was published in the fall of 1905. As an interesting side light on the way it was 'edited' by M. Paléologue, then political director at the Quai d'Orsay, it may be noted that he made a special trip to Berlin to give the French ambassador 'explanations' as to what was to be included in the *Livre Jaune*; and that all the documents now printed in the present volume were omitted from the *Livre Jaune*, except two which are reprinted without change and fifteen which were largely suppressed, reworded, or in one case shifted and annexed to a dispatch of a different date."[35] In a 1937 review of another volume of the French documents Fay returned to the subject at greater length, suggesting:

> The biggest revelation in Volume XI is the evidence of the large extent to which documents were "doctored" in the famous French Yellow Book of 1914. The compiler of this propagandist publication ... saw fit ... to alter nearly half the documents – some 70 out of 159 – in order to change the meaning or implication in more or less important ways. Telegrams of the highest importance ... were omitted completely. In many cases inconvenient sentences and paragraphs were deleted before the mutilated document was published in the Yellow Book. In other cases sentences and paragraphs made up out of whole cloth were inserted. Dates were changed and the sequence of documents altered. Space forbids an enumeration of these astounding alterations.... Such were some of the Yellow Book's contributions to the legends of "war guilt."[36]

While by the mid-1930s Fay had come to recognize the possibility that documentary editing might be subordinated to political necessity in a crisis situation, he failed to recognize that German leaders might have felt themselves to be in just such a situation when they launched *Die Grosse Politik*. Moreover, the deceptive editing of the French documents had been perpetrated by non-historians and revealed by professional historians. Thus, he probably saw the revelations regarding the French documents as a confirmation of his trust in the German documents.

Fay's *Origins of the World War* would go on to become the standard account of how the First World War originated.[37] It was not until the pioneering work of Fritz Fischer in the 1960s that Fay's thesis of universal guilt for the outbreak of war was challenged.[38] This prevailing view of the war's roots influenced, not only views on international relations prior to 1914, but also attitudes with respect to the legitimacy of the Treaty of Versailles and, by implication, attitudes to the Nazis, who loudly proclaimed the treaty's moral bankruptcy. Indeed, it is impossible to find many better examples of how a consciously fabricated historical myth influenced subsequent historiography.

¶ The American View of the Origins of the First World War: The "Merchants of Death" Thesis and the Nye Committee

The United States entered the First World War in April 1917 for a combination of reasons. Cultural affinity for Britain, rising anger over the tactic of submarine warfare used by Germany, concern about German territorial ambitions beyond Europe, the awakening sense of America's role in international affairs, and the identification of future American prosperity with the triumph of the anti-German coalition all combined to draw the United States into the conflict.[39] However, a change of outlook quickly took place. First, the difficult economic situation facing rural and small town "old stock" Americans after the First World War revived their long-standing hostility to urban, industrial America, home to banks, railroads and the heavy industries that dominated national economic policy. Second, the high human cost of the war did not seem to bring about the proportionate level of positive change either politically or economically.

The Senate Munitions Investigation, popularly known as the Nye Committee after its chairman, Senator Gerald Nye of North Dakota, sprang from the convergence of these forces. Wartime pacifist groups had attacked the munitions makers and bankers for bringing on the war and demanded a congressional investigation to prove the charges. Such demands had never made much headway in a country enthusiastic for war or in the comparatively tranquil 1920s. But when Japan seized Manchuria, fears of war revived and new demands for an investigation began to be made. These demands found a champion in Senator Nye. In February 1934 he won approval for a Senate investigation of the munitions industry.[40]

Nye brought to his investigation of the munitions industry a well-established set of beliefs about the occult power of Eastern business and finance. He was a Midwesterner who had spent most of his life before the Senate in the atmosphere of small-town newspapers that observed a long crisis for American farmers at close hand. In the last decade of the nineteenth century American farmers had been haunted by the ghost of a "lost agrarian Eden." In 1892, the year of Nye's birth, the Populist Party had lashed out against "capitalists, corporations, national banks, rings, trusts, watered stock, the demonetization of silver and the oppression of the usurers," declaring that a "vast conspiracy against mankind has been organized on two continents and it is rapidly taking possession of the world."[41] At the same time, in North Dakota and Minnesota there arose the National Non-Partisan League, which advocated state ownership of grain shipping and storage facilities, and government financial assistance to farmers in order to break the power of the urban railroads, elevator companies, and banks. As editor and owner of several small papers, Nye had strongly endorsed the Non-Partisan League.[42]

As a senator Nye built a reputation for investigating the influence of money on politics and it seemed to pay political dividends. Appointed to the Senate in 1925 to fill out a term, Nye won election in his own right in November 1926. From the first, Nye's discourse bore a marked resemblance to the rural radical critique of the Populists and the Non-Partisan League. On 23 January 1926, in his first speech to the Senate, he declared that the "money power reigns supreme, is now known as the international banker, has quite thoroughly conquered in America, has wealth aggregated in a few hands, and is now, perhaps, seeking new fields to invade and to mass the wealth, not of one lone nation, but the nations of all the world."[43] During the Teapot Dome scandal – in which he gained considerable notoriety – Nye described the conspiracy, in language meant to evoke Lincoln's Gettysburg Address, as having been "conceived in darkness and selfishness and dedicated to the proposition that the cause of privilege and the privileged must be served."[44] Nye's work only confirmed his prior beliefs about the power of money in politics. His investigations also suited his constituents. As a result, Nye won re-election to the Senate in November 1932 by a landslide.

Nye was hardly alone in his predisposition to convict businessmen and bankers of skullduggery. His investigation parallelled campaigns against the "interests" by Father Coughlin and Huey Long.[45] Nye found his own niche with the investigation of the "merchants of death." In March 1934 important journals of opinion on both left and right took up the cause of controlling the munitions industry; *Fortune* published a much-read article, "Arms and the Men" and the *New Republic* published the briefer but more direct "Hucksters of Death." While these stories concentrated on the European arms producers, they set the stage for an examination of the American munitions industry. Nye combined his own resolution with the one championed by Arthur Vandenberg to eliminate war profits. The new combined resolution was approved by the entire Senate on 12 April 1934. The tide of publicity and accusation kept running during 1934. Book-length treatments of the role of munitions makers in politics came out on the heels of these first forays. Among the most notable of these was *Merchants of Death* by H. C. Engelbrecht and F. C. Hanighen.[46]

Nye's Senate Munitions Investigating Committee held highly publicized hearings from September 1934 to February 1936.[47] From the beginning of the investigation Nye held to essentially the same line of analysis he had laid out earlier. On 15 January 1935 the *Washington Post* reminded its readers that it was the sixth anniversary of Senate approval of the Kellogg-Briand Pact "outlawing" war. Nye took the occasion to argue that the munitions industry "has played with people and with the fate of nations as men play with checkers upon a checkerboard."[48] Later that same year he stated that "When Americans went into the fray [in 1917–18], they little thought that they were there and fighting to save the skins of American bankers who had bet too boldly on the outcome of the war and had two billions of dollars of loans to the Allies in jeopardy."[49]

The voluminous evidence compiled by the committee completely invalidated the thesis that America had gone to war in 1917 through the machinations of bankers and arms dealers.[50] Nevertheless, after the investigation had been completed, Nye continued to hold to the same line of argument and to favour the same remedies that he had already elaborated before the investigation began. On 5 June 1936 another committee report lamented Woodrow Wilson's inability to resist the forces of militarism in America's slide toward war in 1917, asserting that "President Wilson ... was caught up in a situation created largely by the profit-making interests in the United States, and such interests spread to nearly everybody in the country." On 18 January 1937 Nye told a national radio audience that:

The discretionary kind of [neutrality] policy had its trial back in 1914–1915. Then our neutrality policy was left quite wholly at the discretion of the President. He was a strong President too. His determination to stay out of Europe's war is well recognized. But our neutrality crumbled because of the chance given selfish interests to bring to bear such pressure as no man could possibly stand up under. Step by step this pressure broke down our policy of neutrality then. We ought never again leave a President up against such odds as Woodrow Wilson found in his path in those days.[51]

Only a policy of strict neutrality with no room for presidential discretion could prevent the "merchants of death" from exercising their evil influence once again.

Nye did show a fitful caution. On 9 February 1936 he claimed that "It would not be fair to say that the House of Morgan took us to war to save their investment in the Allies, but the record of facts makes it altogether fair to say that these bankers were in the heart and centre of a system that made our going to war inevitable."[52] In July 1939 Nye told the Senate that "No member of the Munitions Committee to my knowledge has ever contended that it was munitions makers who took us to war." However, he stuck by the Committee's determination that "it was the war trade and the war boom, shared in by many more than the munitions makers, that played the primary part" in bringing the United States into World War I.[53]

What impact did the Nye hearings have on popular understanding of America's intervention in the First World War? Each one of the Nye Committee's seven reports were printed and widely distributed. Read or unread, these reports formed the Bible of the neutralist/pacifist movement in the later 1930s.[54] Popular media versions of the committee reports have tended to leave out the qualifications and to emphasize the role of the "merchants of death." This version of the Nye Committee's findings made a strong impression on a country predisposed to question the wisdom of American participation in the last war and suspicious of the machinations of bankers and industrialists in the midst of the

Depression. "Mass Murderers, in Person," proclaimed the *New Republic* after the first round of hearings.[55] An editorial in the *Philadelphia Record* in 1935 was typical in declaring that "We were pulled into the World War because American bankers and American manufacturers tried to profit from the world holocaust." In January 1936 an editorial in *America* damned the "insidious wiles of the extreme capitalist classes who with their usual folly see in war only an opportunity to revive business," a charge with real meaning in the midst of the Depression.[56]

Nye was widely perceived as one of the most vigilant opponents of those who would entangle America in foreign affairs. In the increasingly isolationist 1930s his reputation grew as the international situation deteriorated. On 16 February 1936, Nye received the Cardinal Newman Award from the Cardinal Newman Foundation at the University of Illinois. The citation lauded him for "investigation of financial interests in drawing this country into the World War" and declared that "Senator Nye presents a refreshing example of a public servant who penetrates beyond current shibboleths and party labels and brings before the eyes of the great masses of our citizens the hidden factors which make for war and menace the peace of the world."[57]

Historian Charles A. Beard also helped disseminate the beliefs of the isolationists regarding the economic origins of American intervention in 1917. His 1936 book, *The Devil Theory of War*, based much of its analysis on the evidence generated by the Nye Committee.[58] Although Beard began by arguing that society as a whole, and not a few bankers and statesmen, had led America into war in 1917, he still concluded that neutrality legislation was essential "to prevent the bankers and politicians from guiding the nation into calamity as in 1914–17."[59] Beard then supported Nye in his successful 1938 re-election campaign.

The Nye Committee's findings helped further arouse the forces of isolationism. Beginning in late June 1935, the Roosevelt administration waged a determined struggle to block the mandatory, non-discretionary legislation favoured by Nye and his colleagues. They made some headway, but the forces favouring strict neutrality in the country were powerful and the White House had to accept temporary compromise legislation in August 1935. This legislation was renewed in March 1936 and made permanent in May 1937. The *New York Herald Tribune* captured the essence of the neutrality legislation by suggesting that it should have been called "an act to preserve the United States from intervention in the war of 1914–18."[60]

¶ Conclusion

What lessons can we derive from these two attempts to shape the interpretation of how two countries entered the First World War? One thing that is abundantly clear is that both cases speak to the issue of "collective memory." In the 1920s the French sociologist Maurice Halbwachs advanced the idea of a "collective memory" of specific events whose shifting content and the meaning attributed to the event reflected the changing preoccupations of those doing the remembering. "Collective memory" is an artifact of a particular period as much as is a document. The "collective memory" of an event is not the same thing as the "history" of an event. Halbwachs postulated that "memory" differed from "history" in the tendency of the former to simplify, to de-contextualize, and to render eternal some past event. Conversely, history is scholarly, the product of a body of knowledge, adopts a critical stance, and claims to encompass all forms of human activity.[61]

Halbwachs' theories have gained a new currency in the past several decades and, to some extent, historians of memory stand on common ground. How we think about ourselves is a function, in part, of the stories we have to tell about ourselves. Thus, historians may study "memory" like any other historical experience, by tracing how and why people have chosen to represent aspects of the past. The aim of memory is to simplify in the interest of clarity and accessibility; it relates episodes of the past to contemporary concerns – often about the self-definition of communities – and centres on evocative symbols. However, different groups within society may construct a memory of an event that differs not only from the memory constructed by other groups, but also from the "dominant" or officially sanctioned memory. Thus, there can be both "official" and "dissident" memories.[62]

Scholars have disagreed on how to implement these insights. Broadly speaking, two strands of thought may be discerned on the subject of "collective memory." On the one hand stand the Freudians. They see some events as "traumatic" – too intense to elicit a response at the moment

– and "repressed." Repression inevitably gives rise to the "return of the repressed" as the traumatic memories boil over in surprising places and at unexpected times. Henry Rousso's examination of the French memory of German occupation and French collaboration from 1940 to 1944 offers a good representation of the Freudian interpretation.[63]

Dismissing Freudian explanations based on "trauma" and "repression," Peter Novick argues that people reflect on the historical significance of events central to their own experience soon after they occur. The gradual fading of events in popular awareness is not due to repression necessarily but to increasing distance between the events in question and those who experienced them.[64] Novick, who applies Halbwachs' idea to the American memory of the Holocaust, finds it puzzling that American interest in the Holocaust arose at all and notes that, when it did arise, it followed the opposite trajectory.[65] Novick concludes that there was silence about the Holocaust in postwar America because of its irrelevance to the United States. Americans had not caused it or perpetrated it; Jews constituted only a tiny portion of the American population and were preoccupied with their integration into a larger society; and regnant cultural ideals emphasized the resilient, taciturn survivor while disparaging the victim. By the 1970s, however, a victim culture had shouldered aside the victor culture of the post-war years; American Jewry seemed threatened by the loss of a common identity thanks to the success of earlier efforts at integration; and the Holocaust could be variously interpreted as providing "lessons" for both the left and right in American politics.[66] Thus, both the forgetting and the remembering of the Holocaust by Americans reflected a changing cultural context.

While eschewing the Halbwachian theory, Paul Cohen makes a similar argument to that of Novick with regard to the shifting interpretations of the anti-foreign Boxer Rebellion in China. Cohen takes the different interpretations of the Boxer Rebellion as expressions of the changing concerns of the interpreters at crucial moments in Chinese history. In the wake of the rebellion, Chinese cultural critics regarded the rebels with some ambiguity. Although they commonly derided the Boxers as a characteristic expression of a primitive China that had to change, they shared the hostility to foreign imperialism. Throughout the 1920s the rising power of Chinese nationalism led some people to interpret the Boxers in a far more positive light, while others sought to tar nationalism with the Boxer brush. During the Cultural Revolution the Boxers were re-interpreted once again. The Chinese Communist government imposed a celebration of the Boxers as enemies of both imperialist foreigners and their purported domestic allies.[67]

The great difficulty in attempting to apply the Freudian approach is the very limited number of historical experiences that can be labelled as authentically "traumatic" and subject to "repression." No historical event is an unmixed blessing, yet people manage to absorb most experiences without repressing them. Many of these events can enter into some form of accessible collective memory. Far more useful is Paul Cohen's argument that what survives in the collective memory are the events that continue to resonate with following generations.[68] As Cohen and Novick demonstrate, memory can survive, be re-configured, and be invoked to serve changing collective needs. Inter-war America offers several good examples of this process in the reception of the revisionist historical analysis of Sidney Bradshaw Fay and the investigative discoveries of Gerald Nye. Fay "revealed" that the sole guilt assigned to Germany by wartime propaganda and the Versailles Treaty had no basis in the documentary record. This view conformed to and confirmed the prevailing disillusionment with America's first major foray into international affairs. It also accorded well with the reaction against Woodrow Wilson's decade of black-and-white idealism. Gerald Nye "revealed" that bankers and industrialists exerted an undue influence in the halls of government. This view conformed to – while simultaneously confirming – the prevailing hostility to businessmen when the "New Era" of the Republican 1920s gave way to the "Hard Times" of the 1930s. In both cases, the First World War served as a crucial point of reference for those seeking to navigate a course for America in a troubled new century.

Yet none of the scholars who have considered the problem of "collective memory" have considered the problem of fraudulent efforts to shape or impose memories. Scholarly knowledge is a central pillar of modern democracies. But what if the knowledge is false, not merely erroneous, but knowingly misrepresented to serve some political end?

In this regard, the cases studied in this essay suggest several useful lessons. First, control of the archives matters. The German government shaped future historiography by selective publication of a documentary record before any other country. Similarly, the Nye Committee fought for access to previously closed public and private archives in order to find the material needed to support its thesis. Those who would seek to concoct a particular view of any given historical event must exercise control of the archival material in order to bolster the credibility of their work in the public eye and to prevent access to documents on the part of those who do not subscribe to their views.[69]

Second, the "historical fictions" briefly sketched above were rooted in social and political power struggles. They were not the products of individual actors. These "lessons of history" were created as elements in those struggles. Sometimes the interpretation of history can be more politically charged than at other times. The inter-war years were such a time because the traumatic effect of historical events left people more highly sensitized to historical explanations. Inter-war German elites deployed their campaign against the "war guilt" clause of the Versailles Treaty as a means of regaining freedom of manoeuvre in international affairs. Given Wilhelmine Germany's externalization of domestic tensions and the failure of the Weimar Republic to purge itself of anti-democratic forces, the assault on historical truth had important implications for domestic political struggles as well. In the United States, the Nye Committee essentially rehearsed a long-standing agrarian critique of Eastern industry and finance. Nye's investigation added to the already strong distrust of involvement in international affairs at a moment when the United States had to play a decisive role in resolving a global crisis. Doubtless there is no historical interpretation that is entirely "innocent" or apolitical. However, the interpretations offered by the editors of *Die Grosse Politik* and the members of the Nye Committee consciously sought to command the past in order to shape the future. The contemporary "lesson" is that we should never underestimate the importance of situating events – real or invented – in their larger historical context. Finally, control of the historical record matters. The German government used the falsified record to create a broadly accepted historiography that undermined a peace settlement it was determined to topple. The Nye Committee used the record to support legislative efforts to restrict executive discretion and limit American entanglements abroad. German historical editing helped discredit the Versailles peace settlement. American legislative investigation helped discredit internationalism. As it happened, together, the "historical fictions" regarding German and American entry into the First World War contributed to the forces making the Second World War possible. In a final "twist of history," deliberate historical fabrications had genuine historical consequences.

Endnotes

1 Fictions are "Statements or concepts that are known to be false or pretense but treated by general agreement as if they were true because such treatment serves some felt need." (see *Encyclopedia Britannica*, IX, 238; see also Morris Cohen, "Fictions," *Encyclopedia of the Social Sciences* 6 (1931), 225 for an argument that "many 'fictions' represent...aspects of reality.").
2 Witness, for example, the interpretation of English law underlined by both Nancy Wright and Andrew Buck in this volume (Wright, "Reading the Past: The Dispossession of the Poor and the Aborigines in Colonial New South Wales," and Buck, "Understanding Property in Australian History"). These interpretations, if not outright confections, were certainly slanting the facts in a way that was advantageous to those who sought to legitimize the dispossession of both the economically disadvantaged and indigenous peoples.
3 Holger H. Herwig, "Clio Deceived: Patriotic Self-Censorship in Germany after the Great War," *International Security* 12:2 (Fall 1987): 6–7.
4 Ibid., 9.
5 Ibid., 9–12.
6 Ibid., 13.
7 Ibid., 42–43.
8 Ibid., 9.
9 Quoted in Catherine Ann Cline, "British Historians and the Treaty of Versailles," *Albion* 20:1 (Spring 1988): 48.
10 Johannes Lepsius, Albrecht Mendelssohn Bartholdy und Friedrich Thimme, *Die Grosse Politik der Europaischen Kabinette, 1871–1914: Sammlung der Diplomatischen Akten des Auswartigen Amtes* (Berlin: Verlagsgeschellschaft für Politik und Geschichte, 1922–1927).
11 Even before the end of the Second World War voices were raised in warning. In 1932 the German liberal historian Hermann Kantorowicz criticized the apologetic campaign for Imperial Germany in *The Spirit of British Policy and the Myth of the Encirclement of Germany*. In 1935, and again in 1942, E. L. Woodward complained that *Die Grosse Politik* had been treated with an "extraordinary lack of critical examination in English-speaking countries." After the war, these same issues were debated in the *Times Literary Supplement*, in August, September, and October 1953. Meanwhile, in 1960 Franz Lassner defended a Ph.D. dissertation at Georgetown University entitled "The Historiographic Propaganda of the German Foreign Office during the Weimar Republic" and in 1970 Hermann J. Wittgens defended a Ph.D. dissertation at the University of Washington entitled "The German Foreign

Office Campaign Against the Treaty of Versailles: An Examination of the Activities of the *Kriegsschuldreferat* in the United States." Thus, Herwig's "Clio Deceived" Cline's "British Historians and the Treaty of Versailles" represent simply two of the more recent contributions to a debate that has been engaged for a considerable period of time.

12 Herwig, "Clio Deceived," 14–17.
13 Cline, "British Historians and the Treaty of Versailles," 47–48. Criticism of the Treaty should not be attributed solely to the success of German policy. The desire to avert another similar conflict also underlay much of the opposition to the Versailles.
14 Quoted in Martin Gilbert, *The Roots of Appeasement* (New York: New American Library, 1966), 121.
15 Quoted in Cline, "British Historians and the Treaty of Versailles," 47, 50, 51.
16 Ibid., 53. Soon after publication of *Recent Revelations*, British Prime Minister, Ramsay MacDonald, described Gooch to Foreign Office official Sir Eyre Crowe as "by far and away our ablest historian." Quoted in Cline, 52–53.
17 Gilbert, *Roots of Appeasement*, 23, 25.
18 Quoted in Raymond Sontag, *A Broken World, 1919–1939* (New York: Harper and Row, 1971), 53. Fay announced his views in three successive issues of the *American Historical Review* [hereafter *AHR*], "New Light on the Origins of the World War, I. Berlin and Vienna, To July 29," 25:4 (July 1920): 616–39; "New Light on the Origins of the World War, II. Berlin and Vienna, July 29 to 31," 26:1 (October 1920): 37–53; and "New Light on the Origins of the World War, III. Russia and the Other Powers," 26:2 (January 1921): 225–54.
19 Ibid., 28:3 (April 1923): 543–48; quotes on 544.
20 Ibid., 30:1 (October 1924): 136–41; quotes from 136–37.
21 Ibid., 31:1 (October 1925): 130–33; see also *AHR* 31:3 (April 1926): 520–24.
22 Ibid., 34:2 (January 1929): 340–42; 34:3 (April 1929): 599–602; 34:2 (January 1929): 343–44; and 35:4 (July 1930): 863–65.
23 Ibid., 33:3 (April 1928): 648.
24 Ibid., 33:1 (October 1927): 126–34.
25 Ibid.
26 Ibid., 34:2 (January 1929): 336–40.
27 Fay's reviews of the *British Documents on the Origins of the War, 1898–1914* (London: H.M. Stationery Office, 1926–1938), appear in *AHR* 32:3 (April 1927): 600–603; 33:3 (April 1928): 648–51; 34:2 January 1929) 340–42; 34:3 (April 1929): 599–602; 35:1 (October 1929): 110–12; 36:1, (October 1930): 151–55; 38:2 (January 1933): 332–35; 38:4 (July 1933): 760–61; 40:2 (January 1935): 338–40; 41:3 (April 1936): 544–46; 41:4 July 1936): 751–53; 42:2 (January 1937): 332–36; 44:3 (April 1939): 626–27.
28 *AHR* 33:4 (July 1928): 878. For Fay's reviews of various volumes of *Documents Diplomatiques Français*, 1871–1914 (Paris: Imprimerie Nationale, 1929–1939), see: *AHR* 35:4 (July 1930): 863–65; 36:3 (April 1931): 592–94; 37: 4 (July 1932): 759–61; 38:3 (April 1933): 554–57; 39:1 (October 1933): 128–29; 40:3 (April 1935): 510–13; 41:3 (April 1936): 544–46; 42:2 (January 1937): 332–36.
29 *AHR* 33:3 (April 1928): 648.
30 Ibid., 33:3 (April 1928): 649.
31 Ibid., 34:3 (April 1929): 602.
32 Ibid., 36:4 (July 1931): 822.
33 Ibid., 35:4 (July 1930): 863.

34 Ibid., 36:4 (July 1931): 821.
35 Ibid., 41:3 (April 1936): 545.
36 Ibid., 43:1 (October 1937): 134.
37 Furthermore, Fay popularized his interpretation with a much larger audience among the educated public through writing for journals of opinion. See his "Serbia's responsibility for the World War," *Current History Monthly* 23 (October 1925): 41–48; "M. Poincaré and war responsibility," *New Republic* 44 (14 October 1925): 197–200; "Black Hand plot that led to the World War," *Current History Monthly* 23 (November 1925): 196–207; "Who started the War? New light from Chancellor Marx" *New Republic* 45 (6 January 1926): 185–86; "Revelations in latest British war documents," *Current History* 29 (January 1929): 644–49; "Secrets of British prewar diplomacy," *Current History* 30 (April 1929): 115–22; and "Sarajevo fifteen years after," *Living Age* 336 (July 1929): 374–79.
38 Fischer caused a major commotion among historians with the 1961 publication of his first book, *Griff nach der Weltmacht* (translated as *Germany's Aims in the First World War*), in which he argued that Germany, driven by economic interests, sought world power.
39 Ernest R. May, *The World War and American Isolation, 1914–1917* (Cambridge, MA: Harvard University Press, 1959).
40 Manfred Jonas, *Isolationism in America, 1935–1941* (Chicago: Imprint Publications, 1990), 142–43; Wayne S. Cole, *Senator Gerald P. Nye and American Foreign Relations* (Minneapolis: University of Minnesota Press, 1962), 69.
41 See Harold U. Faulkner, *Politics, Reform and Expansion, 1890–1900* (New York: Harper and Brothers, 1959) 56, 58.
42 John D. Hicks, *Republican Ascendancy, 1921–1933* (New York: Harper and Row, 1960), 20.
43 Ibid., 61.
44 Cole, *Senator Gerald P. Nye*, 48.
45 Alan Brinkley, *Voices of Protest: Huey Long, Father Coughlin, and the Great Depression* (New York: Alfred A. Knopf, 1982).
46 Jonas, *Isolationism in America*, 140–43; Cole, *Senator Gerald P. Nye*, 249, n. 15.
47 Cole, *Senator Gerald P. Nye*, 73, 79; Jonas, *Isolationism in America*, 144.
48 *Congressional Record*, 74th Congress, 1st session, *1935*, 79, part 1, 444–45.
49 Charles Seymour, *American Neutrality 1914–1917* (New Haven: Yale University Press, 1935), 85.
50 Senate Document 944, "Report of the Special Senate Committee on the Investigation of the Munitions Industry," 74th Congress, 2nd Session.
51 Seymour, *American Neutrality*, 94, 102; *Congressional Record 75th Congress, 1st Session (1937)*, Appendix, 121–22.
52 Seymour, *American Neutrality*, 87.
53 Ibid., 91–92, 94, 102, 115, 96.
54 Cole, *Senator Gerald P. Nye*, 97.
55 Jonathan Mitchell, "Mass Murderers, in Person," *New Republic* 80 (26 September 1934), 178, cited in Wayne S. Cole, *Senator Gerald P. Nye*, 250, n. 35.
56 Quotes from Jonas, *Isolationism in America*, 147–48.
57 *Congressional Record, 74th Congress, 2nd Session (1936)*, 2, 616.
58 Jonas, *Isolationism in America*, 153.
59 Charles A. Beard, *The Devil Theory of War* (1936), quoted in Richard Hofstadter, *The Progressive Historians: Turner, Beard, Parrington* (Chicago: University of Chicago

Press, 1968), 332. Interestingly, Beard had joined in the war-guilt debate. See his reviews "Viscount Grey on war guilt," *New Republic* 44 (7 October 1925): 172–75, and "Heroes and Villains of the World War: A Review of the Genesis of the World War, by H. E. Barnes," *Current History*, 24 (August 1926): 730–35.

60 See Cole, *Senator Gerald P. Nye*, 83, 101–6, 109–10; the *Herald-Tribune* quote can be found in William Leuchtenberg, *Franklin D. Roosevelt and the New Deal* (New York: Harper and Row, 1963), 225.

61 Maurice Halbwachs, *La Mémoire collective* (Paris: Presses Universitaire de France, 1968). For more recent works demonstrating the importance of memory, see Pierre Nora, ed., *Realms of Memory: The Construction of the French Past*, 3 vols., trans. Arthur Goldhammer (New York: Columbia University Press, 1997) and Jay Winter, *Sites of Memory, Sites of Mourning: The Great War in European Cultural History* (Cambridge: Cambridge University Press, 1995).

62 Compare Henry Rousso, *The Vichy Syndrome: History and Memory in France since 1944*, trans. Arthur Goldhammer (Cambridge, MA: Harvard University Press, 1991), 3–4, with Peter Novick, *The Holocaust in American Life* (New York: Mariner Books, 2000), 3–4.

63 Rousso, *The Vichy Syndrome*, 1–10. In Rousso's interpretation, from 1944 to 1954 France "mourned," dealing directly with the memory of Vichy; from 1954 to 1971 France moved on by repressing the memory of Vichy; between 1971 and 1974 this repression of memory broke down; and since 1974 France has been "obsessed" with the memory of Vichy, an obsession which appears in the revival of Jewish memory and the prominent place of Vichy in French political discussion.

64 Novick, *The Holocaust in American Life*, 1.

65 Ibid., 2.

66 Ibid., 6–13.

67 Paul A. Cohen, *History in Three Keys: The Boxers as Event, Experience, and Myth* (New York: Columbia University Press, 1997), 217, 237, 259–62.

68 Cohen, *History in Three Keys*, 212, 292.

69 The issue of the emphasis to be placed on archival work is explored elsewhere in this volume. Compare Peter Farrugia, "Navigating the River of History," 18 with Leo Groarke, "Teaching History: The Future of the Past," 67.

Bibliography

American Historical Review, July 1920–April 1939.

Beard, Charles A. "Viscount Grey on war guilt." *New Republic* 44 (7 October 1925): 172–75.

———. "Heroes and villains of the World war: a review of The Genesis of the World war, by H. E. Barnes." *Current History* 24 (August 1926): 730–35.

Brinkley, Alan. *Voices of Protest: Huey Long, Father Coughlin, and the Great Depression*. New York: Alfred A. Knopf, 1982.

Cline, Catherine Ann. "British Historians and the Treaty of Versailles." *Albion* 20:1 (Spring 1988): 43–58.

Cohen, Morris. "Fictions." *Encyclopedia of the Social Sciences*, 6.

Cohen, Paul A. *History in Three Keys: The Boxers as Event, Experience, and Myth.* New York: Columbia University Press, 1997.
Cole, Wayne S. *Senator Gerald P. Nye and American Foreign Relations.* Minneapolis: University of Minnesota Press, 1962.
Congressional Record, 74th and 75th Congresses.
Documents Diplomatiques Francais, 1871–1914. Paris: Imprimerie Nationale, 1929–1939.
Faulkner, Harold U. *Politics, Reform and Expansion 1890–1900.* New York: Harper and Brothers, 1959.
Fay, Sidney B. "Black Hand plot that led to the World war." *Current History Monthly* 23 (November 1925): 196–207.
———. "M. Poincaré and war responsibility." *New Republic* 44 (14 October 1925): 197–200.
———. "Revelations in latest British war documents." *Current History* 29 (January 1929): 644–49.
———. "Sarajevo fifteen years after." *Living Age* 336 (July 1929): 374–79.
———. "Secrets of British pre-war diplomacy." *Current History* 30 (April 1929): 115–22.
———. "Serbia's responsibility for the World War." *Current History Monthly* 23 (October 1925): 41–48.
———. "Who started the War? New light from Chancellor Marx." *New Republic* 45 (6 January 1926): 185–86.
Fischer, Fritz. *Germany's Aims in the First World War.* New York: W. W. Norton, 1967.
Gilbert, Martin. *The Roots of Appeasement.* New York: New American Library, 1966.
Gooch, G. P. *Recent Revelations of European Diplomacy.* London: Longmans Green, 1927.
Halbwachs, Maurice. *La Memoire collective.* Paris: Presses Universitaire de France, 1968.
Herwig, Holger H. "Clio Deceived: Patriotic Self-Censorship in Germany after the Great War." *International Security* 12:2 (Fall 1987): 5–44.
Hicks, John D. *Republican Ascendancy, 1921–1933.* New York: Harper and Row, 1960.
Hofstadter, Richard. *The Progressive Historians: Turner, Beard, Parrington.* Chicago: University of Chicago Press, 1968.
Jonas, Manfred. *Isolationism in America, 1935–1941.* Chicago: Imprint Publications, 1990.
Kantorowicz, Hermann. *The Spirit of British Policy and the Myth of the Encirclement of Germany.* Trans. W. H. Johnston. New York: Oxford University Press, 1932.
Lassner, Franz. "The Historiographic Propaganda of the German Foreign Office during the Weimar Republic" Ph.D. dissertation, Georgetown University, 1960.
Lepsius, Johannes, Albrecht Mendelssohn Bartholdy und Friedrich Thimme, *Die Grosse Politik der Europaischen Kabinette, 1871–1914: Sammlung der Diplomatischen Akten des Auswartigen Amtes.* Berlin: Verlagsgeschellschaft für Politik und Geschichte, 1922–1927.
Leuchtenberg, William. *Franklin D. Roosevelt and the New Deal.* New York: Harper and Row, 1963.
May, Ernest R. *The World War and American Isolation, 1914–1917.* Cambridge, MA: Harvard University Press, 1959.
Nora, Pierre, ed. *Realms of Memory: The Construction of the French Past.* 3 vols. Trans. Arthur Goldhammer. New York: Columbia University Press, 1997.
Novick, Peter. *The Holocaust in American Life.* New York: Mariner Books, 2000.
Rousso, Henry. *The Vichy Syndrome: History and Memory in France since 1944.* Trans. Arthur Goldhammer. Cambridge, MA: Harvard University Press, 1991.

Senate Document 944, "Report of the Special Senate Committee on the Investigation of the Munitions Industry," 74th Congress, 2nd Session.

Seymour, Charles. *American Neutrality 1914–1917*. New Haven: Yale University Press, 1935.

Sontag, Raymond. *A Broken World, 1919–1939*. New York: Harper and Row, 1971.

Winter, Jay. *Sites of Memory Sites of Mourning: The Great War in European Cultural History*. Cambridge: Cambridge University Press, 1995.

Wittgens, Hermann J. "The German Foreign Office Campaign Against the Treaty of Versailles: An Examination of the Activities of the *Kriegsschuldreferat* in the United States." Ph.D. dissertation, University of Washington, 1970.

7

Being Present, Owning the Past, and Growing into the Future: Temporality, Revelation and the Therapeutic Culture[1]

JEFFREY BROWN

When people tell their stories in twelve-step groups they generally follow the tried and true Alcoholics Anonymous format: "What was it like? What happened? What is it like now?" This is a template for organizing personal history that increasing numbers of North Americans have encountered. Its proliferation is fueled by its efficacy for countless numbers of alcoholics, addicts, and others. It seems to work, in short, for purposes of "recovery." But the *recovery* of a past that may be usefully deployed in the service of recovery from addiction is not all that is involved here. The rubric is as much a plan for building as it is a map for digging. As with all historical methodologies, the narratives it yields are pieced together only partly from "recovered" fragments of the past. The rest is new construction, configured by the tools and materials of the moment. In this case, the organizing tool provided by AA is of paramount importance. One can easily imagine even small modifications in the template leading to radically different results. The questions might be reversed in sequence – "What is it like now? What happened? What was it like before?" – and so weighted toward the present at the expense of the past. Or they might be reframed in moralistic terms – "What was wrong with you? What did you do? What set you straight?" – and so freighted with the presupposition of guilt. It is precisely such 'loaded' questions that the AA rubric seeks to supplant. The custom presupposes that the histories we make as individuals are determined by the questions we ask of our pasts, and that these histories can matter a great deal. For those battling addictions, replacing a deficient narrative with one that works in the cause of abstinence may be a matter of life or death.

How ironic then, that the historical discourse which attempts to explain the cultural context that has sustained and been shaped by the twelve step movement has been so heavily influenced by the sort of jaundiced narrative that AA members are encouraged to reject. This narrative delineates the rise of a pervasive and pernicious "therapeutic culture," both agent and expression of the self-absorbed individualism of twentieth century consumer capitalism. Like the flawed and profitless personal histories of addicts and alcoholics, however, the cultural history of the therapeutic has outlived its usefulness, and now stands in need of extensive reworking. I will make a start at this shortly, following the revisionist plot of the AA template. The therapeutic turn, I will suggest, is best understood as a reverberation of fundamental shifts in the way history is conceived and experienced by individuals. To begin with, however, it will be useful to review the interpretive trend that gave rise to the "therapeutic culture" in the first place.

Philip Rieff coined the term in his 1966 book, *The Triumph of the Therapeutic*, the chronicle of a sweeping and apparently irrevocable shift in the moral and social values of modern Americans. Rieff portrayed the new ethos with a scorn that oscillated between alarm and resignation. And who would not find a cultural degeneration of the nature and scale that Rieff described disturbing? "The therapeutic man," he proclaimed, had disavowed "all binding engagements" to those systems of religious and communal purpose that had previously insured the "internalization of moral demands." With the marginalization of traditional symbolic orders of commitment and self-denial came the emergence of new "religious psychologies of release and social technologies of affluence" that refused to temper liberation with "a fresh imposition of restrictive demands." Under the therapeutic dispensation, Rieff memorably concluded, the "sense of well-being has become the end, rather than a by-product of striving after some superior communal end."[2]

Thirteen years following the publication of *Triumph* – with the movement anthems of the sixties now replaced by the soft, atonal strains of seventies' quests for "consciousness," "liberation," and "human potential" – Rieff's ominous report was powerfully amplified in Christopher Lasch's, *The Culture of Narcissism*. "Plagued by anxiety, depression, vague discontents, [and] a sense of inner emptiness, the 'psychological man' of the twentieth-century seeks neither individual self-aggrandizement nor spiritual transcendence but peace of mind," Lasch declared. His "principal allies" on this quest are therapists, to whom "he turns ... in the hope of achieving the modern equivalent of salvation, 'mental health.'" In a society that "gives no thought to anything beyond its immediate needs," however, mental health is reduced to the "fulfillment of ... immediate emotional requirements." The idea that one might "subordinate his needs and interests to those of others, to someone or some cause or tradition outside the self" had become unthinkable to the new narcissist. "[Such] sublimations strike the therapeutic sensibility as intolerably oppressive," Lasch maintained. The purpose of post-Freudian therapists, their popularizers, and converts, was "to liberate humanity from such outmoded ideas of love and duty." "Mental health" for them, Lasch lamented, meant "the overthrow of inhibitions and the immediate gratification of every impulse."[3]

By the mid-eighties, with the contextualizing efforts of Warren Susman and Jackson Lears, the major arguments for the historical emergence and current ascendancy of the therapeutic, and against its efficacy as an ethical ideal and mode of selfhood, were well established. Working from the symptomatology of Rieff and Lasch, Susman and Lears produced a compelling historical etiology of the therapeutic ethos, locating its onset in the psychic dislocations of late-nineteenth- and early-twentieth-century American modernity. They correlated the transition from a "heroic," production-based, scarcity-plagued, proprietary capitalism to a corporate consumer-driven variety retooled for abundance, with the eclipse of inner-directed "character" by other-directed "personality."[4] Secularizing trends, especially those enmeshed in a liberalizing Protestantism, shredded the moral and theological ground beneath the feet of the Victorian autonomous agent, who now scrambled for stability, lunging between the pursuit of worldly success, the allure of intense experience, and the evanescent promise of self-realization held forth by a new "therapeutic elite." Unburdened of the weight of nineteenth century repression, the therapeutic self celebrated its new moral agility decked out in surface attire fashioned to restyle with the ever-shifting opportunities for social and business advantage afforded in the new urban-bureaucratic environment.[5]

I cannot begin to do justice here to the multifaceted and often subtle and incisive rendering of the therapeutic frame of mind and culture that took shape at the hands of these historian-critics, much less consider the numerous parallel and connecting projects that augmented the interpretive boom in this area. I do, however, want to emphasize the formative place of the work of these scholars in the rise of the therapeutic as an object of analysis, and to call particular attention to the rather sinister cast of their fabrication. The erection of the therapeutic, with all its appurtenances — psychological man, the protean and the minimal self, expressive individualism, the emotivist ethic, the narcissistic personality, etc. — was undertaken from a platform of disillusion and indignation. Its architects left no doubt about which side of the psycho-historical divide their sympathies lay.

The proclivity is at its most pronounced in the work of Rieff, who predicted in his 1973 book, *Fellow Teachers*, that violence, "the therapy of therapies," would eventually be the spawn of a culture in which the rebellion against authority yielded to no new authority and the campaign against the interdicts of tradition ended not with the setting of new limits, but rather with the abrogation of their very idea: "a conclusive freedom," as Rieff put it. "With the end of authority," he warned, "no violence will be illegitimate"; and the "nightmare history" of the twentieth century may prove only a "promontory flash" to the coming catastrophes of the therapeutic epoch.[6] Though such "exaggerated apprehensions," as Lasch would later call them, are not representative of the genre in its entirety, they nonetheless reflect something of this discourse's unmistakable penchant for the prophetic.[7] Max Weber's famous portent about "specialists without spirit [and] sensualists without heart" serves as epigraph for two of its foundational texts.[8] Only Rieff believed that the "nullity" Weber had foreseen was headed for the apocalypse, but all the historian-critics were deeply impressed by the sociologist's astonishing prescience; and all sought to explain how the sorry state of affairs Weber had augured at the beginning of the twentieth century had actually come to pass in its closing decades.

The historian-critics of the therapeutic were animated, then, both by presentism and prejudgment; indeed, these postures prescribed the single leading question from which the entire enterprise proceeded: "what," in a word, "went wrong?" No one can deny that the flood of explanation that followed shed a great deal of light on the cultural and psychic history of modern America. But the polemical purposes of the historian-critics overrode their analytical ones, and material that was not readily assimilable to the critical agenda was relegated to the margins or passed over altogether. It is no surprise that recent investigations have rendered the demarcation of psycho-cultural "modal-types," the blueprint for Susman and Lears's historical explication of the therapeutic, highly suspect. There seems, to put it bluntly, to have been plenty of personality in the putatively heroic age of character before 1890, and no lack of character in the post-1920 era of allegedly unbridled personality.[9] My own investigations corroborate the latter of these observations. Indeed, I think that central components of the therapeutic culture are precisely about making character, and that this endeavor has proceeded through modes of thought and action which, though ungrounded in the sort of religious conviction and institutional authority that may once have served to calibrate the internal gyroscopes of moral agents, can foster ethical rigor, social responsibility, and civic engagement nonetheless.

While there are several ways in which one might approach this argument, I want to attend to it while considering a largely overlooked but uniquely revealing dimension of the therapeutic turn: its temporal dimension. What does the idea and experience of time have to do with the coalescence of the therapeutic around the turn of the twentieth century? The irruption of the therapeutic into the cultural mainstream coincided with a profound destabilization both in historical time and in the idea of a divine creator standing outside history. Deeply rooted assumptions about the "time of the world" and the "time of the soul," to borrow the terms of philosopher Paul Ricoeur, became widely problematic during these years. The operative dynamic here is best described with the unwieldy but useful term, "immanentization."[10] Atemporal, external, and supernatural sources of revelation were replaced by temporal, indwelling, and organic ones; and the special knowledge – the revelation – once believed to be the exclusive province of the former, was now diligently sought in the latter.[11]

Immanentization took two forms that are especially pertinent to the question at hand. In modernist Protestantism and Catholicism, in radically empiricist, neo-idealist, and vitalist philosophy, and in the host of popular spiritual practices associated with the New Thought movement, the eternal and transcendent God of the fathers was brought down to earth and made natural, accessible, and ever-present here and now. Correspondingly, in the new empirical and psychodynamic psychology, in the psychotherapeutic movement, and especially in psychoanalysis, the past was made immanent in the present. The primal source of behavior, belief, identity, morality, and that new attribute, "mental health," was uprooted from its customary dwelling in the divinely inscribed reason of the mind, and from its more recent materialistic lodgings in the neurons and germ plasm of the brain and body, and relocated in the vicissitudes of individual history. Viewed as a moral and cultural expression of this biform immanentization, the "triumph of the therapeutic" looks considerably less smooth and complete than it is depicted by the historian-critics.

What, then, was it like? The intimacy of the temporal dimension, its commonplace familiarity as the frame that life stretches over, and its embeddedness in the methodological foundations of the social and human sciences, have fostered its comparative invisibility. It has figured as an unacknowledged basis for inquiry far more often than an object of inquiry in its own right.[12] There are signs, however, of a shift in this historic trend. Temporality has undergone an intense, perhaps unprecedented, round of analysis in recent years.[13] The scrutiny has produced a complex image of temporal perspectives in the nineteenth century, a long revolutionary epoch which saw the culmination in the West of a project begun with the paradigmatic formulations of Isaac Newton: time's rationalization and the naturalization of the system that resulted.[14]

The major substantive steps of this process between 1789 and 1914 are recited easily enough: the effective universalization and ongoing refinement of industrial work-time discipline, the mass production and consumption of clocks and watches, the standardization of national times and the adoption, in 1913, of a world standard.[15] More germane to the present discussion, however, is the delineation of the dominant temporal presuppositions – both scientific and religious – that grounded the worldview of the educated classes. One might summarize this set of premises as follows: time is an objective reality independent of consciousness; time is linear, sequential, continuous, uniform, predictable, and universal in nature; the Christian God, His revelation, and the moral laws He decreed, exist eternally, above and beyond the time of His creation; this transcendent deity once ordained and now superintends the temporal world of nature, a world that operates rationally and in accordance with a divine plan and purpose; human beings are self-determining temporal agents, with stable, conscious centers grounding the convictions and volitions by which they pursue their destinies in accordance with God's plan; omniscient design and human efforts are at their most harmonious in the work of moral and economic progress.[16]

Of course, this rudimentary enumeration is far from comprehensive. Notions of the size of the interval between humanity and the divine, and of the prospects for its bridging, were diverse and fluctuating in this epoch as in others. The coexistence in nineteenth-century America of such incongruous Gods as the remote, rational, and benevolent "Architect and Governor of the Universe" of the New England Unitarians, the austere and omnipotent Judge of the New Divinity Calvinists, and the processive, all-pervasive "Oversoul" of the Transcendentalists, does not preclude the general point, however. Of importance here is not the heterogeneity of conceptions of time and eternity, but the cultural preeminence, by and large, of a single constellation of understandings.[17]

So what happened? The disintegration of dominant temporal forms, manifest particularly in metaphysics and psychology, proceeded with marked intensity between, roughly, 1880 and 1920. During these years a cross-denominational liberal Protestantism acquired sufficient cultural and institutional prominence to confer unprecedented legitimacy on an immanentism affirming God's intrinsic presence in human affairs. Liberal Protestants sought to square accounts with Darwin by locating the guiding hand of the divine in biological evolution. The development of civilization seemed, in this view, to represent conclusive evidence of God's beneficent immediacy. Progress, accordingly, became a near euphemism for the realization of His Kingdom on Earth. The same optimism, moreover, obtained in the personal project of spiritual self-realization, at bottom a matter of the recognition by the individual consciousness of its own inherent cognate divinity.[18]

It was a short but momentous step – documented with peerless sagacity by William James in his 1903 work, *Varieties of Religious Experience* – from the intellectual conviction of divine immanence to its unmediated apprehension. While James's account legitimated all sorts of unconventional spiritual phenomena, it was in no respect more radical than in its respectful treatment of the controversial teachings of the New Thought. This burgeoning movement in popular spiritual psychotherapeutics cohered loosely around the premise that the material world was a transitory and subsidiary reverberation of an infinite realm of spirit in whose energy it was suffused.[19] It was less the speculative heterodoxy of New Thought cosmology, however, than the eccentricity of its practice that distinguished it from Liberal Protestantism. The New Thought was above all a system of "practical metaphysics,"[20] a fashionable oxymoron around the turn of the century that boiled down to a single tantalizing proposition: if human beings could begin to think outside the conceptual grid within which they habitually experienced reality, they would discover intuitive pathways to an incalculably richer and wider spiritual reality. The notion was accompanied by the potentially subversive corollary that thinking in overly materialistic and mechanistic terms was the gravest of metaphysical errors. And while the New Thought did not itself discernibly impede the advance of mechanism and materialism, or, for that matter, the technological, industrial, and commercial juggernaut they underwrote, it did help set the tone for a diffuse anti-rationalism that found its first measure of cultural and political expression among the young urban avant-garde of the pre-war 1910s.[21]

Widely heralded metaphysical developments in American and European philosophy seemed to corroborate in high theory much of what the New Thought had arrived at through individual experiment and popular practice. Josiah Royce, G. H. Howison, Borden Parker Bowne, and Rudolf Eucken recast idealism as a dynamic and personal philosophy of life; vitalism became acutely critical and intriguingly compensatory in the work of Henri Bergson and Hans Driesch; and empiricism was made pragmatic, radical, and pluralistic by William James and F.C.S. Schiller. Diverse currents in transatlantic intellectual culture had churned into what James, in 1904, termed a "great unsettlement" in Western ideas.[22]

The "unsettlement," whether in established religious traditions, new spiritual movements, or academic philosophy, amounted to much the same thing: the discovery of the close proximity of an indwelling, elementally temporal, metaphysical reality and the adumbration of various means – all involving the evasion or transformation of linear time – by which one might gain access to it.[23]

The immanentization of psychological conceptions, like that of metaphysics, was both a theoretical and a practical phenomenon. Psychodynamic interpretations of mental illness emphasized the role of the personal past in accounting for present disorders. And psychodynamic psychotherapeutics formulated methodologies of recognition and retrieval by which this immanent domain became accessible. These developments ushered in a series of propositions that simultaneously complicated and illuminated the distinctive histories of individual selves.[24] The past was suddenly of interest not solely for what was remembered about it, but also for what was forgotten. And what had slipped the mind was no longer lost; it was still there, present, but unavailable to cognition under ordinary circumstances. The great novelty conferred on the "modern sensibility" by the new mental therapeutics was "the idea," as Ian Hacking has put it, "that what has been forgotten is what forms our character, our personality, our soul."[25] Recovering the forgotten, untangling idiosyncratic history from the tentacles of fantasy and repression, and so accounting for the action of the moment and the implications of its projection into the future, had suddenly become both a scientific mandate and an individual responsibility.

Notions of the past's determinations, its irrefragable immediacy, and its plasticity for purposes of "moving on," moreover, were not strictly the purview of psychodynamic theory and therapeutics; ideas such as these issued from multiple sources, including some that championed metaphysical immanentism as well. In 1900 the symbolist poet and playwright Maurice Maeterlinck, for example, wrote of the past as a "buried temple," the very "hot-bed of our existence, ever in movement," where one might "extract unexpected treasure from … wreckage" and find that "the dead themselves will annul their verdicts in order to judge afresh a past that today has transfigured and endowed with new life."[26] And Bergson, an intellectual who, as Ruth Leys has observed, "hovered about these prewar developments" in mental therapeutics like a "talismanic figure,"[27] construed that aspect of memory which gathered "pure perception" and stored it in an ever expanding reservoir of "images" as the very source of freedom and the spiritual life.[28] Such conjunctions of psychological and metaphysical immanentism have played an exemplary role in the consolidation and fomentation of therapeutic ideas and approaches. Self-consciously modern Americans revered Maeterlinck and Bergson as prophets early in the twentieth century because their writings brought together two of the day's most enigmatic and compelling intellectual tendencies. Subsequent avatars of the therapeutic have followed suit, the breadth of their influence seemingly linked to the intensity of their association of the psychological and the spiritual.[29]

What is it like now? The mandala that adorns the front of Ram Dass' bible of the consciousness counterculture is girded by the words "Be Here Now," but parallel with each of the four edges of the book's square purple cover are the white letters, "Remember."[30] The two adjurations fittingly represent the twofold immanentism of the therapeutic culture, an immanentism constitutive of the complex tangle of discourse, practice, and sensibility that is such a pervasive aspect of contemporary life. Approaching the therapeutic along its temporal roots permits a fuller and more conscientious exploration than those that begin in the branches. From this primary region it is impossible, first and foremost, to ascribe determinate moral, social, or political consequences to any bough or sprout of the therapeutic tree. That is not to say that the therapeutic, like other complex social phenomena, is not fraught with moral and political implications, but rather that the nature of such implications are fundamentally ambiguous.

"Being here now," for example, readily lends itself to the impulsive worship of the "moment" that so eagerly heeds the market's call to immediate gratification. More rigorously conceived, however, it may form the basis of a systematic discipline of withdrawal from linear time, or a habitual mindfulness of time as the experience of passage, both hardly in keeping with the exchange of work/time for money or the spending of time/money in the work of consumption to which North Americans are so insistently enjoined.[31] At the same time, if awareness of the past's immanence can be imagined to feed into a self serving species of introspection dedicated to the flight from responsibility – a disposition entirely susceptible to the manipulations of mass consumer culture – it might just as readily contribute to an entirely different sort of engagement with memory, one in which the past is laboriously combed for self-serving illusions and denials, then reappropriated, or "owned," precisely for the purpose of complete accountability and personal integrity.

Both "being present" and "owning the past" are cardinal precepts of twelve-step recovery, the therapeutic configuration that has suffered the most heated denunciation since the seventies vogue for "human potential" faded from view.[32] Rising in response to the proliferation of twelve-step doctrine in chemical dependency treatment and self-help literature, this criticism attempts to apply and extend the work of the historian-critics. But it exposes the weaknesses of the critical discourse of the therapeutic far more impressively than it builds upon its strengths. Such anti-recovery blasts as Stanton Peele's *Diseasing of America*, Charles Sykes' *A Nation of Victims*, Stan Katz and Aimee Liu's, *The Codependency Conspiracy*, and Wendy Kaminer's *I'm Dysfunctional, You're Dysfunctional*, sound the shrill and strident tones of an argument extended far beyond the conditions that once gave it credence.[33] There are some keen and useful insights in this literature, but all sink, eventually, into tendentious mire.

Consider, for example, the influential 1991 essay, "Victims All? Recovery, co-dependency, and the art of blaming somebody else" by David Rieff, son of historian-critic patriarch, Philip Rieff.[34] As the title of his piece would suggest, Rieff's objection to twelve-step recovery has much to do with what his father liked to call "remission," the abjuration by the individual of inherited moral interdicts. The recovery movement, according to David Rieff, has become a pervasive and pernicious agent of remission. It is now "taken for granted," he writes, "that no blame for ... addictions or dependencies can be assigned to those who exhibit them."[35] Blame, rather, is placed upon the authority figures charged with establishing the "interdictory symbolism" by which addictive behavior becomes blameworthy to begin with – to parents, then, and to those agencies of culture and tradition responsible for the moral and emotional apparatus of guilt and shame making. Even the language of blame, terms such as "'character,' 'weakness,' and 'individual responsibility,' are no longer deemed appropriate" in a society in which "nearly everyone is identified ... as some sort of psychological cripple."[36] Epitomizing the generational trend, David Rieff characterizes twelve-step recovery as society's primary manufacturer of "victimhood," the newest strategy of a self-obsessed therapeutic mind-set fixated on shirking responsibility – whether individual or social and civic.

The "desperate creed" Rieff portrays would be alarming if it took the form he describes in anything like the ubiquity he suggests. This has not been the case, however. One wonders, indeed, how addiction and recovery could possibly have become "our central [cultural] metaphors," as Rieff asserts, if one cannot even assume that they are the "central metaphors" of individuals who read recovery books and go to twelve-step meetings. Cultures, like individuals, are complex affairs. It would be a gross underestimation of either to claim, as have Rieff and others, that commitment to one category of activities – say, to individual growth and change in a recovery group – prohibits other sorts of commitments, to social justice or political engagement for example.[37] More troubling than this sort of obvious polemical overextension, however, is the flagrant misrepresentation of recovery principles typical of second-generation critiques. Rieff, for his part, presumes to portray the twelve-step "movement" without considering its programmatic core, the twelve steps themselves. The omission is telling. For the steps offer instruction in scrupulous honesty and painstaking accountability, both as a means of atonement and as a guide to continuing moral conduct, that belies the image of recovery as the nexus of blame shifting and self-exoneration conveyed by its detractors.[38]

Neither have the subtleties of the much maligned "disease concept of addiction" interested the critics. Stanton Peele's book is filled with derisive references to the "AA disease view" but empty of any discussion of the richly polysemic nature of this view. In the AA tradition, "disease," or "dis-ease," has operated as a metaphor signifying, most fundamentally, the inveteracy of a repetitive and destructive pattern of thought and behavior that defies individual efforts at control. Far from reducing the "condition" to biology, and so casting the "diseased person ... as a victim of infectious agents who ... has no responsibility for its onset,"[39] the "disease" of AA doctrine is a physical, mental, and spiritual malady for which the alcoholic must become accountable in order to stay sober.[40]

Taking responsibility for the consequences of choices freely made is at the core of the twelve-step program of recovery. Becoming responsible, however, is thought to require the paradoxical acceptance of powerlessness over the addictive habit. This sort of "surrender" does not conduce to remission, however, but to a kind of heroic realism. It is the illusion of control, of omnipotence, that lies at the heart of the addictive personality in the AA view. Surrendering to limits and humbly accepting human fallibility is the "antidote" to a "disease" of deep-seated self-obsession. The ritual admission of powerlessness at twelve-step meetings, the imperative to take frequent "searching and fearless moral inventory," and the necessity of coming to believe in a "power greater than the self" are all, in this respect, modes of renunciation, articles in the surrender of a contorted and belligerent ego.

Seen in this light, the therapeutic regime of the twelve steps appears dramatically out of sync with the therapeutic culture it is purported to sustain and exemplify. Indeed, the sentiment expressed by a speaker at AA's twenty-fifth anniversary conference in 1957, that those in recovery were fortunate not only for refusing to succumb to their addictions, but also for escaping "enslavement to the false ideas of a materialistic society" in which "millions" exist in shallow "illusory worlds, nurturing the basic anxieties and insecurities of human existence rather than facing themselves with courage and humility," remains a common one in twelve-step circles.[41] One might, in fact, make a plausible argument to the effect that twelve-step fellowships are profoundly, perhaps uniquely, *counter*cultural. Unlike the youth counterculture of the sixties and seventies, whose "rebellion" intensified the hedonistic and transgressive dynamic already inherent within the commodity culture of market capitalism, the culture of twelve-step recovery is rooted in a sober recognition of limits and a repudiation of the logic of immediate gratification.[42]

I have no interest in developing such an argument here, however. It would ensnarl me in a reductionism of the sort I am contending against; for neither twelve-step recovery nor the therapeutic culture in which it is embedded readily submit to ethical-political categorization. Indeed, it is in its refractory pluralism that the twelve-step movement is most reflective of its therapeutic cultural context. There are currently, as the second-generation critics snidely observe, twelve-step programs for any number of "diseases," or, more properly, for the welter of symptoms issuing from the ur-disease of addiction. There is a massive ancillary industry in recovery-related publications and twelve-step-based treatment. And there is the wide expanse of spiritual and psychotherapeutic discourse and practice – the therapeutic culture at large – crowded with countless sects and disciplines, orientations, traditions, therapies and institutions, enthusiasms, fads, fakes, and fancies. Large swathes of this space are void of socially redeeming features. Yet the desolation is by no means interminable.

The arrogation to the present self of sources of revelation formerly beyond time and will – immanentization – carries a variety of implications. Simultaneously advancing and redressing the long depreciation of transcendent foundations that is the hallmark of modernity, this process is conservative in the sense that it impedes the slide to nihilism by attempting to shore up meaning and authority in the self. However, making the human and the temporal the primary locus of revelation gives rise to an apparently endless cycle of irresolution and contention. The move comes with the promise that what has been taken away in security and certitude may be recouped in realism and responsibility, but human beings have generally been unable to make much of this potential. The confusion of the therapeutic is in part a reflection of the difficulty of meeting such challenges, a confusion manifest, not least, in the retreat from realism and responsibility altogether.

Twelve-step programs, if nothing else, are rooted in principles that have tended to militate against the latter possibility. The immanentism of recovery is exhibited in the spiritual exercise of living "one day [hour, minute, breath] at a time," in the metaphysical premise that a "higher power" inheres in the loving and caring interactions of individuals, and in the moral discipline of "owning the past" through an ongoing, deliberative and exhaustive, evaluation of one's personal history. But there are crucial vestiges of non-immanent beliefs in the twelve-step tradition. The "higher power," however intimately known, remains irrevocably higher. "God's will" and "self will," accordingly, are frequently and emphatically distinguished in recovery rhetoric. It is the abiding struggle of the recovering addict to observe this distinction in the vicissitudes of his or her daily experience.

It seems, then, that in the final analysis what it is like now is rather difficult to determine. And this is precisely the point. For all their keen insight, the historian-critics and their successors were too hasty in their classification and judgment of the cultural phenomena gathered under the rubric of "the therapeutic." It may be, indeed, that the term has now become too reprobative to designate an area for impartial exploration.

Perhaps it is time to remove it from our analytical maps. In any event, the modest sketch of twelve-step recovery attempted here demonstrates that there is nothing *necessarily* passive or remissive or antisocial about the modes of thought and practice encountered in this region. Any effort to understand and interpret its morals and customs ought at least to begin with this recognition. The varieties of therapeutic experience may never find their William James, but they are long overdue a measure of Jamesian open-mindedness. If dispassion in matters emotional and partisan is a prerequisite for such an inquiry, passionate precision in matters historical is equally imperative. The therapeutic culture and sensibility – assuming it makes sense to continue to speak in such abstractions – needs elucidation both in its constitutive complexity and in its thick entanglement in an even more complex historical context. Much more work is needed before firm conclusions can be drawn. Yet it is perhaps not too early to hazard the prediction that fair-minded inquirers will one day resolve that the "the therapeutic" was, and is, less an agent of such lamentable trends as the culture of consumption, the narcissistic personality, and the fall of public man, than a highly variegated and deeply ambivalent response to them.

Endnotes

1. I am indebted to Paul Antze, Daniel Borus, James I. Campbell, Joan Shelley Rubin, and Robert Westbrook for reading and commenting upon various earlier incarnations of this essay.
2. Philip Rieff, *The Triumph of the Therapeutic: Uses of Faith After Freud* (New York: Harper and Row, 1966), 242–61.
3. Christopher Lasch, *The Culture of Narcissism: American Life in an Age of Diminishing Expectations* (New York: W. W. Norton, 1979), 42–43. Also see his, *Haven in a Heartless World: The Family Besieged* (New York: Basic Books, 1977) and *The Minimal Self: Psychic Survival in Trouble Times* (New York: W. W. Norton, 1984).
4. Sociologist David Riesman's landmark work on inner and other directed character types, *The Lonely Crowd: A Study of the Changing American Character* (New Haven: Yale University Press, 1950), provided the theoretical framework for Susman and Lears.
5. Warren Susman's signal essay, "'Personality' and the Making of Twentieth-Century Culture," in *New Trends in Intellectual History*, eds. John Higham and Paul K. Conklin (Baltimore: John Hopkins University Press, 1979), 212–26 marked the inauguration of the historical elaboration of the therapeutic. T. J. Jackson Lears extended the project in his, *No Place of Grace: Antimodernism and the Transformation of American Culture, 1880–1920* (New York: Pantheon, 1981) and, "From

Salvation to Self-Realization: Advertising and the Therapeutic Roots of the Consumer Culture, 1880–1930," in *The Culture of Consumption: Critical Essays in American History, 1880–1980*, eds. Richard Wightman Fox and T. J. Jackson Lears (New York: Pantheon, 1983).

6   Rieff, "Observations on the Therapeutic," in *Psychological Man*, ed. Robert Boyers (New York: Harper and Row, 1975), 22–23.

7   Lasch, "Philip Rieff and the Religion of Culture," *The Revolt of the Elites and the Betrayal of Democracy* (New York and London: Norton, c.1995), 225.

8   "For of the last stage of this cultural development, it might well be truly said: 'Specialists without spirit, sensualists without heart; this nullity imagines that it has attained a level of civilization never before achieved.'" (Weber, *The Protestant Ethic and the Spirit of Capitalism*, trans. Talcott Parsons [London: Counterpoint, 1985], 182).

9   Richard Fox has detected a far more complicated dialectic between "personality" and "character" in his "The Culture of Liberal Protestant Progressivism, 1875–1925," *Journal of Interdisciplinary History* 23:3 (Winter, 1993): 639–60; and Eugene McCarraher, in "Heal Me: 'Personality,' Religion, and the Therapeutic Ethic in Modern America," *Intellectual History Newsletter* 21 (1999): 31–40, has found "character" in the mid-twentieth century work of liberal Protestant social thinker Paul Tillich, and "personality" in the hard-bitten neo-orthodoxy of Reinhold Niebuhr.

10 Paul Ricoeur, *Time and Narrative*, trans. Kathleen McLaughlin and David Pellauer (Chicago: University of Chicago Press, 1984). "Immanentization" is from Fox "The Culture of Liberal Protestant Progressivism," 645.

11 See Angus Nicholls' perceptive remarks on this topic, "The Secularization of Revelation from Plato to Freud," *Contretemps* 1 (September 2000): 62–70.

12 Brent D. Slife, *Time and Psychological Explanation* (Albany: State University of NewYork Press, 1993), 1–29.

13 See Johannes Fabian, *Time and the Other: How Anthropology Makes its Object* (New York: Columbia University Press, 1983); Fredric Jameson, *The Seeds of Time* (New York: Columbia University Press, 1994); Norbert Elias, *Time: An Essay* (Oxford: Blackwell, 1992); and Helga Nowotny, *Time: The Modern and Postmodern Experience*, trans. Neville Plaice (Oxford: Blackwell, 1994).

14 See Richard Terdiman, *Modernity and the Memory Crisis* (Ithaca: Cornell University Press, 1993); and Pierre Nora, "Introduction," *Realms of Memory* vol. 1 (New York: Columbia University Press, 1960).

15 See Michael O'Malley, *Keeping Watch: A History of American Time* (New York: Viking Penguin, 1990); Stephen Kern, *The Culture of Time and Space, 1880–1918* (Cambridge: Harvard University Press, 1983); and E. P. Thompson, "Time, Work-Discipline, and Industrial Capitalism," *Past and Present* 38 (December 1967): 86.

16 This list is a compression and adaptation of two others: Bertrand Helm's, in *Time and Reality in American Philosophy* (Amherst: University of Massachusetts Press, 1985), 2; and Brent Slife's, *Time and Psychological Explanation*, 28–29.

17 Sidney E. Ahlstrom, *A Religious History of the American People* (New Haven: Yale University Press, 1972), 391.

18 For the immanentism of American liberal Protestantism circa 1870–1930 see Fox, "The Culture of Liberal Protestant Progressivism, 1875–1925"; Ahlstrom, *A Religious History of the American People*; William Hutchison, *The Modernist Impulse in American Protestantism* (Cambridge and London: Harvard University Press, 1976); and Martin Marty, *Modern American Religion*, vol. 1: *The Irony of it All, 1893–1919* (Chicago: University of Chicago Press, 1986).

19 See James's famous chapter, "The Religion of Healthy-Mindedness," in *The Varieties of Religious Experience* (New York: Collier, 1961), 78–113. On the New Thought see Beryl Satter, *Each Mind a Kingdom: American Women, Sexual Purity, and the New Thought Movement, 1875–1920* (Berkeley: University of California Press, 1999).

20 "Practical metaphysics," in fact, was the title of a flagship New Thought journal of the late 1890s edited by Horatio Dresser, the movement's leading author and publicist.

21 I am thinking of the "young intellectuals" Waldo Frank, Van Wyck Brooks, Randolph Bourne, and Lewis Mumford (the group elucidated in Casey Blake's *Beloved Community: The Cultural Criticism of Randolph Bourne, Van Wyck Brooks, Waldo Frank, and Lewis Mumford* [Chapel Hill: University of North Carolina Press, 1990]), and of such fellow traveling leftist bohemians as John Reed, Emma Goldman, Max Eastman, and William English Walling, who articulated a distinctive brand of anti-materialist cultural and political radicalism in the 1910s.

22 James's observation is contained in "A World of Pure Experience" (1904), *The Writings of William James: A Comprehensive Edition*, ed. John J. McDermott (New York: Random House, 1967), 194–214. It is worth noting that in addition to the insurgency of Western immanentisms and subjectivisms, Eastern metaphysics made its first major incursion into the United States around this time.

23 I discuss this topic at length in "Vitalism and the Modernist Search for Meaning: Subjectivity, Social Order, and the Philosophy of Life in the Progressive Era" (PhD Dissertation, University of Rochester, 2001).

24 See Eric Caplan, *Mind Games: American Culture and the Birth of Psychotherapy* (Berkeley: University of California Press, 1998).

25 Ian Hacking, "Memory Sciences, Memory Politics," in *Tense Past: Cultural Essays in Trauma and Memory*, eds. Paul Antze and Michael Lambek (New York and London: Routledge, 1996), 70. Also see Stephen G. Brush, "Scientific Revolutionaries of the Twentieth Century," in *Rutherford and Physics at the Turn of the Century*, eds. Mario Bunge and William Shea (New York: Dawson and Science History Publications, 1979), 140–71.

26 Quoted in E. Hermann, *Eucken and Bergson: Their Significance for Christian Thought* (Boston: The Pilgrim Press, 1912), 70–71.

27 Ruth Leys, "Traumatic Cures: Shell Shock, Janet, and the Question of Memory" in *Tense Past*, 112.

28 See Henri Bergson, *Matter and Memory* [1908], trans., Nancy Margaret Paul and W. Scott Palmer (New York: Zone Books, 1988) 235.

29 Hence Carl Jung tops the list of twentieth-century therapeutic visionaries, a list that includes such names as D. H. Lawrence, Edgar Cayce, G. I. Gurdjieff, Wilhelm Reich, Aldous Huxley, Alan Watts, Carl Rogers, Rollo May, Werner Erhard, and Ken Wilber.

30 Richard Alpert (into Baba Ram Dass), *Be Here Now* (San Cristobal, NM: Hanuman Foundation, 1971).

31 For an alternative to this linear view, see Carol Duncan's exploration of *travessao* consciousness, "*Travessao*: African Diasporic Migratory Subjectivity and the Making of History," in this volume.

32 Twelve-step recovery began with the creation of Alcoholics Anonymous in the mid-1930s, an organization founded on the revelation of two recently dry alcoholics, Bill Wilson and Dr. Bob Smith, that their sobriety depended on helping other alcoholics achieve the same. The steps were developed to guide the freshly sober

Jeffrey Scott Brown

to a new way of life and have since been adapted to serve drug addicts, the loved ones of alcoholics and addicts, and those plagued by behaviors associated with the "addictive process."

33 Stanton Peele, *Diseasing of America: How We Allowed Recovery Zealots and the Treatment Industry to Convince Us We Are Out of Control* (New York: Lexington Books, 1989); Charles J. Sykes, *A Nation of Victims: The Decay of the American Character* (New York: St. Martin's Press, 1992); Stan Katz and Aimee Liu, *The Codependency Conspiracy* (New York: Warner Books, 1991); Wendy Kaminer, *I'm Dysfunctional You're Dysfunctional: The Recovery Movement and Other Self-Help Fashions* (Reading, MA: Addison Wesley, 1992). Also see Jeffrey Schaler, "Drugs and Free Will," *Society* 28:6 (September/October, 1991): 42–49.

34 David Rieff, "Victims All? Recovery, co-dependency, and the art of blaming somebody else," *Harper's Magazine* (October 1991), 49-56.

35 Ibid., 49.

36 Ibid.

37 For this observation, and my discussion of twelve-step recovery in general, I am indebted to friends and acquaintances who are members of twelve-step fellowships. Also see Craig Reinarman's nuanced discussion of the political implications of the recovery movement in his "The Twelve-Step Movement and Advanced Capitalist Culture: The Politics of Self-Control in Postmodernity," in *Cultural Politics and Social Movements*, eds. Marcy Darnovsky, Barbara Epstein, and Richard Flacks (Philadelphia: Temple University Press, 1995), 90–109.

38 The tendency to underestimate the pivotal role of the twelve steps is also evident in recent academic studies of the "codependency" variant of the twelve-step movement. See, Cary Greenberg, *The Self on the Shelf: Recovery Books and the Good Life* (Albany: State University of New York Press, 1994); John Steadman Rice, *A Disease of One's Own: Psychotherapy, Addiction, and the Emergence of Co-Dependency* (New Brunswick, NJ: Transaction Publishers, 1996); and Leslie Irvine, *Codependent Forevermore: The Invention of Self in a Twelve Step Group* (Chicago: University of Chicago Press, 1999).

39 Quoted in Sykes, *A Nation of Victims*, 137.

40 Ernest Kurtz offers an acute discussion of the "disease" of addiction as a metaphor for the "threefold" – physical, mental, and spiritual – "subjective condition of modernity" (202), in his intellectual history of AA, *Not God: A History of Alcoholics Anonymous* (Center City, MN: Hazelden, 1979), 199–204. Also see Mariana Valverde's perceptive discussion of AA's "ambiguous pragmatism" in *Diseases of the Will: Alcohol and the Dilemmas of Freedom* (Cambridge: Cambridge University Press, 1998). The history of interpreting, regulating, and treating addictions is laid out in encyclopedic fashion by William L. White, *Slaying the Dragon: The History of Addiction Treatment and Recovery in America* (Chestnut Health Systems/Lighthouse Institute, 1998).

41 Quoted in Paul Antze, "Symbolic Action in Alcoholics Anonymous," in *Constructive Drinking: Perspectives on Drink from Anthropology*, ed. Mary Douglas (Cambridge: Cambridge University Press, 1987), 168.

42 Ironically, twelve step fellowships seem to embody many of the characteristics that Philip Rieff associated with "positive" communities (see McCarraher, "Heal Me," 31–32, for a useful clarification of this aspect of Rieff's thought).

Bibliography

Ahlstrom, Sidney E. *A Religious History of the American People*. New Haven: Yale University Press, 1972.

Alpert, Richard. *Be Here Now*. San Cristobal, New Mexico: Hanuman Foundation, 1971.

Bergson, Henri. *Matter and Memory*. Trans. Nancy Margaret Paul and W. Scott Palmer. New York: Zone Books, 1988.

Blake, Casey. *Beloved Community: The Cultural Criticism of Randolph Bourne, Van Wyck Brooks, Waldo Frank, and Lewis Mumford*. Chapel Hill: University of North Carolina Press, 1990.

Brown, Jeffrey S. "Vitalism and the Modernist Search for Meaning: Subjectivity, Social Order, and the Philosophy of Life in the Progressive Era." Ph.D. dissertation, University of Rochester, 2001.

Brush, Stephen G. "Scientific Revolutionaries of the Twentieth Century." In *Rutherford and Physics at the Turn of the Century*, edited by Mario Bunge and William Shea, 140–71. New York: Dawson and Science History Publications, 1979.

Caplan, Eric. *Mind Games: American Culture and the Birth of Psychotherapy*. Berkeley: University of California Press, 1998.

Elias, Norbert. *Time: An Essay*. Oxford: Blackwell, 1992.

Fabian, Johannes. *Time and the Other: How Anthropology Makes its Object*. New York: Columbia University Press, 1983.

Fox, Richard. "The Culture of Liberal Protestant Progressivism, 1875–1925." *Journal of Interdisciplinary History* 23:3 (Winter 1993): 639–60

Greenberg, Cary. *The Self on the Shelf: Recovery Books and the Good Life*. Albany: State University of New York Press, 1994.

Hacking, Ian. "Memory Sciences, Memory Politics." In *Tense Past: Cultural Essays in Trauma and Memory*, edited by Paul Antze and Michael Lambek, 67–87. New York and London: Routledge, 1996.

Helm, Bertrand. *Time and Reality in American Philosophy*. Amherst: University of Massachusetts Press, 1985.

Hermann, E. *Eucken and Bergson: Their Significance for Christian Thought*. Boston: Pilgrim Press, 1912.

Hutchison, William. *The Modernist Impulse in American Protestantism*. Cambridge and London: Harvard University Press, 1976.

Irvine, Leslie. *Codependent Forevermore: The Invention of Self in a Twelve Step Group*. Chicago: University of Chicago Press, 1999.

James, William. "The Religion of Healthy-Mindedness." In *The Varieties of Religious Experience*, 78–113. New York: Collier, 1961.

———. "A World of Pure Experience." In *The Writings of William James: A Comprehensive Edition*, edited by John J. McDermott, 194–214. New York: Random House, 1967.

Jameson, Fredric. *The Seeds of Time*. New York: Columbia University Press, 1994.

Kaminer, Wendy. *I'm Dysfunctional You're Dysfunctional: The Recovery Movement and Other Self-Help Fashions*. Reading, MA: Addison Wesley, 1992.

Katz, Stan, and Aimee Liu. *The Codependency Conspiracy*. New York: Warner Books, 1991.

Kern, Stephen. *The Culture of Time and Space, 1880–1918*. Cambridge: Harvard University Press, 1983.

Kurtz, Ernest. *Not God: A History of Alcoholics Anonymous.* Center City, MN: Hazelden, 1979.
Lasch, Christopher. *Haven in a Heartless World: The Family Besieged.* New York: Basic Books, 1977.
———. *The Culture of Narcissism: American Life in an Age of Diminishing Expectations.* New York: W. W. Norton, 1979.
———. *The Minimal Self: Psychic Survival in Trouble Times.* New York: W. W. Norton, 1984.
———. "Philip Rieff and the Religion of Culture." In *The Revolt of the Elites and the Betrayal of Democracy.* New York and London: W. W. Norton, c1995.
Lears, T. J. Jackson. *No Place of Grace: Antimodernism and the Transformation of American Culture, 1880–1920.* New York: Pantheon, 1981.
———. "From Salvation to Self-Realization: Advertising and the Therapeutic Roots of the Consumer Culture, 1880–1930." In *The Culture of Consumption: Critical Essays in American History, 1880–1980*, edited by Richard Wightman Fox and T. J. Jackson Lears. New York: Pantheon, 1983.
Leys, Ruth. "Traumatic Cures: Shell Shock, Janet, and the Question of Memory." In *Tense Past: Cultural Essays in Trauma and Memory*, edited by Paul Antze and Michael Lambek, 103–45. New York and London: Routledge, 1996.
Marty, Martin. *Modern American Religion* vol. 1: *The Irony of it All, 1893–1919.* Chicago: University of Chicago Press, 1986.
McCarraher, Eugene. "Heal Me: 'Personality,' Religion, and the Therapeutic Ethic in Modern America." *Intellectual History Newsletter* 21 (1999): 31–40.
Nicholls, Angus. "The Secularization of Revelation from Plato to Freud," *Contretemps* 1 (September 2000): 62–70.
Nora, Pierre. "Introduction." In *Realms of Memory*, vol. 1. New York: Columbia University Press, 1960.
Nowotny, Helga. *Time: The Modern and Postmodern Experience.* Trans. Neville Plaice. Oxford: Blackwell, 1994.
O'Malley, Michael. *Keeping Watch: A History of American Time.* New York: Viking Penguin, 1990.
Peele, Stanton. *Diseasing of America: How We Allowed Recovery Zealots and the Treatment Industry to Convince Us We Are Out of Control.* New York: Lexington Books, 1989.
Reinarman Craig. "The Twelve-Step Movement and Advanced Capitalist Culture: The Politics of Self-Control in Postmodernity." In *Cultural Politics and Social Movements*, edited by Marcy Darnovsky, Barbara Epstein, and Richard Flacks, 90–109. Philadelphia: Temple University Press, 1995.
Rice, John Steadman. *A Disease of One's Own: Psychotherapy, Addiction, and the Emergence of Co-Dependency.* New Brunswick, NJ: Transaction Publishers, 1996.
Ricoeur, Paul. *Time and Narrative.* Trans. Kathleen McLaughlin and David Pellauer. Chicago and London: University of Chicago Press, 1984.
Rieff, David. "Victims All? Recovery, co-dependency, and the art of blaming somebody else." *Harper's Magazine* (October 1991): 49–56.
Rieff, Philip. *The Triumph of the Therapeutic: Uses of Faith After Freud.* New York: Harper and Row, 1966.
———. "Observations on the Therapeutic." In *Psychological Man*, edited by Robert Boyers, 18–26. New York: Harper and Row, 1975.
Riesman, David. *The Lonely Crowd: A Study of the Changing American Character.* New Haven: Yale University Press, 1950.

Satter, Beryl. *Each Mind a Kingdom: American Women, Sexual Purity, and the New Thought Movement, 1875–1920*. Berkeley: University of California Press, 1999.

Schaler, Jeffrey. "Drugs and Free Will," *Society* 28:6 (September/October, 1991): 42–49.

Slife, Brent D. *Time and Psychological Explanation*. Albany: State University of New York Press, 1993.

Susman. Warren. "'Personality' and the Making of Twentieth-Century Culture." In *New Trends in Intellectual History*, edited by John Higham and Paul K. Conklin, 212–26. Baltimore: John Hopkins University Press, 1979.

Sykes, Charles J. *A Nation of Victims: The Decay of the American Character*. New York: St. Martin's Press, 1992.

Terdiman, Richard. *Modernity and the Memory Crisis*. Ithaca: Cornell University Press, 1993.

Thompson, E. P. "Time, Work-Discipline, and Industrial Capitalism," *Past and Present* 38 (December 1967): 56–97.

Valverde, Mariana. *Diseases of the Will: Alcohol and the Dilemmas of Freedom*. Cambridge: Cambridge University Press, 1998.

Weber, Max. *The Protestant Ethic and the Spirit of Capitalism*. Trans. Talcott Parsons. London: Counterpoint, 1985.

White, William L. *Slaying the Dragon: The History of Addiction Treatment and Recovery in America*. Chestnut Health Systems/Lighthouse Institute, 1998.

8

Travessao: African Diasporic Migratory Subjectivity and the Making of History

CAROL B. DUNCAN

I believe there are a few events in my life which have not happened to many. It is true the incidents of it are numerous; and did I consider myself an European, I might say my sufferings were great: but when I compare my lot with that of most of my countrymen, I regard myself as a particular favourite of Heaven, and acknowledge the mercies of Providence in every occurrence of my life.

– Olaudah Equiano

¶ Introduction

Can we learn from history? Do we make history? These questions, while deceptively straightforward in their formulation, upon closer examination yield a myriad of possible responses which are themselves open to inquiry: Whose history is it, anyway? By what processes is "it" made and for what purposes? Who are the historians and what is their relationship to the subjects of history? These questions, broad, provocative, and

195

controversial, inform my discussion of the *travessao*, a spirit-traveler and intermediary figure, to whom I was introduced in my research on the lives of Spiritual Baptists, members of an African-Caribbean religion, who have emigrated to Toronto.

In this essay, I discuss the significance of the *travessao*, with specific reference to two Spiritual Baptist women's narratives about their individual and familial lives and the religion's history. Relatedly, I also extend my analysis to an exploration of the *travessao* as a trope in the writings of African-Caribbean and African-American women writers. This discussion emerges out of an ongoing concern with the ways in which individuals and communities in the African Diaspora in the Americas created, and continue to create, histories about themselves and their communities in the face of a legacy of both actual and perceived[1] misrepresentation and omission in mainstream historical narratives. While my focus is specifically on Spiritual Baptists in this essay, this discussion is contextualized within a larger conversation which includes post-colonial, feminist and post-modernist discussions concerning the construction of knowledge and its political and cultural implications.

As evinced by the quote from the 1789 *Narrative of Olaudah Equiano*, in the slave narratives – the genre which constitute the earliest writings by Africans in the Americas about their own experiences – we can see a reflection on the way in which black life experiences are differentially accounted for. This essay aims to contribute to this dialogue by examining one of the ways in which practitioners of an African-Caribbean religious tradition treat multiple localities and temporalities in personal and collective narrative accounts of experiences. By extension, I then examine a similar impulse in the writing of black women writers, Paule Marshall and Dionne Brand, as a way of exploring the significance of the *travessao* figure for scholarly analysis on the African Diaspora.

In exploring the figure of the *travessao* within the Spiritual Baptist Church, I engaged the religion's oral tradition. Here, oral traditions including prayer, testimony, sermon, song and dance represent a repository of the religion's history. In this sense, history is both theory and practice as Leo Groarke suggests in his essay,[2] in which he argues persuasively for the teaching of history. My own essay can be read, in part, as a counterpoint to his and Robert Wright's papers, through its engagement with the underlying problematic of the political stakes involved in historical accounts and a process of national identity building which is expressed in popular historical narratives. The arena in which I address these issues, however, shifts from the North American academy, mass media and popular culture to the ways in which practitioners of an African-Caribbean religion tell their own history, utilizing a narrative framework which presents an alternative approach to the theoretical and methodological approaches of "history" in the academy. In doing so, my essay also resonates with explorations of the factual/fictional divide in the construction of history.[3] In this way, I underscore the ways in which these multiple renderings of story often involved accounts that varied, not only from teller to teller, but also among different tellings by the same speaker.

¶ Methodology

My reflections are based primarily on participant/observer field research and in-depth interviews conducted with Spiritual Baptist Church members in Toronto over a five-year period from 1992 to 1997. This essay, therefore, grows out of the explication of a hermeneutic as enacted in religion's oral traditions as well as the explanations provided during interviews with practitioners. Chief amongst these ritual practices is "mourning," a period of prayer and fasting in which the pilgrim – as the one who mourns is designated – "travels," spiritually, and experiences visions and receives messages.

I sought, in doing my research, an interpretive framework which bridged "here" and "there." This framework is firmly rooted in the Spiritual Baptist worldview that posits an inextricable link between the spiritual and the material worlds. As expressed in the theology of the religion, "so carnally, so spiritually" or "so spiritually, so carnally," the events of the temporal, material world exist in a series of complex relationships to those of another ontological reality, the world of spirit.

This theory of interpretation is based on the *travessao*, a figure which emerges from Spiritual Baptist cosmology. The *travessao* represents a form of consciousness and way of being in the world which is fluid in its movements across boundaries of physical space and time as well as between different religious contexts. It validates fluidity, movement and the sometimes contradictory perspectives which emerge from telling stories from different vantage points as the basis of a critical perspective. I suggest here that the figure of the *travessao* represents the internal hermeneutic of Spiritual Baptist experiences, especially in the context of migration to Canada. The *travessao*, as a traveler, a spirit walker, is particularly responsive to stories which are told in transition and which reflect the restlessness and flexibility of the storytellers' vantage point.

I propose, then, that the *travessao* can be considered an intermediary, trickster figure like the Yoruban *orisha*, Eleggua or Elegba, Anansi the spider in the Caribbean tale-telling tradition and the signifyin' monkey in the folk traditions of Southern African-Americans. Henry Louis Gates in *The Signifyin' Monkey* and Joyce Jonas in *Anancy in the Great House* drew on these figures to define theories of literary criticism which emerged from within New World black story-telling traditions. Gates, in the preface to *The Signifyin' Monkey*, notes that "The challenge of my project if not exactly to invent a black theory, was to locate and identify how the black tradition had theorized about itself."[4] He further remarks that the reactions of a colleague and various students' to his work "confirmed my hope that I had at last located within the African and Afro-American traditions a system of rhetoric and interpretation that could be drawn upon both as figures for a genuinely 'black' criticism and as frames through which I could interpret, or 'read,' theories of contemporary literary criticism."[5]

My project mirrors Gates' in that I seek to locate the internal critic within the Spiritual Baptist tradition itself. I am concerned with locating the ways in which the members of the religion created an intrinsic theoretical tradition and produced their own narrative strategies, techniques of interpretation and accounts of their own history. This discernment happened largely within the context of face-to-face interpersonal communication, both in interviews with Spiritual Baptists in Toronto and Trinidad, and in the worship experience itself. I had to take a self-conscious look at Spiritual Baptist oral traditions of testifying, witnessing, preaching, praying and singing – the cornerstones of the religion's worship experience – as the locus of this system of critique.

I should note that this discernment was by no means a smooth process; I experienced an acute awareness of the disjuncture between the richness of the church members' often dialogic accounts about their own experiences and my attempts to represent those multiply-expressed experiences in a written format based on an assumption, initially, of the value of a single, one-voiced, expression. My tongue-tied status at the outset of my research on Spiritual Baptists was manifested in an awareness of the gap between my analytical categories, linear narrative directive, and my literary approach to "history" and the ways in which people's stories had actually emerged in complex oral narrative strategies often characterized by seemingly discontiguous and fragmented bits and pieces, which nevertheless constituted a whole story from the individuals' perspectives. The solution, or better stated, communicative and interpretive strategy, that I eventually employed was to *listen* carefully to the forms of oral communication which church members used and in which I myself was engaged, and to attempt to represent the oral accounts with all of their contradictions. In engaging this strategy, consciously, I found the figure of the *travessao* a useful analogy.

¶ *Travessao* Movement: "You in everyting"

The *travessao* transgresses barriers between dualistic pairs such as past/present; black/white; listener/speaker. The *travessao* can be conceptualized as an inhabitant of the borderlands, the territory Gloria Anzaldúa points to as *la frontera*.[6] The *travessao* is an expression of what Anzaldúa calls "mestiza consciousness," which she describes as a third, intermediary space that embraces contradictions. For Anzaldúa, this consciousness was born out of her life as a Latina in the United States facing contradictions of "race," colour, language, and nation.[7]

In the following excerpts from a conversation between Queen Mother Ruby and myself she discusses the figure of the *travessao*, noting its "cosmopolitan" and "mixed" nature enabling travel to "many nations":

A *travessao*? Well that is when they [have] many nations now. You in everyting. Yes. And sometimes … sometimes, they claim, the people who would do wickedness and they want to find you, they can't find you. [laughter] So now it come like if somebody looking for you and even though you were safe and when dey come here, dey ain' see you. They want to know wey you gone. Becor dey know you was here.... It have many um, spiritual people ... well some a' dem wouldn' [say] *travessao*, they say, "mixed nations." You're Indian. You could be still Chinee. You understan'? Mmmhmm. So in every country, you could be fin' dere. But is only who would know you would be able to fin' you out. Because it come ... let us say, I know you and maybe if I leave here now and go out from where you may dress up ... serve ting dat I wouldn' make you out. But with you now, you will ...'Dis ain't Mother Ruby?' Becor' through curiosity, you will [say] "Come, ain't your name is Mother Ruby?" Ah say, "Well, yes." "But you ain" remember me?' Ah say, "No." "Aah, is Carol." We goin' to greet! Because you know me and I know you! So when we leave dere now, you go on 'bout your business and I gone 'bout mine.[8]

While the terminology used by Queen Mother Ruby is different than that used by Anzaldúa, the meaning is synonymous.

In the following excerpt, Mother Yvonne, a church leader in Toronto, relates her experience of being a "nation mother" as a *travessao* experience precisely because of the notion of "mixed nations":

It's on the Orisha ... it means that you would be in all different aspects of the spiritual world. When we talk of versatility as like for me ... I'm gonna use myself again as an example. I'm what they call a nation mother. I work out of India. I work the – the nation, all the nations. I was given Mother of the Twelve Tribes. I was given my colours to represent that. I receive it. Some people receive it in flags. I receive it in cords of twelve different colours. So, when it was thrown on my shoulders, that's like, every cord was a pound. On my shoulder. Because I'm nation representing every nation, this is what we call a *travessao* of the spirit. You know, you're anywhere. Anywhere spiritually. You could be found.[9]

The figure of the *travessao* is identified with mobility, and "versatility," to use Mother Yvonne's term. Both Mother Yvonne and Queen Mother Ruby, who identify with *travessao* experiences, have "mixed nation" ancestry in their family histories. Queen Mother Ruby's parents emigrated from Barbados and St. Vincent to Trinidad while Mother Yvonne's father's family came from Grenada to Trinidad. As Queen

Mother Ruby remarked: "Well, my mother was a Barbadian. And me faada was a Vincentian. So, I wasn' born in Trinidad! [laughter with C]. [Coughs] So sometime I does sit down and – and ask meself what ah really is."

These women's life histories mirror the multiple migrations within the region and especially Trinidad and Tobago in the early decades of the twentieth century, when people from smaller islands in the Eastern Caribbean migrated to Trinidad and Tobago in search of work. Coupled with their stories, it was my own experience of multiple migration[10] that prompted Queen Mother Ruby to identify *travessao* experiences with my research. This identification, based on my personal and familial migratory history from the Caribbean to England and then to Canada, inspired me to think in a self-conscious way about how this movement and migration had influenced the construction and relaying of knowledge both in written and oral rhetorical forms. The experience also prompted me to think self-consciously about my own agency in writing rather than to focus solely on Mother Yvonne and Queen Mother Ruby's agency as the subjects/objects of research.[11]

¶ *Travessao* Consciousness

Is the *travessao* a figure with an ontological reality? The use of the term by Queen Mother Ruby, and Mother Yvonne and other Spiritual Baptists with whom I spoke, pointed to a "*travessao* of the spirit" as a way of being, seeing and interacting in the world which encompasses movement, fluidity and contradictions. To say, then, that an experience is *travessao* is to indicate its multi-locality and movement; it is to point to discontinuous locations and identities and – importantly – to the ability to skilfully navigate and negotiate these differences and contradictions. As Mother Yvonne noted, in the excerpt from our conversation, a *travessao* of the spirit would be "versatile"and furthermore, "People would not be able to handle you." In this way, the figure of the *travessao* defies one, singular definition and is a figure of resistance. This is clear in the following observation made by Queen Mother Ruby: "So now it come like if somebody looking for you and even though you were safe and when dey come here, dey ain' see you. They want to know wey gone. Becor dey know you was here." However, this multi-faceted identity does not mean ontological insecurity. As Queen Mother Ruby indicated, *travessao*, while having the ability to travel to "other" environments and locales, maintain a knowledge of who they really are, a knowledge of an authentic self which is recognizable to others – safe others rather than enemies.

The *travessao* is born of the history of movement and migration within and outside of the Caribbean region. It is a figure that emerges from the discontinuous landscapes of the Caribbean and its littorals. Benitez-Rojo notes that as a "meta-archipelago":

it has the virtue of having neither a boundary nor a center. Thus the Caribbean flows outward past the limits of its own sea with a vengeance, and its *ultima Thule* may be found on the outskirts of Bombay, near the low and murmuring shores of Gambia, in a Cantonese tavern of circa 1850, at a Balinese temple, in an old Bristol pub, in a commercial warehouse in Bordeaux at the time of Colbert, in a windmill beside the Zuider Zee, at a café in a barrio of Manhattan, in the existential saudade of an old Portuguese lyric. But what is it that repeats? Tropisms, in series; movements in approximate direction. Let's say the unforeseen relation between a dance movement and the baroque spiral of a colonial railing.[12]

Benitez Rojo's discussion of the Caribbean archipelago as a "repeating island" helps us construct the imaginary geography of *travessao* consciousness.

Carole Boyce Davies' discussion of the Caribbean also echoes Benitez Rojo's notion of the Caribbean as a "meta-archipelago" while cautioning against the invocation of "race" and "colour"-based hierarchies in pointing to notion of a "mixed" identity:

Caribbean identities then are products of numerous processes of migration. As a result, many conclude that the Caribbean is not so much a geographical location but a cultural construction based on a series of mixtures, languages, communities of people. Thus some speak of "creolization" or "metissage" as a fundamental defining of the Caribbean. Still, "creole" and "mestizo" carry their own negativities and associations with positions in racial hierarchy, if used in relation to Black populations in certain countries like Brazil.[13]

As Davies cautiously notes, "some" – not all – speak of "creolization" and "metissage" as defining characteristics of the Caribbean. Her comments here point to the existence of other possibilities for conceptualizing and understanding the history of the region. The metaphor of the *travessao* creates a space for those multiple imaginings.

¶ Boundary Crossing and Displacement

Travessao shifts of time and place involve a remembering, for as Queen Mother Ruby's and Mother Yvonne's comments intimated, the movements are purposeful as well as exploratory. As noted by Carole Boyce Davies, acts of reconnecting are representative of African people's political, cultural and social experiences because of a history of separation:

Because we were/are products of separations and dislocations and dismemberings, people of African descent in the Americas historically have sought reconnection. From the "flying back" stories which originated in slavery to the "Back to Africa" movements of Garvey and those before him, to the Pan-Africanist activity of people like Dubois and C.L.R. James, this need to reconnect and re-member, as Morrison would term it, has been a central impulse in the structuring of Black thought.[14]

The experiences of *travessao* encompass this desire to reconnect and remember through time and space. Thus, the *travessao* is simultaneously historian, cartographer and geographer, drawing and re-drawing discontinuous maps while creating narrative accounts. Both Queen Mother Ruby's and Mother Yvonne's descriptions of the *travessao* imply cross-cultural and cross-religious boundary crossing. However, Carole Boyce Davies reminds us of historian and singer Bernice Johnson Reagon's assertion that "any crossing of boundaries can mean occupying space belonging to someone else."[15] Questions of appropriation and disenfranchisement are implied here. This notion of displacement takes on an additional significance for the relationship between researchers and the individuals and communities with whom they are working.

Figures like the Watchman and the Prover and Diver in the Spiritual Baptist tradition operate as boundary keepers. They are the self-conscious way in which a religious tradition that embraces boundary crossing checks and balances itself. The leadership roles or church offices of Prover, Diver, and Watchman point to the ways in which the Spiritual Baptist Church has developed its own internal system of critique. If the *travessao* is the figure that is able to simultaneously exist in multiple locations, the Watchman, Prover and Diver are the capacities that address veracity and dissemination of knowledge.

In the following, Queen Mother Ruby describes the role of the Prover and Diver with reference to Spiritual Baptist churches in Trinidad in her past experience. She notes: "But in does days, people couldn' do anyting, anyhow and come in a Baptist church. Becor di Prover dere to Prove you. Di Diver dere to dive you out." The Prover serves as a kind of moral compass of the religious community: "well, let us say as how tiefin' is rampant and all dis, now. You couldn' do all dese tings and come in a churchlong time and get off wid it. Dey will know you. 'Cor dey have di Provers dey. Dey'll only watch you and according to whatever inspire within dem, what dey get, dey will come and dey kick you out."

These church offices, regarded by members as spiritual "gifts," point to a multi-faceted system of knowledge production and verification within the Spiritual Baptist Church. The usefulness from a critical, theoretical viewpoint is to employ this "internal" critique as a viable, constructive way of accounting for "what happened." It points to a theory of knowledge which allows for multiple interpretations and questioning in the construction of history.

I am not, however, suggesting a reformulated diasporic, Caribbean variant of a *laissez faire*, cultural relativist approach. What I am suggesting in pointing to multiple points of origin and multiple temporalities is an alternative orientation to conceptualizing history. My task here is not to suggest a wholesale application of Spiritual Baptist ways of knowing within an academic context, but to show the intrinsic, self-defined ways of knowing which proved useful for discussing the history of the church and the experiences of its members in Toronto. Self-conscious adaptation of this perspective in doing research on the Spiritual Baptist community in Toronto provided many occasions in which I was "proven," "taught," "dove out" as well as "prophesied to" within both observation of ritual contexts and in conversational interviews. How can this perspective be useful in scholarly analysis? In the following, I will address this question with reference to the writing of Paule Marshall and Dionne Brand.

¶ *Travessao* in the writing of Paule Marshall and Dionne Brand

Travessao consciousness is evident in the writing of writers Paule Marshall and Dionne Brand. Both women's life histories bridge the Caribbean and to North America. Paule Marshall is the American-born daughter of Barbadian immigrants while Brand, herself, emigrated to Toronto from Trinidad. In Paule Marshall's *Praisesong for the Widow* and Dionne Brand's *In Another Place Not Here* we are presented with the female protagonists Avatara "Avey" Johnson, and Verlia and Elizete. These black women's personal transformations are profoundly affected by their physical and spiritual movements between the Caribbean, Africa and North America. In each of these novels, the narrative shifts between past and present with projections into the immediate future. These novels are all "historical" in that they address the history of Africans and their descendants in the Americas through an intimate telling of personal and familial stories. A discussion of these novels is necessary here for they demonstrate a way in which a text can be produced employing the strategies of *travessao* consciousness in moving between the spirit and the material, the seen and unseen and "here" and "there," the spoken and the written and the past and the present.

In *Praisesong*, Avey Johnson, a middle-class black woman approaching elderhood, completes the circle of recognition and reintegration of a fragmented self through her participation in a Big Drum ceremony on the island of Cariaccou. This ritual resonates with the Shouter ring dances she witnessed with her Great Aunt Cuney as a child on summer holidays in a Gullah community. Marshall's novel is representative of *travessao* consciousness in Avey Johnson's movements between past and present, waking and dreaming, the North American mainland and Cariaccou in the Caribbean.

In the following passage, the reader is told of the beginning of Avey Johnson's voyage of reintegration. The series of events that lead to Avey's disembarking from the cruise ship before the end of her journey is precipitated by an encounter with her Great Aunt Cuney in a dream. This occurrence is representative of the simultaneous present- and past-tense existence of *travessao* consciousness:

And then three nights ago, in the dream, there the old woman had been after all those years, drawn up waiting for her on the road beside Shad Dawson's wood cedar and oak. Standing there unmarked by the grave in the field hat and the dress with the double belts, beckoning to her with a hand that should have been fleshless bone by now: clappers to be played at a Juba.[16]

In fact, the story that Great Aunt Cuney had passed on to Avey – the one whose importance she came back to underline for her – demands a *travessao* consciousness in accepting its veracity. This is the story of the Africans who walked back across the water when the slave ship landed at Ibo Landing. The story has a double resonance. The first one is that the Africans who turned and walked into the waters of the Atlantic drowned in a collective act of suicide. The second resonance is a telling which posits that they walked across the water, all the way home to Africa in a feat as miraculous as that of Jesus. This meaning is made clear by Great Aunt Cuney answering a ten-year-old Avey's question wondering why they had not died with the question: "Did it say Jesus drowned when he went walking on the water in that Sunday School book your momma always send with you?"[17] Her inference is that this story – like the story of Jesus walking on the water – should be accepted as a matter of faith.

It has been suggested that this story and its location, Ibo Landing, held religious significance for Great Aunt Cuney: "People in Tatem said she had made the Landing her religion after that [her expulsion from the religious community for dancing in church as distinguished from the intricate, rhythmic steps of the shout]."[18] Great Aunt Cuney recounted this "miracle" of the Ibo summer after summer to Avey as a child. The story embodied the "necessary distance" and connectedness with Africa needed for survival amongst communities of Africans in the Diaspora. This "distance" and "connectedness" were symbolized in Great Aunt Cuney's stance: "Her body she always usta say might be in Tatem, but her mind, her mind was long gone with the Ibos."[19]

With reference to Avey Johnson's connectedness to Diasporic African cultures as a child, Marshall referred to an image of threads, reminiscent of umbilical cords, which weave in and out of the child and the others in her community. The passage, excerpted at length is as follows:

Boat rides up the Hudson! Sometimes, standing with her family amid the growing crowd on the pier, waiting for the Robert Fulton to heave into sight, she would have the same strange sensation as when she stood beside her great-aunt outside the church in Tatem, watching the elderly folk inside perform the Ring Shout. *As more people arrived to throng the area beside the river and the cool morning air warmed to the greeting and talk, she would feel what seemed to be hundreds of slender threads streaming out from her navel and from the place where her heart was to enter those around her.* And the threads went out not only to people she recognized from the neighbourhood but to those she didn't know as well, such as the roomers just up from the South and the small group of West Indians whose odd accent called to mind Gullah talk and who it was said were as passionate about their rice as her father.[20]

Avey then realizes that her connectedness to others is two-way and that the threads also emanate from "their navels and hearts to stream into her." Threads were "lifelines" on which Avey could pull for help: "*She visualized the threads as being silken, like those used in the embroidery on a summer dress, and of a hundred different colors.*"[21]

Note Mother Yvonne's earlier description of her role as a "nation mother" – symbolized by the spiritual "gift" of twelve multi-coloured "cords" – echoed here in Marshall's novel as the childhood Avey's "threads" of many hues. It is interesting to remark that Avey's threads simultaneously emanate from, and enter, her heart and her navel symbolizing both "heart-felt" emotional, affective as well as "birth" and blood relative connections. Mother Yvonne's cords are also linked to her body. For her, however, they are resting on her shoulder. This passage even references the function of the Diver discussed earlier in pointing to the threads as "lifelines," which could be pulled should she venture into the deepest of "waters." Here the waters of the Hudson River symbolize life experiences including those which are most threatening.

Shifting northwards and southwards, Dionne Brand's *oeuvre*, including essays, short stories, and her novel *In Another Place, Not Here*, interrogates the tension experienced by immigrant African-Caribbean women of being "here" in Canada and "there" in the Caribbean. In her collection of essays, *Bread Out of Stone*, Brand moves in *travessao* form from her past as a child in Trinidad, interpreting the proverbs of the adults around her in "Bread Out of Stone" and "Water More than Flour," to her contemporary reality of adulthood in Toronto. In these essays she reflects on her childhood in Trinidad, her adult life in Toronto and the politics of "race," gender, class and sexuality.

In "Just Rain, Bacolet," Brand reflects on movement and migration, noting the significance of travelling for Africans in the Diaspora:

Traveling is a constant state. You do not leave things behind or take them with you, everything is always moving; you are not the centre of your own movement, everything sticks, makes you more heavy or more light as you lurch, everything changes your direction. We were born thinking of traveling back. It is our singular preoccupation, we think of nothing else. I am convinced. We are continually uncomfortable where we are. We do not sleep easily, not without dreaming of traveling back. This must be the code written on the lining of my brain, go back, go back, like a fever, a pandemic scourging the Diaspora – Go back, the call waiting for an answer. How complicated they can get, all the journeys to the answer, all the journeys, physical and imaginary, on airplane, on foot, in the heart and drying on the tongue.

Faith and I glimpse it here. We first get off the airplane and slip into our skin, the gravity of racial difference disappears. *But it is this and more, a knowledge we slip into, a kind of understanding of the world which will get us through.* Here we only have to pay attention to what we do. One night Vi called, said, Do you want to see a leather-back turtle? She's laying her eggs on Turtle Beach. We went. I felt called as I do for every event here. Surrounded so by spirits, history, ancestors, I give over to their direction. I realize that I live differently in Canada. I live without connection to this world with its obligations, homage, significance, with how you are in the soul.[22]

In the above excerpt, Brand makes explicit reference to that which characterizes *travessao* consciousness: movement both physical and spiritual, fluidity and restlessness. Significantly she notes that there is a "kind of understanding of the world which will get us through" which comes out of this experience. I suggest that this "kind of understanding" which allows one to get through is *travessao* consciousness.

In her novel, *In Another Place, Not Here*, this "kind of understanding" is evident in the narrative flow of the story between Toronto and Trinidad. The story takes place in the liminal spaces between the real and the imaginary[23] in Toronto and Trinidad in the lives of Elizete and Verlia, two women who become lovers and who are motivated by a deep longing for change in their lives. Elizete longs for escape from Trinidad and life with her husband Isaiah. Verlia arrives in Elizete's community looking for change through revolution. This story of love between Verlia and Elizete is also a story of multiple migration of the spirit, body and mind in the fruition of a diasporic dream of flight. Elizete is attracted to Verlia's *travessao* qualities of movement. She thinks to herself: "I like it how she leap. Run in the air without moving. I watch she make she way around we as if she was from here, all the time moving faster than the last thing she say. It come so I know where she standing in the field without looking for she. Because she moving, moving, moving all the time without moving. If I didn't like it she would frighten me."[24] The *travessao* qualities are Verlia's ability to blend in: "I watch she make she way around here we as if she was from here" and her constant "moving, moving all the time without moving." These observations by Verlia, a Trinidadian woman character created by Brand, a woman herself from Trinidad, echo Trinidadian Spiritual Baptist elder Queen Mother Ruby's earlier comments in which she pointed to the abilities of *travessao* to disguise themselves. She noted: "So now it come like if somebody looking for you and even though you were safe and when dey come here, dey ain' see you."

When the reader encounters Elizete at the opening of the novel, she is a woman who dreams of flight from her life. However, both the dream and possibility of this flight are blocked:

Nobody here can remember when they wasn't here. I come here with Isaiah. He show me the room and he show me the washtub and the he show me the fire and he show me the road. He tell me never let him catch me at the junction. I didn't believe him but I find out soon when I catch the end of his whip. That was long time now. No need to remember. I don't even remember when I stop trying to run away, stop trying to make that junction. It was long. He would always be at that junction when I get there. I tried for a long time. I think to myself one day he is going to miss, one day. One day when he think I train, he is going to miss. But I stop. He get his way. When I see that it was his play, I resign. He stop watching me but then I remember why I was trying to get there. Didn't have no place to go anyway when I think of it. Trying to get to the junction so much I forget where I was going. I know every track leading to it but when I get there and see Isaiah, I come like he was the end of it. I used to have some place in mind I know but.... One time, I plotting my way through the mangle, one of these old ones I never expect ask me "Where you running running so all the time?" The spite of the thing hit me and it take me by surprise, and I suppose I didn't have nowhere in mind except not here. Cold water just run in my feet then. You trust old people to know better. Why they wouldn't want good for me? If you can't see a way for yourself, see it for somebody else nah? So all of that is how I wear away.[25]

In this passage, Elizete reveals her dream of flight, her thwarting by Isaiah and the recognition by an elder of her ability to "run." Elizete feels blocked by the refusal of the old one to envision a place not here even if it is a place for someone else. Meeting Verlia and imagining the possibility of migration to Canada make the "not here" a possibility. Elizete's desire for flight echoes the desire for flight in African cultures throughout the Diaspora. Expressed in song, religious tradition and dance, the desire for flight politically, culturally and physically from enslavement is embodied by the *travessao*.

¶ Conclusion

Let us return to some of the initial questions asked at the outset of this essay concerning history. These questions were aimed at examining history as process, involving both methodological and theoretical assumptions, as well as the authorship of history. In the foregoing discussion of the *travessao* figure as discussed by Spiritual Baptist women, Queen Mother Ruby and Mother Yvonne, and as manifested in the works of African-Caribbean and African-American women writers, the female protagonists serve emphatically as both historical subjects *and* historians. They also embody fluidity, multiple realities, and discontinuity as opposed to linearity and monolithic reality. Their stories introduce a way of critically analyzing Caribbean narratives which bridge both the oral and the literary, the factual and the fictive, "here" and "there," through the figure of the *travessao*.

In the same way that aboriginal notions of space differ from European conceptions,[26] so too the *travessao* notion of time and reality varies from the dominant western view. Thus, through the *travessao*, we the reading audience view historical accounts as storied happenings that are at once specific, local and general in their telling. Shifts between a Caribbean past and a Toronto present, dreams and everyday waking life, a mythic African and biblical past and contemporary political reality are a part of the weaving of the historical. Past, present and future are not discrete but inextricably linked, and events – even the seemingly mundane – potentially have wider resonance and significance. The *travessao*, from this perspective, is both witness and narrator of history. And perhaps, if we are concerned, both to truly make history meaningful to a wider audience and to be sensitive to the actors in the dramas we write, the *travessao*, with its multiple locations in time and space, is the ideal guide.

Endnotes

1. I have noted the legacy of "actual *and* perceived" misrepresentation and omission, for while the works of contemporary historians of Africans and their descendants in the Americas (for example David St. George Walker, Philip S. Curtin, Barbara Bush, Barry David Gaspar and Nell Irvin Painter) have aimed at providing accurate and complex accounts, I think that it is plausible to argue that an awareness of the weight of previous generations' misrepresentations and omissions fuels, in part, popular discourse in black communities about the history of Africans in the Diaspora.
2. See Leo Groarke, "Teaching History: The Future of the Past," in this volume.
3. A divide also explored by John Hill in this collection (see John S. Hill, "Historical Fictions: The Invention of Historical Events for Political Purposes"). Interestingly, Hill concludes that the fabrications he explores often end up having unexpected consequences beyond the control of the manipulators.
4. Henry Louis Gates, Jr., *The Signifying Monkey: A Theory of Afro-American Literary Criticism* (New York and London: Oxford University Press, 1988), ix.
5. Ibid.
6. See Gloria Anzaldúa, *Borderlands: The New Mestiza* (San Francisco: Aunt Lute, 1987).

7 See Gloria Anzaldúa, "La conciencia de la mestiza: Towards a New Consciousness," in Anzaldúa ed., *Making Face, Making Soul: Haciendo Caras: Creative and Critical Perspectives by Feminists of Color* (San Francisco: Aunt Lute Books, 1990), 377–89.
8 Queen Mother Ruby, Interview by author, Movant, Trinidad, 29 August 1995.
9 Mother Yvonne, Interview by author, Toronto, Canada, 11 November 1994.
10 As a British-born black woman of Antiguan and Guyanese parentage who spent her early childhood in Antigua before moving to Canada, the notion of migratory subjectivity is something which has not only fascinated me as a researcher but has also informed my familial history and, indeed, ways of perceiving identity in relationship to history.
11 For a fuller discussion, see my essay, "'This Spot of Ground': Migration, Community and Identity Amongst Spiritual Baptists," in Nuzhat Amin et al., eds. *Canadian Woman Studies: An Introductory Reader* (Toronto: Inanna Publications and Education Inc., 1999), 471–77.
12 Antonio Benitez-Rojo, *The Repeating Island: the Caribbean and the Postmodern Perspective* (Durharm: Duke University Press, 1992).
13 Carole Boyce Davies, *Black Women, Writing and Identity: Migrations of the Subject* (London and New York: Routledge, 1994).
14 Ibid., 17.
15 Ibid., 18.
16 Paule Marshall, *Praisesong for the Widow* (New York: Penguin Books, 1983), 40.
17 Ibid.
18 Ibid., 34.
19 Ibid., 39.
20 Ibid., 190 (my emphasis).
21 Ibid., 191 (my emphasis).
22 Dionne Brand, *Bread Out of Stone: Recollections, Sex, Recognitions, Race, Dreaming, Politics* (Toronto: Coach House Press, 1994), 58–59 (my emphasis).
23 I have purposely not used the term "magic realism" because in many ways it suggests a monolithic literary genre lumping together significantly different world views and socio-historical cultural contexts in ways that may not be particularly useful for critical analysis. It can also signal the reader that this text is not only "unreal" but it is "unreal" in a way that other "fiction" is not. In other words, it is *more* unreal and therefore more easily dismissed than other fictive or "real" texts.
24 Dionne Brand, *In Another Place Not Here* (Toronto: A. A. Knopf Canada, 1996), 7.
25 Ibid., 8–9.
26 See John McLaren, "The Memory of Property: The Challenge of Using the Past to Enlighten the Lawyers of the Future," in this volume.

Bibliography

Anzaldúa, Gloria. *Borderlands: The New Mestiza.* San Francisco: Aunt Lute, 1987.

———. "La conciencia de la mestiza: Towards a New Consciousness." In *Making Face, Making Soul: Haciendo Caras: Creative and Critical Perspectives by Feminists of Color,* edited by Gloria Anzaldúa, 377–89. San Francisco: Aunt Lute Books, 1990.

Benitez-Rojo, Antonio. *The Repeating Island: the Caribbean and the Postmodern Perspective.* Durharm: Duke University Press, 1992.

Brand, Dionne. *Bread Out of Stone: recollections, sex, recognitions, race, dreaming, politics.* Toronto: Coach House Press, 1994.

———. *In Another Place Not Here.* Toronto: A. A. Knopf Canada, 1996.

Davies, Carole Boyce. *Black Women, Writing and Identity: Migrations of the Subject.* London and New York: Routledge, 1994.

Duncan, Carol B. "'This Spot of Ground': Migration, Community and Identity Amongst Spiritual Baptists." In *Canadian Woman Studies: An Introductory Reader,* edited by Nuzhat Amin et al., 471–77. Toronto: Inanna Publications and Education, 1999.

Gates, Jr., Henry Louis. *The Signifying Monkey: A Theory of Afro-American Literary Criticism.* New York and London: Oxford University Press, 1988.

Marshall, Paule. *Praisesong for the Widow.* New York: Penguin Books, 1983.

Mother Yvonne. Interview by author. Toronto, Canada, 11 November 1994.

Queen Mother Ruby. Interview by author. Movant, Trinidad, 29 August 1995.

IV

Future History: Technological Development and Historical Change

"History is more or less bunk. It's tradition. We don't want tradition. We want to live in the present and the only history that is worth a tinker's damn is the history we made today."
– Henry Ford

"History cannot give us a program for the future, but it can give us a fuller understanding of ourselves, and of our common humanity so that we can better face the future"
– Robert Penn Warren

9

Canada's Lost Tradition of Technological Criticism

JAMES GERRIE

In studying the philosophical critiques of modern society of three pioneering Canadian technology theorists, Harold Innis, Marshall McLuhan and George Grant, I found myself facing a peculiar situation as a philosopher. The more I investigated, the more I found I needed more information about their biographies in order to fully understand their philosophical work. This represented a peculiar situation because much of my philosophical training generally involved strong inducements to focus solely on the ideas of the great thinkers I was examining and subtle discouragement not to look too closely at their lives and the historical context of their intellectual activity.

Such investigation did not come naturally, but it was absolutely necessary because the three figures I was examining each had not only contributed influential writings to the academic world, but had played prominent leadership roles in both the academy and various public institutions. This fact alone would have warranted some interest on my part in their biographies, but it was a purely theoretical requirement that clinched the necessity for the inclusion of such investigation in my analysis of the philosophical implications of their work on technology. The following, therefore, represents not only a defence of a distinctive philosophical approach to technology that I feel is shared by these three prominent twentieth-century Canadian intellectuals, but an account of my discovery, as a professional philosopher, of the importance of the work of professional historians.

Many in the field of the Philosophy of Technology consider Martin Heidegger's 1953 lecture "The Question Concerning Technology," and Herbert Marcuse's 1941 article "Some Social implications of Modern Technology" as seminal writings in the emergence of this new sub-discipline of philosophy. In these writings one finds expressions of philosophical critiques of technology that emphasize the intimate relationship between technology and everyday human practice.[1] Around the same time that Heidegger and Marcuse were forming their groundbreaking perspectives on modern technological civilization, three pioneering Canadian technology theorists, Harold Innis, Marshall McLuhan and George Grant, were also developing critical practice-based understandings of technology. In Innis' deep concern about "the mechanization of knowledge" presented in his 1948 address to the Conference of Commonwealth Universities at Oxford, reprinted in *The Bias of Communication*, Grant's 1948 essay on "The Philosophy of Francis Bacon" and McLuhan's concept of the medium as message, first presented in 1951 in *The Mechanical Bride: The Folklore of Industrial Man*, one finds non-artifact based understandings of technology, which emphasize the danger that technology poses to our civilization. Over the course of their careers each of these three thinkers also argued that our ordinary involvement in technological practice can create a dependence on a technological approach to life and that meeting the ethical challenges of technology must involve an appropriate awareness of this kind of dependence.

Arthur Kroker's seminal work on these three figures, however, emphasizes the dissimilarities of their positions on the ethical implications of technology.[2] According to Kroker, McLuhan is an optimistic herald of the new information age, Grant is a dark prophet of technological society, and Innis a practical-minded intermediary between these two visions of our technological future. John Goyder, on the other hand, argues that there is a certain similarity between the perspectives of Grant and

McLuhan, but this shared perspective results not in a critical attitude towards technology but, according to Goyder, "a state of fascinated ambivalence."[3] The following essay argues that a fundamental unity can be found in the varied responses of Innis, McLuhan and Grant to the ethical challenges of technology and that their general ethical approaches to technology are significantly more critical of technological development than either Kroker or Goyder acknowledge.

Innis, McLuhan and Grant are generally acknowledged as engaged public intellectuals. Unlike some of their colleagues, they did not avoid involvement in public life. According to Daniel Drache:

More than any other Canadian scholar in recent times, Innis's prodigious writings on political economy shaped the views of his contemporaries, from Donald Creighton, one of Canada's most eminent historians, to Marshall McLuhan, a world figure in communications theory. As a leading university administrator, Innis was a moving force in the founding of the Social Sciences Research Council of Canada and a key figure in public life while Dean of Graduate Studies at the University of Toronto. Throughout much of his adult life, Harold Adams Innis was Canada's pre-eminent thinker and theoretician. He had the stature of a Galbraith in public policy; governments beat a path to his door for advice and counsel.[4]

McLuhan and Grant were similarly involved in the world around them. McLuhan played the role of public intellectual and "was a worldwide celebrity by the late 1960s, an overnight sensation created by the same forces that his work described."[5] Grant wrote books for wide public audiences in Canada, such as *Lament for a Nation*, which was highly praised both by nationalist conservatives and members of Canada's new left movement in the late sixties. As a result, as Rawlinson and Granatstein note in their survey of Canada's most prominent twentieth century intellectuals, "Grant's influence on the public and the politicians was immense. Even today in a much more integrated North America, Grant's lament continues to rally the nationalist Tories, the left-Liberals, and the social democrats."[6] What is puzzling is that, despite their willingness to play a public role, in all of their extensive writings on technology there is a strange silence about the practical matter of how to best go about making practical judgements about technologies and technological issues.

Carl Berger suggests that an impractical or even determinist approach to social and political issues was an integral part of Innis' outlook throughout his career. He notes that "for reformers, Innis appeared to dwell excessively on what men could not do.... He had an anti-reformist bias.... He often seemed more impressed – one might almost say overwhelmed – with the intractability of the forces at work than with the prospects for precise solutions."[7] And although Innis served on several commissions of the national government of Canada, "he tended to be scornful of those academics who were eager to serve governments at every opportunity. Scholars should teach and research, not be policy makers."[8]

Philip Marchand similarly notes that one of the persistent forms of criticism levelled at McLuhan was "that he was complacent about the phenomena he described and indifferent to matters of social justice."[9] Even a sympathetic colleague, Abraham Rotstein, could observe: "the march of modernity in seven league boots to some imminent global unity was equally mesmerizing [to McLuhan].... But he offers no systematic social or philosophical critique beyond a present critical vigilance and a future benign anticipation."[10] McLuhan is popularly held to have been one of the twentieth century's most provocative thinkers about modern communications technologies. And yet no practical program for dealing with the negative effects of these technologies is generally recognized as having emerged from his work. As Northrop Frye notes, "he has come down as a kind of half-thinker who never worked out the other part of what he was really talking about."[11]

It has also been noted of Grant that, while he was a strong critic of technological civilization, he was largely silent about practical responses to specific issues. Ian Box argues that "specifically, he offers little in the way of systematic criticism of technological civilization, and no constructive alternatives to our present disorder are put forward for consideration."[12] William Christian, on the other hand, argues that one can at least find indications of "an implicit and positive teaching in his writings."[13] Others have noted in Grant's work a pervasive attitude of despair in the face of the problems of modern life, as can be seen in the titles of articles such as John Muggeridge's "George Grant's Anguished Conservatism," William Christian's "George Grant and the Terrifying

Darkness," Edwin and David Heaven's, "Some Influences of Simone Weil on George Grant's Silence" and Dennis Lee's "Grant's Impasse."[14]

Why should three of Canada's most notable twentieth-century technological critics, who were generally not hesitant about publicly expressing their views, seem so reticent when it came to making suggestions about how we should deal with a subject which came to dominate their academic work? In his later work Innis shifted his interest from economic history to the dynamic of technological change. As Drache notes, "the point he repeatedly emphasized was that everyone had to be conscious of the contradictory potential of each new technology."[15] Grant came to see technology in Heideggerian terms as the "endeavour which summons forth everything to give its reasons, and through the summoning forth of those reasons turns the world into potential raw material, at the disposal of our 'creative' wills."[16] Or as he puts it elsewhere, technology is the merging of two fundamental types of human activity, "knowing and making," in which "both activities are changed by their co-penetration."[17] For him, technology is more a process than product, and this process is most fundamentally concerned with "the domination of man over nature through knowledge and its application."[18] For McLuhan dependency involves a "subliminal and docile acceptance" of technology.[19] This docile attitude is a result of a distinctive form of unconsciousness that he thinks attends most of our technological activities. The problem is not one of false consciousness or false needs, but a lack of consciousness at all of the changes that technology brings in oneself and society. The result is that "a man is not free if he cannot see where he is going."[20]

While each of these thinkers was known for having misgivings about the course that technological civilization was taking, none of them undertook to describe anything in the way of a systematic approach to responding to the kinds of ethical challenges that technology can present. Their silence in this regard is a mystery worth considering. It could be suggested that they were simply detached, ivory tower academics. However, their willingness to participate in public debate seems to belie such a claim. My counter-hypothesis is that for them the challenge of technology was located in the very nature of technology itself, as a distinctive and pervasive form of human activity, and that this perspective explains their refusal to advocate a systematic response to the challenges of technological civilization. I will argue against the claim that these three prominent Canadian intellectuals generally advocated a neutral or ambivalent position on the issue of technology. I will argue, instead, that they would have greatly appreciated, for instance, the critical examination of road planning techniques provided by Carl Simpson in this section.[21]

At the core of the silence of Innis, McLuhan and Grant is a shared understanding of the technological phenomenon as encompassing all formalized and systematic problem-solving practice. Technology is any kind of formalized practice we can habitually engage in, whether in the form of a technique or technique-and-artifact, to respond to commonly encountered difficulties. Each sees proper awareness of this aspect of technological practice as being essential to our understanding of technology. They share the position of rejecting a search for a systematic ethical or political approach because such a search can too easily turn into the very kind of habitual technological response they wished to put into question. Each dealt with this realization in a different way: Innis with his eventual refusal to serve governments as a policy consultant;[22] McLuhan with his renunciation after the publication of *The Mechanical Bride* of "the error of critical moralism;"[23] and Grant with his refusal to act as apologist for the political programs of either the left or the right.[24]

We can see the first glimmerings of Innis' understanding of the centrality of habit for technological practice in his address, at the Conference of Commonwealth Universities at Oxford University in 1948. He began:

> I propose to adhere rather closely to the terms of the subject of this discussion, namely, "a critical review, from the points of view of an historian, a philosopher and a sociologist, of the structural and moral changes produced in modern society by scientific and technological advance." I ask you to try to understand what that means. In the first place, the phrasing of the subject reflects the limitations of Western civilization. An interest in economics implies neglect of the work of professional historians, philosophers, and sociologists. Knowledge has been divided to the extent that it is apparently hopeless to expect a common point of view. In following the directions of those responsible for the wording of the title, I propose to ask why Western civilization has reached the point that a conference largely composed of university administrators should unconsciously

assume division in points of view in the field of learning and why this conference, representing the universities of the British Commonwealth, should have been so far concerned with political representation as to forget the problem of unity in Western civilization, or, to put it in a general way, why all of us here together seem to be what is wrong with Western civilization.[25]

For Innis, the assumption of conference organizers that an academic conference on the future of the university should be structured along the lines of academic specialization was a manifestation of the kind of technological mindset he wished to combat. William Westfall notes that for Innis the university in the post war period had "become synonymous with specialization and departmentalization" and that "with a professionalised university we have succumbed to the very pressures that Innis had worked so hard to oppose."[26] John Watson sees Innis as a tragic figure because "the sad truth is that the continuing struggle he waged against specialization in the social sciences and for an authentically indigenous school of scholarship has largely been lost since his death."[27] The influence that ingrained beliefs, or bias as Innis called such beliefs, was to become the essential focus of Innis' understanding of technology.

The emphasis on the aspect of unconscious habit or bias in technology is common to all three of these scholars. Grant puts this point bluntly when he states "We are technique."[28] Technology is for him a process in which all people participate so intensely through the actions of their "hourly existing" that it is almost impossible to conceive of them bringing this process under any kind of sustained ethical scrutiny. He comments that "every moment our existence is so surrounded by the benefits of technology that to try to understand the limits to its conquest, and also its relation to human excellence, may seem the work of neurotic seeking to escape from life into dream."[29] According to Grant, the fact that technological activity has come to dominate the lives of most modern individuals presents them with a unique dilemma. Since this fundamental way of acting has become taken for granted, when it comes to addressing issues which might suggest possible limits to this kind of activity, their tendency is to engage in this kind of activity rather than to consider its limitation. Or as he puts this point, "we are at the mercy of the technological machine we have built, and every time anything difficult happens, we add to that machine."[30]

James Gerrie 223

For McLuhan our intimate engagement with technologies also prevents our proper awareness of the ethical implications of these technologies. In his book *Understanding Media*, he describes at length how the intensity of the process of technological change can "numb" one's sensitivity to this process.[31] The origin of this numbness is in the nature of technology. According to McLuhan all technologies are "extensions of some human faculty – psychic or physical."[32] And so, in the same way that most people are normally unaware of thought when they are thinking, or of their hands when they are grasping, or of their mouths when they are speaking, they are normally unaware of the technologies in their regular use. In most natural and unmediated human activities one's focus is on the task itself and one's goals and not the means being used to achieve those goals. This means that it is precisely the "tools" with which we are most familiar that we will be most blind too, in the same way that a medium of communication, such as a television, fades into the background when we are focussed on the message it is conveying.

McLuhan sees two reasons for this normal lack of awareness. The first is the result of the simple intimacy that is an integral characteristic of technology as an extension of oneself. His suggestion is that in our technological actions, just as in our unmediated actions, we are normally unconscious of the various parts of our functioning body and mind. He declares: "The principle of numbness comes into play with electric technology, as with any other. We have to numb our central nervous system when it is extended and exposed, or we will die."[33] As McLuhan suggests on many occasions, it is only when technologies have passed from normal use that they typically become objects of conscious appreciation, such as when they become objects in museums. It is for this reason that McLuhan compares most attempts at understanding the ethical impact of technologies to an attempt at driving a car by way of its rear-view-mirror.[34]

However, there is one further source of the general lack of consciousness of our technologies and their effects. According to McLuhan it is also the habitual nature of most technological activities that contributes to the tendency to overlook these activities. As he puts this point, "It is this continuous embrace of our own technology in daily use that puts us in the Narcissus role of subliminal awareness and numbness in relation to these images of ourselves. By continuously embracing technologies, we relate to them as servomechanisms."[35] All technologies involve us in routine forms of practice. From the grain pounding mill of rural villages in developing nations, to the procedures of airways management of large airline hubs in the developed world, routine procedure is the name of the game when it comes to technology. And this very routineness can, according to McLuhan, contribute to a lack of awareness of the implications of such practice.

Innis, McLuhan and Grant are each concerned with understanding unconscious social processes. As Leslie Pal notes, "The subject matter which Innis retained for social science was habit or bias. [In choosing this subject,] Innis was suggesting that while some human activity is consciously and spontaneously directed much of it appears to be the result of unreflective and ingrained behaviour."[36] Grant's fundamental philosophical approach to technology, as Philip Hanson describes it, was to become "a spectator, waiting and listening to the speeches, rituals, and strivings of a society dominated by technique."[37] McLuhan writes that "man is not only a robot in his private reflexes but in his civilized behaviour and in all his responses to the extensions of his body, which we call technology."[38] They each look past the obvious and sometimes grandiose failures of technology to the nature of technological action itself.

Each of these three men saw a need to develop an approach to technology in which the character of technological action as habit is consciously examined. However, each also suggests that the deep-rootedness of the technological approach to difficulties can even lead us to habitually seek technological solutions to this problem. Innis presents this dilemma in the following fragmentary note taken from his *Idea File*:

Mankind is continually being caught in his own traps – [once specialist] language and systems [are] developed [they become] difficult to break down.... [The ancient] Greeks had the advantage of debating without control but the development of a written tradition [strengthened the power of specialist language and systems. An emphasis on] control [by way] of systems followed – [the legal code] used by [the] Romans [being one example]. [Early written] communication [was] limited to a small number – [resulting in a] hierarchy of philosophy – [Humankind's] egoism makes it more difficult to secure relief

James Gerrie 225

[from the tyranny of specialist language and systems because] – mankind's belief in his own contrivances [prevents him from questioning his commitment to these contrivances].[39]

As Innis points out, our dependency on technologies and technological problem-solving practice is augmented by the fact that every technology is also a source of power.

For Innis, any new form of technological capability creates a definable group who will benefit from the application of that capability. These "elites," as Innis calls them, have an interest in maintaining a situation conducive to the development and continued use of the technologies that benefit them. The term "elite," as used by Innis, is not meant to carry the notion that such groups will necessarily be privileged minorities. His use of this term is meant, instead, to suggest, in a manner similar to the work of Foucault, that any new technology always results in the creation of a definable group that gains an advantage from the use of a technology and also a group that does not. Technologies must, according to Innis, inevitably set up distinct bodies of individuals, ranging from immensely large to immensely small, and these can come into political conflict. He suspects that whole nations/linguistic groups emerged because of their commitment to certain technological conventions. For example "The Dutch language had an existence separate from Germany because it was fixed early in writing."[40]

Innis' later work focused on what he called "monopolies of knowledge," which he describes as "channels of thought" and practice that emerge in civilizations through the adoption of new technologies.[41] As Arthur Kroker notes, "Long before the French philosopher, Michel Foucault, said that *power* is the locus of the modern century, Innis in his studies of neotechnical capitalism had already revealed exactly *how* the power system works: by investing the body through capillaries of diet, lifestyle, and housing."[42] Innis uses the term "monopoly or oligopoly of knowledge" to describe any situation of a specific group of people benefiting from a technology.[43] New technologies unleash changes in societies because they disrupt existing elites and knowledge monopolies. As new challenges arise which cannot be addressed by existing elites, new technologies and new elites arise. These new elites, however, inevitably support the creation of new knowledge monopolies, which help give rise to new forms of rigidity and disequilibrium in society in the face of changing circumstances. These strains in the social framework create the need for new technologies. Like Innis, McLuhan was aware of the dynamic at work between technology and society. He describes a process similar to the one articulated by Innis when he suggests that "It is the accumulation of group pressures and irritations that prompt invention and innovation as counter-irritants … physiologically, man in the normal use of technology is perpetually modified by it and in turn finds ever new ways of modifying his technology."[44]

Watson argues that Innis' later work focuses almost exclusively on "an examination of how a different dialectic [than that of Marx], the dialectic of power and knowledge, was played out in human history using communications systems as a focus for analysis of this process.… The effect which Innis predicted was a tendency away from critical thinking and towards following orders on a mass scale."[45] One reason that critical thinking can be threatened by the ordinary process of technological practice, according to Innis, is that seeking to manage this process can itself become a source of power. He notes that "constant change in capitalist society – compels administration to keep constantly alert to protect themselves against and to take advantage of any particular change."[46] Professional innovators, facilitators of innovation, can become engaged in the project of "development" and in this way be considered to constitute a technological elite with an interest in encouraging and directing technological change in general. Such a broad conception of technology's influence obviously puts the ability to think freely about technology at a premium.

Innis felt that the university was the only place from which to expect any understanding of the influence of bias to emerge. He believed that it was the only place dedicated in principle to producing authentic social criticism of the application of human knowledge and creativity. As he puts it: "[The] Place of learned class [and] universities [is] to prevent domination of various groups – church, army, state – [universities should foster] appreciation of [the] necessity of limit[ing the] power of groups."[47] This belief in the university as a special haven for critical inquiry is perhaps why "some of his choicest epigrams of dispraise were reserved for those academics who, far from retaining a tentativeness about their subject bred of an awareness of limits, proceeded to expound final solutions."[48] Innis knew from personal experience how tempting it was for social scientists to accede to "appeals to utility and immediate application" to the detriment of the ceaseless task of understanding the nature and implications of such action.[49]

Grant explicitly asks the question of how one can make judgements about technology that are not biased by one's practical dependence on a vast array of technologies and the general approach of technological problem-solving in his discussion of the "will to technology" in his book *Technology and Empire*.[50] He develops the idea further in *Technology and Justice* when he examines the comment of a computer scientist colleague that "the computer does not impose on us the ways it should be used."[51] He uses this comment to illustrate how difficult it is for even thoughtful people to avoid an unconscious bias towards adopting a technological problem-solving approach to most problems, including ethical issues. According to Grant, most people simply believe in the dogma that "all human problems can be settled by technical skill" even when "some of the dogma's formulations are shown to tend toward immoral practice."[52]

In response to his colleague's remark he points out the simple fact that computer use is dependent on the existence of investment-heavy machines that require large commercial institutions for their production and hence "at the simplest factual level, computers can be built only in societies in which there are large corporations."[53] Also, computers have certain operating constraints, one of these being the need to classify data, and as Grant suggests, "It is the very nature of any classifying to homogenise."[54] He concludes that contrary to what his colleague would have him believe, computer technology does impose on its users how it should be used because it imposes a certain "destiny" on any society in which that technology is used. One cannot have computers without countenancing a certain kind of industrial development and one will, in using computers, necessarily become involved in actions of classification. The computer scientist's remark that the computer "does not impose" reveals that he is either ignorant of these social implications or that he believes that any difficulties, ethical or otherwise, that might arise can be dealt with without having to ethically question the uses of a computer. In either case, the remark illustrates an unquestioned faith that further technological activity will be sufficient for dealing with any difficulties that might arise from the application of computer technology and that technological innovations do not, in any meaningful sense, increase the burden of moral judgement that people must bear.

But Grant also insists that it would be a mistake to think technology is just the purview of technicians such as his computer scientist colleague. For him technology is a process in which all people participate through a multitude of everyday actions. The result is a "package deal," as he puts it.[55] He questions how we can be expected to make judgements about technologies if we are so continuously engaged in the process of technological development. Grant expresses the dilemma that arises from this situation as follows: "The result of this is that when we are deliberating in any practical situation our judgement acts rather like a mirror, which throws back the very metaphysic of the technology which we are supposed to be deliberating about in detail. The outcome is inevitably a decision for further technological development."[56] If the general approach of creative technological problem-solving itself becomes a standard and habitual way of responding to the problems created by such action, what practical action can be undertaken to face this problem that will not simply exacerbate the problem? According to Grant, in the process of bringing technology into ethical consideration, one can even slip into a search for new technologies or techniques to address the problem of slipping too easily into a search for new technologies or techniques.

Like Grant, Innis also points out that an uncritically positive attitude towards a technological problem-solving approach has come to dominate in Western societies. As he puts it, "The form of mind from Plato to Kant which hallowed existence beyond change is proclaimed decedent. This contemporary attitude leads to the discouragement of all exercise of the will or the belief in individual power."[57] But he does not outline a programmatic way to address this problem. Innis' approach to communications studies simply attempts to make his reader aware of the possibility for such bias. Or, as William Westfall remarks, "The fact that one studies bias does not make one immune from it. Consequently, Innis incorporated into his analysis of bias a study of the specific context in which the observer existed and in which scientific analysis took place."[58] But does this reluctance to make practical suggestions for dealing with technology and technological bias imply that it is completely impossible to escape their influence? As Grant attempts to put the problem succinctly, "technique is ourselves,"[59] or as McLuhan describes the fundamental predicament of modern individuals: "Man becomes, as it were, the sex organs of the machine world, as the bee of the plant world, enabling it to fecundate and to evolve ever new forms. The machine world reciprocates man's love by expediting his wishes and desires, namely, in providing him with wealth."[60] How can we respond to technological dependency if the task of developing a specific ethical or political program for offsetting its inherent tendencies is to be avoided?

What Innis, Grant and McLuhan's analyses of technology seem to suggest is that there is a way of responding to any issue brought about by technological change that does not simply fall into the pattern of technological dependency. One must seek a proper balance between novel technological practice and the critical ethical suspension of one's participation in certain forms of such practice, when dealing with technological issues. In other words, when we are "deliberating in any practical situation" as Grant describes this fundamental choice, we can either choose the route of "technological development" or we can critically reject some form of technological development in which we are participating. McLuhan suggests that such a fundamental choice is always a possibility when he states that "we can if we choose, think things out before we put them out."[61] Innis seems to describe such a possibility when he notes that "civilization [is] a struggle between those who know their limitations and those who do not."[62] Their analyses of technological dependency all seem to indicate that, when seeking to respond ethically to practical problems in which technology has played some part, the *choice is always between innovation and discrimination about innovation*. Their critical theories of technology argue for a more balanced application of these two fundamental approaches.

The source for this fundamental choice is in the inherent nature of the technological process to create new problems, or "irritants," and new forms of imbalance in power. Since it is impossible, according to Innis, McLuhan or Grant, for humanity to ever attain a state of technological completion, any new technology will always bring with it certain harmful effects in addition to benefits; these will also be distributed unevenly in a society. Thus, the technological process perpetually creates new technological issues that can be responded to either by seeking some new form of technological power or by way of the critical rejection of some problematic technology. Or as McLuhan describes this dynamic:

"Response to the increased power and speed of our own extended bodies is one which engenders new extensions. Every technology creates new stresses and needs in human beings who have engendered it. The new need and the new technological response are born of our embrace of the already existing technology – a ceaseless process."[63] The ongoing potential for bias toward technological action to respond to novel problems is based in this dynamic. Since we are talking about two fundamentally different categories of possible response to any practical difficulty in which technology plays some part, unless the human capacity for action is unlimited, then one's life will always have to consist of a certain ratio between these two kinds of action. But it is obvious that without some conscious effort to maintain this ratio at some appropriate level, the ratio could skew dramatically in one direction or the other. And the strongest tendency will be towards the technological side because technological activity always involves us either in habitual ways of acting or in the intense pursuit of such ways, which can themselves become habitual responses. And technological action not only creates an ongoing need for such action but it can, by its very nature, help denude one's ability to engage in thoughtful reflection on, and judgement of, such need. All technological action can involve a largely unconscious self-reinforcing tendency in virtue of the fact that such action always involves its own distinctive way of resolving the problems that it helps produce. Thus, this way can compete with alternative ways of addressing such problems, such as the simple reflective rejection of specific technological actions.

According to Grant, the activity of reflecting on the ethical import of our technological choices can therefore be increasingly excluded from a life dominated by technology. As he puts it, "as an end in itself, [technology] inhibits the pursuit of other ends in the society it controls."[64] There is a very simple reason for this tendency. According to Grant, technology involves such a tendency because it cannot itself encompass contemplation and deliberation about ends. It cannot encompass these types of activity because it is the active pursuit to satisfy specified ends, taken as already given. It can be coupled with the activities of contemplation and deliberation about ends, but it need not, and this inherent possibility of disjunction means that, not only can it potentially escape ongoing ethical scrutiny, but it can displace such activity.[65] Innis describes this inherent tendency as follows: "Constant changes in technology …

increase the difficulties of recognizing balance let alone achieving it."[66] Or, as he also notes about writing: "Absorption of energies in mastering the technique of writing left little possibility for considering implications of the technique."[67] McLuhan cites in at least five places Alfred North Whitehead's statement: "The greatest invention of the nineteenth century was the invention of the method of invention."[68] Coupling this notion with his understanding of the inherent nature of all technologies to escape our critical awareness indicates that he felt it equally important to be critically aware of our use of the technological problem-solving approach. In the opinion of each of these Canadian critics of technology it would appear that if one was unwilling to question one's commitment to habitual forms of technological practice, including the general approach of technological problem-solving, one would fail to fully meet the ethical challenge of technology.

In line with their call for greater skepticism about innovation, it is not surprising that Innis, McLuhan and Grant eschewed calls for novel ethical approaches to meet the challenges of our technological future. They suggest instead that we might already be equipped well enough with appropriate ethical tools and that what is lacking is simply a willingness to put these tools to use in the restriction of specific technological activities. Perhaps this emphasis on the strength of tradition is why many commentators have considered them to be impractical when it comes to addressing our technological future. Certainly, a variety of commentators have expressed a common disappointment with their work in this regard. We are told that "Innis never believed in an easy dissolution of such biases, especially as he perceived more clearly their operation in our own time, nor did he advance any special vision of the future"[69]; McLuhan has been faulted for realizing "the mechanical bride marries us to the power of the state and its industrial economy" but preferring "not to lift the veil [of power]"[70]; Grant has been taken to task because he "ultimately refuses to follow through on the hard implications of his philosophy"[71] and he has also been accused of "providing few solutions to the profound problems he raised. To 'lament,' after all, is to imply that it is already too late to do much.... One might wish that he had been able, or had been more inclined, to couple his deep analyses and profound faith with plans for action."[72] According to such commentators one should expect some kind of innovative theoretical approach to the ethical and political challenges of technology from such reputedly insightful critics of our technological age.

That no such novel approaches were proffered has puzzled such commentators, but the silence of Innis, McLuhan and Grant makes sense in light of their discussions of the dangers of technological dependency. Part of their message might be that we should be cautious about experts and novel theories, avoid the search for ethical and political reform programs or ideologies and feel confident that we can actually make choices about the technologies in our own lives right now. As Arthur Kroker has pointed out about McLuhan, "Over and over again in his writings, McLuhan returned to the theme that only a sharpening and refocusing of human *perception* could provide a way out of the labyrinth of the technostructure."[73] As Grant puts it, "those of us who at certain times look to grasp something beyond history must search for it as the remembering of a negated tradition."[74] Innis writes "It is to be expected that you will ask for cures and for some improvement from the state of chaos and strife in which we find ourselves in this century. There is no cure except the appeal to reason and an emphasis on long-run considerations – on the future and on the past."[75] The implication of the ethical critiques of technology of Innis, McLuhan and Grant is that one should not avoid actually making choices about one's technological actions because one is preoccupied with the development of better ethical or policy tools.

This idea is exemplified in the lives of these men. They practised what they preached. As one commentator notes of Innis:

His own bias, as he so often stated, valued a culture characterized by balance, order, and the oral tradition. His analysis of the problem and his attachment to these human, non-technological values set a course that a number of Canadian nationalists would follow. He beheld the decline and fall of a meaningful culture, and he was bitter as he faced defeat. One can hear the echoes of his lamentations in the work of George Grant, Donald Creighton and Dennis Lee.[76]

Innis could make comments like the following because his stance towards technology encourages not only innovation but also the possibility of the critical rejection of some innovations. As he pointed out

"Mass production and standardization are the enemies of the West. The limitations of mechanization of the printed and spoken word must be emphasized, and determined efforts to recapture the vitality of the oral tradition must be made."[77] However, it is possible to see in Innis' work strains of determinism, and therefore, the rejection of any possibility of actively seeking a balance between the various technological forces that allow for the stability of empires.[78] It is also possible to see in his work a call to create novel technological forms in an attempt to achieve the type of balance he felt could be found in the civilization of Byzantium.[79] Both these perspectives fail to fully capture the position of Innis because his position also encompasses the possibility for the critical rejection of technologies, such as the rejection of print in favour of face-to-face discourse. As Dennis Duffy observes, "his own bias, he proclaimed, was for the oral tradition, which he saw involving 'personal contact and a consideration for the feelings of others.'"[80]

McLuhan was also willing to consider the possibility of the critical rejection of technologies. For instance, he states: "The technology of the photo is an extension of our own being and can be withdrawn from circulation like any other technology if we decide that it is virulent."[81] There is a desperate quality to the writings of McLuhan near the end of his life, well documented by his biographers. As Marchand remarks, in his last years McLuhan resigned himself to the "grim role of the seer who is sometimes derided, sometimes petted, but never heeded."[82] But this desperation did not stop him from taking action to fight those aspects of modernity he disliked. Marchand also notes that: "He publicly opposed increased congestion in the heart of the city, whether in the form of new expressways or high-rise apartment buildings, which he particularly despised" and that he "disliked automobiles on principle."[83] It is well known of McLuhan that he could sometimes present himself as an apologist for technological change.[84] However, Marchand suggests that "he was also in the habit of defending his intellectual flank by frequently insisting that his outlining the features of the new media ought to have inspired everyone with sufficient revulsion to avoid them."[85]

The apparent espousal of technological change has brought some of McLuhan's followers to conclude that McLuhan favoured unrestricted experimentation with new technology. Derrick De Kerckhove, for example, interprets McLuhan as championing a form of techno-fetishism:

Where other cultural observers might have cited forces of marketing, McLuhan saw in this phenomenon a purely psychological pattern of narcissistic identification with the power of our toys. I [De Kerckhove] see it as proof that we are indeed becoming cyborgs, and that, as each technology extends one of our faculties and transcends our physical limitations, we are inspired to acquire the very best extension of our own body.[86]

However, others besides Marchand have argued that the position of McLuhan is perhaps more akin to old-fashioned moralism, and even Luddism, than De Kerckhove is willing to acknowledge. As Sam Solecki notes about McLuhan: "He told one reviewer that he was a conservative and hated all change, but given that change was inevitable he was damned if he was going to let it roll over him."[87] Such an interpretation of McLuhan means taking seriously his statement that "we can if we choose, think things out before we put them out."[88] It means considering the possibility, as Marchand recommends, that some of McLuhan's seemingly positive statements about technological change were meant more as rhetorical overstatements aimed at eliciting scepticism.[89] For McLuhan, stopping the use of a technology quite clearly does not commit a person to the complete rejection of all technology but to an intelligent readjustment of technological choices. He states that the "amputation of such extensions calls for as much knowledge and skill as are prerequisite to any other physical amputation."[90] Rejecting a technology may mean filling the space left in one's capabilities with another existing technology or it may mean simply choosing to do different things altogether. "To resist TV," McLuhan writes, "one must acquire the antidote of related media like print."[91]

If the positions of Innis, McLuhan and Grant leave them open to accusations of vagueness and impracticability, this may be intended, for their positions were founded on the conviction that the elaboration of a novel "ethical program" was probably the last thing needed in a society in which so many seem hooked on seeking novel programs of one sort or another. Instead, we must look to what they refused to do in order to chart a proper course into the technological future. We can see a critical approach to technology in Grant's positions on abortion and the growing influence in the humanities of the scientific paradigm of research, and in his call for the recovery of ancient political philosophy.[92]

For Innis, a critical approach can be seen in his misgivings about the expansion of "the price system" and his battles against the "mechanization" of knowledge and the increasing tendency of economists to become consultants to governments and business.[93] He often criticized social scientists for being too enamoured with "elaborate calculating machines" and "refinements in mathematical techniques."[94] He was skeptical about whether the new media of communication would contribute to improving human awareness and understanding, as can be seen in the following note from the *Idea File*: "Improved communication smothers ideas and restricts concentration and development of major ideas. Mechanization and sterility of knowledge [result]."[95] Innis, like McLuhan and Grant, includes a certain degree of anti-reformism in his approach to technology. How else can one make sense of a comment such as this: "Belief in [a] prosperity cult [is a] part of increased advertising – [the] emphasis [is always] on [seeking a] better world and [the] avoidance of problem[s]."[96] The fundamental point each makes through his programmatic silence but willingness to engage in the critical rejection of specific modern trends is that one's response to the challenges of technology should not become overly focussed on finding some systematic way of ameliorating the effects of technological change.

Innis, McLuhan and Grant each argue that such technological proposals for political action are not enough and that they can easily become mere public relations exercises, distracting us from wrestling with our own contribution to the technological causes of many social ills. Innis suggests that the rise of modern mass-communication media encourages such an escapist tactic. As he puts it: "[Modern politics is characterized by a] necessity of stressing continuous political and legal change as a device for dominating news."[97] Even guided by the best intentions, some calls for systematic political reform can produce unforeseen consequence such as reinforcing technological dependency by defusing public pressure for the critical re-examination of individual technological practices. What is required is that, in addition to creating innovative political action, one must also consider the possibility of eschewing certain technological actions that have contributed to the creation of particular social problems. As McLuhan expresses this dual ethical task: "What we seek today is either a means of controlling these shifts in the sense ratios of the psychic and social outlook, or a means of avoiding them altogether."[98] Ethically addressing technology should not simply involve seeking ways to mange or control the effects of technological change. It must also involve the critical analysis of the negative effects of one's own technological choices.

The life of renowned architectural critic, city planner, and environmentalist Jane Jacobs provides a good example of someone attempting to live a life in which technological action is properly balanced by action focused on the reconsideration of particular technological activities. Jacobs is perhaps more renowned for the actions she has rejected than those which she has endorsed. She was "instrumental in preventing the wholesale devastation of neighbourhoods [in Toronto] by various misguided crosstown expressway proposals," such as the Spadina Expressway.[99] One commentator notes that she "rejected the prevailing credo of wide highways, big [housing] projects and single-purpose zoning."[100] As she herself recounts, "When David Crombie was mayor he consulted me about getting housing downtown.... One of the biggest problems we had to deal with was old bylaws."[101] She also has commented "If the car has become a source of evil, it is because it has been made to fill too many niches."[102] And she recounts: "I was born and raised in a suburb, when I went to New York at the age of 18, I was enchanted. I've never been tempted to go back to live in a suburb."[103] Her main impact has not been in espousing a specific political program but rather in rejecting and advocating for the rejection of specific technological practices. As Alan Littlewood, a Toronto City planner put it "Jane was never prescriptive. There were no formulas, no 'how-to' books."[104]

Innis, McLuhan, and Grant were most likely silent on the question of how to fashion public policy for the control of technology because their understandings of technology involved seeing such a project as a manifestation of technological habit. Their response is a case of the medium being the message. The message of their silence is that a search for a specific ethical approach to technology, whether in the form of a novel ethical theory or a specific "critical theory of technology" may be just another way of ethically responding to technology that ultimately distracts us from ethically questioning any of our own specific habitual technological practices. This conclusion suggests that philosophical hopes, like those of Andrew Feenberg, of finding some kind of "politics of technological transformation" or some "structural basis for understanding the operations in which the dominated might resist domination" might be misplaced.[105]

In fact, Feenberg's own discussions of the theories of technology of Heidegger, Marcuse, Foucault, and Ellul, and his concerns about the "fatalism" of their conclusions, and in particular the political "impasse" he finds in Heidegger's thought, seem to parallel my own analysis of the thought of Innis, McLuhan and Grant.[106] The apparent pessimism to which many of these thinkers seem prone could indicate that they also may have shared a belief that the thoughtful rejection of specific technological actions using the ethical "tools" one already had "on hand" could be an adequate response to the ethical challenge of technology. In other words, all of these thinkers might have agreed with Iain Thomson's suggestion concerning Heidegger, that "the critical theorist of technology can learn much from the Amish, who are no 'knee-jerk technophobes,' but rather 'very adaptive techno-selectives who devise remarkable technologies that fit within their self-imposed limits.'"[107]

Innis, McLuhan and Grant all point toward the need to include such limits in one's life. That they remained largely silent about how to respond systematically to technology's challenges indicates the extent to which one must go in controlling habitual technological response. One can find in their silence a demonstration of the clear alternative to the technological approach – the simple thoughtful rejection of specific technological habits. Their analysis of technology suggests that a proper response to technologically originated issues is to understand the limits of our ability to resolve technological dilemmas through technological problem-solving and to recognize the compelling moral necessity for people to also exercise personal responsibility when it comes to their own technological choices. In other words, we should not always rely first and foremost on novel legal mechanisms, political programs, ethical theories or any other such "plans for action" to resolve the ethical dilemmas raised by technology, but realize that technology must also be responded to by the ethical judgement of human individuals. Such a position is similar to one increasingly suggested by some environmentalists in regards to environmental issues, such as climate change. Their calls for people to make radical changes in lifestyle echo the suggestion of Innis, McLuhan and Grant that there may be instances in which technology creates challenges that can only be met adequately by individuals making moral judgements about their own complicity in the processes they see as negative.

Innis, McLuhan and Grant exhort us to be more vigilant critics of technological civilization, but because of their analysis of technology they were also forced to conclude that they should not tell us specifically how to do this. Unfortunately, our society, as they each also point out, is increasingly primed only to listen to those who can offer programmatic solutions.[108] But if their final conclusions about technology lead them to a forced silence, then what can we learn of practical interest from these great theorists of technological civilization? We must look to biography, the historical inquiry into their lives, to gain some insight into how they felt technology could be ethically addressed. What one finds in the biographies of Innis, McLuhan, and Grant are accounts of individuals prepared to reject the application of certain tools, both physical and intellectual, based on the thoughtful ethical insight.

Endnotes

1 Martin Heidegger, "The Question Concerning Technology," in *Basic Writings: From Being and Time to The Task of Thinking*, ed. David Farrell Krell (Harper Collins, 1977, 1993), 311; Herbert Marcuse, "Some Implications of Modern Technology," in *Technology, War, Fascism*, ed., Douglas Kellner (London: Routledge, 1998).
2 Arthur Kroker, *Technology and the Canadian Mind: Innis/McLuhan/Grant* (Montreal: New World Perspectives, 1984), 18.
3 John Goyder, *Technology and Society: A Canadian Perspective* (Peterborough, ON: Broadview Press, 1997), 239.
4 Daniel Drache, "Introduction," *Staples, Markets and Cultural Change: Selected Essays by Harold Innis* (Montreal: McGill-Queen's University Press, 1995), xvii.
5 J. Rawlinson and J. L. Granatstein, *The Canadian 100: The Hundred Most Influential Canadians of the Twentieth Century* (Toronto: Little Brown and Co., 1997), 231.
6 Ibid., 188.
7 Carl Berger, *The Writing of Canadian History* (Toronto: Oxford University Press, 1976), 103.
8 Ibid., 96.
9 Philip Marchand, *Marshall McLuhan: The Medium and the Messenger* (Toronto: Vintage Books, 1990), 191.
10 Abraham Rotstein, "Technology and Alienation," Keynote Address Presented at the Opening Session of the Third Biennial Meeting of the Institute for Ultimate Reality and Meaning, Toronto, 23 August 1985.

11 Northrop Frye, "Technology and Society," interview by David Cayley in *Northrop Frye in Conversation* (Concord, ON: House of Anansi Press, 1992), 161.
12 Ian Box, "George Grant and the Embrace of Technology," *Canadian Journal of Political Science* 15 (September 1982): 504 (my emphasis).
13 William Christian, "George Grant and Love: A Comment on Ian Box's 'George Grant and the Embrace of Technology,'" *Canadian Journal of Political Science* 16 (June 1983): 350.
14 John Muggeridge, "George Grant's Anguished Conservatism," in Larry Schmidt ed., *George Grant in Process* (Toronto: House of Anansi, 1978), 40–48; William Christian, "George Grant and the Terrifying Darkness," in *George Grant in Process*, 167–78. In the same anthology, see Edwin and David Heaven, "Some Influences of Simone Weil on George Grant's Silence," (68–78), William Mathie, "The Technological Regime: George Grant's Analysis of Modernity," (157–66). Also enlightening is Dennis Lee's, "Grant's Impasse," in Peter C. Emberley ed., *By Loving Our Own: George Grant and the Legacy of Lament for a Nation* (Ottawa: Carleton University Press, 1990), 11–42.
15 Drache, "Introduction," *Staples, Markets and Cultural Change*, li.
16 George Grant, *English Speaking Justice* (Sackville: Mount Allison University, 1974), 88.
17 George Grant, *Technology and Justice* (Concord, ON: House of Anansi Press, 1986), 13.
18 Ibid., 4.
19 Marshall McLuhan, "from Understanding Media" in *Technology and Man's Future*, 2d ed., ed. Albert H. Teich (New York: St. Martin's Press, 1977), 103.
20 Ibid.
21 M. Carleton Simpson, "Linking the past to the future," in this volume.
22 Donald Creighton, *Harold Adams Innis: Portrait of a Scholar* (Toronto: University of Toronto Press, 1957), 110–11.
23 Judith Fitzgerald, *Marshall McLuhan: Wise Guy* (Montreal: XYZ Publishing, 2001), 78.
24 James Reimer, "George Grant: Liberal, Socialist, or Conservative?" In *George Grant in Process*, 49–57.
25 Harold Innis, *The Bias of Communication* (Toronto: University of Toronto Press, 1964), 190–91. Presumably, this same insight lay behind the creation of a series of interdisciplinary conferences at Laurier Brantford and selection of the "interplay of past, present and future" as the theme of this collection.
26 William Westfall, "The Ambivalent Verdict: Harold Innis and Canadian History," in William H. Melody, Liora Salter and Paul Heyer (eds.) *Culture Communication and Dependency: The Tradition of H. A. Innis* (Jersey City: Ablex, 1981), 45.
27 John A. Watson, "Harold Innis and Classical Scholarship," *Journal of Canadian Studies* 12:5 (Winter 1977): 45.
28 George Grant, *Technology and Empire: Perspectives on North America* (Toronto: House of Anansi Press, 1969), 137.
29 George Grant, *Philosophy in the Mass Age* (Toronto: Copp Clark, 1959, 1966), vi.
30 George Grant and Gad Horowits, "A Conversation on Technology and Man," *Journal of Canadian Studies* 4:3 (August 1969): 3.
31 Marshall McLuhan, *Understanding Media: The Extensions of Man* (New York: McGraw-Hill, 1964), 41.
32 Marshall McLuhan, *The Medium is the Message*, with Quentin Fiore and produced by Jerome Agel (New York: Touchstone Books, 1967), 26.

33 McLuhan, "from Understanding Media" in *Technology and Man's Future*, 106.
34 McLuhan, *The Medium is the Message*, 100.
35 McLuhan, "from Understanding Media" in *Technology and Man's Future*, 105.
36 Leslie A. Pal, "Scholarship and the Later Innis," *Journal of Canadian Studies* 12:5 (Winter 1977): 33.
37 Philip J. Hanson, "George Grant: A Negative Theologian On Technology" in *Research in Philosophy and Technology* vol. 1, ed. Carl Mitcham (Amsterdam: JAI, 1978), 308.
38 Marshall McLuhan, and Quentin Fiore, *War and Peace in the Global Village* (New York: Touchstone Books, 1968, 1989), 19.
39 Harold Innis, *The Idea File of Harold Adams Innis*, ed. William Christian (Toronto: University of Toronto Press, 1980), §6.50.
40 Innis, *The Bias of Communication*, 125.
41 Ibid., 120.
42 Kroker, *Technology and the Canadian Mind*, 120.
43 Innis, *The Bias of Communication*, 64.
44 McLuhan, *Understanding Media*, 46.
45 Watson, "Harold Innis and Classical Scholarship," 58.
46 Innis, *Idea File*, §5.20.
47 Ibid., §2.17.
48 Berger, *The Writing of Canadian History*, 106.
49 Creighton, *Harold Adams Innis: Portrait of a Scholar*, 130.
50 Grant, *Technology and Empire*, 31–32.
51 Grant, *Technology and Justice*, 19.
52 Grant, *Philosophy in the Mass Age*, iii, vi.
53 Grant, *Technology and Justice*, 25.
54 Ibid., 23.
55 Ibid., 33.
56 Ibid.
57 Innis, *The Bias of Communication*, 90.
58 William Westfall, "The Ambivalent Verdict," 44.
59 George Grant, *Time as History* (Toronto: The Hunter Rose Company, 1969), 137.
60 McLuhan, *Understanding Media*, 46.
61 Ibid., 49.
62 Innis, *Idea File*, §5.33.
63 McLuhan, *Understanding Media*, 183.
64 Grant, *Philosophy in the Mass Age*, vii.
65 As Grant states, "Perhaps [as moderns] we are lacking the recognition that our response to the whole should not most deeply be that of doing... but that of wondering or marvelling at what is, being amazed or astonished by it, or perhaps best, in a discarded English usage, admiring it." in *Technology and Empire*, 35.
66 Innis, *The Bias of Communication*, 140.
67 Ibid., 9.
68 Marshall McLuhan, *The Gutenberg Galaxy: The Making of Typographic Man* (Toronto: University of Toronto Press, 1962), 45, 176; "Is it Natural That One Medium Should Appropriate and Exploit Another?", in *Essential McLuhan*, eds. Frank Zingrone and Eric McLuhan (Concord, ON: House of Anansi Press, 1995); reprinted from *McLuhan: Hot and Cool*, ed. Gerald E. Stearn (New York: New American Library, Signet Books, 1967), 187; "The Laws of Media." in *Essential McLuhan*, 383; *War and Peace in the Global Village*, 15.

69 E. Crowley, "Harold Innis and the Modern Perspective of Communication," In *Culture Communication and Dependency*, William H. Melody, Liora Slater and Paul Heyer, eds. (Norwood, NJ: Ablex Publishing, 1981), 240–41.
70 John O'Neill, "McLuhan's Loss of Innis-Sense," *Canadian Forum* (May 1981): 13.
71 Kroker, *Technology and the Canadian Mind*, 49.
72 Robert E. Babe, *Canadian Communication Thought: Ten Foundational Writers* (Toronto: University of Toronto Press, 2000), 205–6.
73 Kroker, *Technology and the Canadian Mind*, 64.
74 Grant, *Time as History*, 49.
75 Harold Innis, "This Has Killed That," *Journal of Canadian Studies* 12:5 (Winter 1977): 5.
76 Westfall, "The Ambivalent Verdict," 47.
77 Harold Innis, *Empire and Communications* (Oxford: Clarendon Press, 1950), 168.
78 Dennis Duffy, "Harold Adams Innis," in *Marshall McLuhan* (Toronto: McClelland and Stewart, 1969), 16.
79 Innis, *The Bias of Communication*, 117.
80 Duffy, *Marshall McLuhan*, 16.
81 McLuhan, *Understanding Media*, 193.
82 Marchand, *Marshall McLuhan*, 228.
83 Ibid., 228, 89.
84 Ibid., 169.
85 Ibid., 170.
86 Derrick De Kerckhove, *The Skin of Culture: Investigating the New Electronic Reality* (Toronto: Somerville House, 1995), 3.
87 Sam Solecki, obituary of "Marshall McLuhan (1911–1980)," *Canadian Forum* (May 1981): 4.
88 Ibid., 49.
89 Marchand, *Marshall McLuhan*, 169.
90 McLuhan, *Understanding Media*, 193.
91 Ibid., 170.
92 Joan O'Donovan, *George Grant and the Twilight of Justice* (Toronto: University of Toronto Press, 1984), 73.
93 Kroker, *Technology and the Canadian Mind*, 118–21.
94 Innis, *The Bias of Communication*, 86.
95 Innis. *Idea File*, §2.7.
96 Ibid., §2.3.
97 Ibid., §5.24.
98 McLuhan, *Understanding Media*, 70.
99 Doug Saunders, "Citizen Jane," *Globe and Mail*, 11 October 1997, C20; McLuhan worked with Jacobs in the resistance to the expressway, which Jacobs recounts in *Who Was Marshall McLuhan? Exploring a Mosaic of Impressions* (Nevitt 1994), 101–2).
100 Christopher Hume, "The city that Jane helped build," *Toronto Star*, 12 October 1997, F1.
101 Ibid., F5.
102 Ibid.
103 Ibid.
104 Ibid.
105 Andrew Feenberg, *A Critical Theory of Technology* (New York: Oxford University Press, 1991), 13, 73.

106　Ibid., 73, 75. Also see: Iain Thomson, "From the Question Concerning Technology to the Quest for a Democratic Technology: Heidegger, Marcuse, Feenberg," *Inquiry* 43 (2000): 203–16; David J. Stump, "Socially Constructed Technology," *Inquiry* 43 (2000): 217–24; Andrew Feenberg, "Constructivism and Technology Critique: Replies to Critics," *Inquiry* 43 (2000): 225–38; Iain Thomson, "What's Wrong with Being a Technological Essentialist? A Response to Feenberg," *Inquiry* 43 (2000): 239–44; Feenberg, "The Ontic and the Ontological in Heideggers's Philosophy of Technology: Response to Thomson," *Inquiry* 43 (2000): 445–50.

107　Thomson, "From the Question Concerning Technology to the Quest for a Democratic Technology," 208.

108　Here, the connection between my study of Canada's leading critics of technology and the wider purpose of this anthology becomes apparent. The struggles of Innis, McLuhan and Grant to articulate a critique of technology that did not itself fall into a pattern dictated by technology can certainly be likened to the struggle to own history. In both instances, we must be alive to the ways in which habits formed over decades and centuries as well as contemporary concerns affecting our judgement influence how we perceive the past and plan for the future.

Bibliography

Babe, Robert E. *Canadian Communication Thought: Ten Foundational Writers*. Toronto: University of Toronto Press, 2000.

Berger, Carl. *The Writing of Canadian History*. Toronto: Oxford University Press, 1976.

Box, Ian. "George Grant and the Embrace of Technology." In *Canadian Journal of Political Science* 15 (September 1982): 503–15.

Christian, William. "George Grant and Love: A Comment on Ian Box's 'George Grant and the Embrace of Technology.'" *Canadian Journal of Political Science* 16 (June 1983): 347–54.

Creighton, Donald. *Harold Adams Innis: Portrait of a Scholar*. Toronto: University of Toronto Press, 1957.

Crowley, E. "Harold Innis and the Modern Perspective of Communication." In *Culture Communication and Dependency*, edited by William H. Melody, Liora Slater and Paul Heyer, 235–46. Norwood NJ: Ablex Publishing, 1981.

de Kerckhove, Derrick. *The Skin of Culture: Investigating the New Electronic Reality*. Toronto: Somerville House, 1995.

Drache, Daniel. "Introduction." In *Staples, Markets and Cultural Change: Selected Essays by Harold Innis*. Montreal: McGill-Queen's University Press, 1995.

Duffy, Dennis. *Marshall McLuhan*. Toronto: McClelland and Stewart, 1969.

Feenberg, Andrew. *A Critical Theory of Technology*. New York: Oxford University Press, 1991.

———. "Constructivism and Technology Critique: Replies to Critics." *Inquiry* 43 (2000): 225–38.

———. "The Ontic and the Ontological in Heideggers's Philosophy of Technology: Response to Thomson." *Inquiry* 43 (2000): 445–50.

Fitzgerald, Judith. *Marshall McLuhan: Wise Guy*. Montreal: XYZ Publishing, 2001.

Frye, Northrop. "Technology and Society." Interview by David Cayley in *Northrop Frye In Conversation*. Concord, ON: House of Anansi Press, 1992.

Goyder, John. *Technology and Society: A Canadian Perspective.* Peterborough, ON: Broadview Press, 1997.

Grant, George. *Philosophy in the Mass Age.* Toronto: Copp Clark, 1959, 1966.

———. *Technology and Empire: Perspectives on North America.* Toronto: House of Anansi, 1969.

———. *Time as History.* Toronto: Hunter Rose, 1969.

———. *English Speaking Justice.* Sackville: Mount Allison University, 1974.

———. *Technology and Justice.* Concord, ON: House of Anansi Press, 1986.

Grant, George, and Gad Horowits. "A Conversation on Technology and Man." *Journal of Canadian Studies* 4:3 (August 1969): 3–6.

Hanson, Philip J. "George Grant: A Negative Theologian On Technology." In *Research in Philosophy and Technology*, vol. 1, edited by Carl Mitcham. Amsterdam: JAI, 1978.

Heidegger, Martin. "The Question Concerning Technology." In *Basic Writings: from Being and Time to the Task of Thinking*, edited by David Farrell Krell, 307–41. Harper Collins, 1977, 1993.

Hume, Christopher. "The city that Jane helped build." *Toronto Star*, 12 October 1997, F1.

Innis, Harold. *Empire and Communications.* Oxford: Clarendon Press, 1950.

———. *The Bias of Communication.* Toronto: University of Toronto Press, 1964.

———. "This Has Killed That." *Journal of Canadian Studies* 12:5 (Winter 1977): 3–5.

———. *The Idea File of Harold Adams Innis*, edited by William Christian. Toronto: University of Toronto Press, 1980.

Kroker, Arthur. *Technology and the Canadian Mind: Innis/McLuhan/Grant.* Montreal: New World Perspectives, 1984.

Lee, Dennis. "Grant's Impasse." In *By Loving Our Own: George Grant and the legacy of Lament for a Nation*, edited by Peter C. Emberley, 11–42. Ottawa: Carleton University Press, 1990.

Marchand, Philip. *Marshall McLuhan: The Medium and The Messenger.* Toronto: Vintage Books Edition, 1990.

Marcuse, Herbert. "Some Implications of Modern Technology," In *Technology, War, Fascism*, edited by Douglas Kellner. London: Routledge, 1998.

Massolin, Philip. "Context and Content: Harold Innis, Marshall McLuhan, and George Grant and the Role of Technology in Modern Society." *Past Imperfect*, 5, (1996), 81–118.

McLuhan, Marshall. *The Gutenberg Galaxy: The Making of Typographic Man.* Toronto: University of Toronto Press, 1962.

———. *Understanding Media: The Extensions of Man.* New York: McGraw-Hill, 1964.

———. *The Medium is the Message*, with Quentin Fiore and produced by Jerome Agel. New York: Touchstone Books, 1967.

———. "from Understanding Media." In *Technology and Man's Future.* 2nd ed., edited by Albert H. Teich. New York: St. Martin's Press, 1977.

———. "Is it Natural That One Medium Should Appropriate and Exploit Another?" In *Essential McLuhan*, edited by Frank Zingrone and Eric McLuhan, 180–88. Concord, ON: House of Anansi Press, 1995.

———. "The Laws of Media." In *Essential McLuhan*, edited by Frank Zingrone and Eric McLuhan, 366–88. Concord, ON: House of Anansi Press, 1995.

McLuhan, Marshall, and Quentin Fiore. *War and Peace in the Global Village.* New York: Touchstone Books, 1968, 1989.

Muggeridge, John. "George Grant's Anguished Conservatism." In *George Grant in Process*, edited by Larry Schmidt, 130–38. Toronto: House of Anansi, 1978.

O'Donovan, Joan. *George Grant and the Twilight of Justice.* Toronto: University of Toronto Press, 1984.

O'Neill, John. "McLuhan's Loss of Innis-Sense." *Canadian Forum* (May 1981): 13–15.

Pal, Leslie A. "Scholarship and the Later Innis," *Journal of Canadian Studies* 12:5 (Winter 1977): 32–44.

Rawlinson J., and J. L. Granatstein. *The Canadian 100: The Hundred Most Influential Canadians of the Twentieth Century.* Toronto: Little Brown, 1997.

Reimer, James. "George Grant: Liberal, Socialist, or Conservative?" In *George Grant in Process*, edited by Larry Schmidt, 49–57. Toronto: House of Anansi, 1978.

Rotstein, Abraham."Technology and Alienation," Keynote Address Presented at the Opening Session of the Third Biennial Meeting of the Institute for Ultimate Reality and Meaning, Toronto, 23 August 1985.

Saunders, Doug. "Citizen Jane." *Globe and Mail*, 11 October 1997, C20.

Solecki, Sam, "Obituary of Marshall McLuhan," *Canadian Forum* (May 1981): 4.

Stump, David J. "Socially Constructed Technology." *Inquiry* 43 (2000): 217–24.

Thomson, Iain. "From the Question Concerning Technology to the Quest for a Democratic Technology: Heidegger, Marcuse, Feenberg." *Inquiry* 43: 203–16.

———. "What's Wrong with Being a Technological Essentialist? A Response to Feenberg." *Inquiry* 43 (2000): 239–44.

Watson, John A. "Harold Innis and Classical Scholarship." *Journal of Canadian Studies* 12:5 (Winter 1977): 45–61.

Westfall, William. "The Ambivalent Verdict: Harold Innis and Canadian History." In William H. Melody, Liora Salter and Paul Heyer *Culture Communication and Dependency: The Tradition of H. A. Innis.* Jersey City: Ablex, 1981.

Zingrone, Frank, Wayne Constantineau and Eric McLuhan. *Who Was Marshall McLuhan? Exploring a Mosaic of Impressions.* Toronto: Comprehensivist Press, 1994.

10

Linking the Past to the Future

M. CARLETON SIMPSON

¶ At Home in the Car

A few years ago a car ad appeared in which a man powers down his car window and, speaking to the camera in public-service-announcement tones, says words to this effect: "This is a message to the people who invented the drive-in theatre, the drive-through burger window and car wash, and drive-up banking: keep up the good work." A more recent ad campaign includes variations of the slogan: "On the road of life there are drivers and there are passengers. Drivers wanted." The primary aim of this ad is to appeal to a general "take charge" mentality, and to infer that being a driver is better than being a passenger or pedestrian. A secondary message is that, specifically, people should *want* to be in cars. This is particularly clear in the subsequent ads of the campaign that state simply: "Drivers wanted." Perhaps not intentionally, both of these campaigns make the assumption that at least some people don't want to get out of their cars; the place they really want to be is in their car. At the same time, many believe that cars kill street life, damage the social fabric of communities, isolate people, foster suburban sprawl, waste energy and natural resources, and cause pollution.[1] Lists of this sort can be found in any number of sources, especially since the 1960s,[2] but also date back to the early days of the automobile.

A third message is that the future is unfolding as it should; that technological progress is inevitable and, at least on balance, desirable. Technological and historical determinism may have been thoroughly debated in academic circles,[3] but there is much evidence of their continued life in the business and manufacturing sectors, and federal and local governments. While these two forms of determinism are seldom discussed conjointly, I wish to do so here, as it seems to me at least that they are inseparably linked by time's arrow. They both predict the future based on past states and events.

If the advertisers are right in their assumption, and are not merely creating a desire to be in cars, we have two conflicting notions of the desirability of the automobile. At the very least, it would seem we have people willfully engaging in a known detrimental activity. In what follows, I will consider the historical underpinnings of several modern justifications of roads – all of which presuppose historical determinism and all of which violate its precepts. I will assess the strength of these justifications and draw conclusions about the ethical merits of the two sides of this conflict. Popularly, we think of this conflict as a relatively recent discovery, something that arose in the late 1960s. This is because the 1950s and early 1960s were marked by near total, uncritical car enthusiasm that reflected the dominance of deterministic thinking. This was the period of the greatest growth in automobile ownership. The year 1955 was the first in which an American business recorded sales in excess of $1 billion and that corporation was General Motors. But we are also familiar with the bucolic family outing shattered, the family terrorized, by the fast, noisy, and carelessly driven horseless carriage – and this scene is based on historic truth. The car is an evolving technology of prosthetic extension; it extends our abilities to move our selves and our goods. But central to its history is the way it has changed the phenomenal world of our experiences. It allows us to do more, but in a radically different world. One of the challenges of this benefit is the infrastructure of roads and the effect these have on our social lives – how and where we meet and interact. By their very nature roads do not exist for those who live adjacent to them. In getting from "A" to "B" we travel past and through "C." While part of any community, a road is also essentially a part of another community. *Commutity* is not merely a necessary movement from one place to another; it is an overwhelming desire to be moving.

The automobile boom in the 1950s that allowed GM to set a world record was the third wave of the car. The first, modest wave began in 1886 with Karl Benz in Germany. Two years after successfully building a tricycle powered by the twenty-five year old internal combustion engine, Benz began selling cars. By 1900, there were 8,000 cars registered in the United States and 6,000 in France, by far the two largest markets. Worldwide, just over 7,000 new cars were manufactured that year.[4] The second wave came in the pre-Depression roaring twenties. At the beginning of the decade, 10.5 million cars were registered in the United States. By 1929, that number had increased to 26.7 million.[5] In U.S. cities in 1915 about one in every sixty citizens had a car. By 1930, that ratio was reduced to one in four.[6]

Each of these waves accompanied similar social demands – urban congestion, programs encouraging first-time home buying, the desire for larger, more open lots and communities – and in the United States each of the three waves followed on the heels of a great war. The story of how we changed our conception of roads and of how we developed two competing visions of social organization is really a story of growth in the United States, for this is essentially a story of how cities have coped with growth. Even at the crest of the third wave, in 1956, the largest Canadian city only had a population of just over one million. Canadian cities were not factors in the first two waves. While the second wave fizzled in the depression, the criticisms that followed the first and third wave were responses to strikingly similar effects. Most notably, congestion increased. One set of problems was replaced with another, seemingly less desirable set.

More attention has been focused on cars than on the roads under them. However, the early history of the automobile demonstrates the need for the latter to facilitate use of the former. While the two are nearly inextricably linked, I want to attend to this concomitant of cars. The automobile has changed the nature of roads – in design, quantity, and function. New modes of transport have always raised demands for new road engineering. The automobile is not alone in presenting this secondary engineering change. However, it directly altered the way all roads are conceived. Of course, road design and planning decisions are based on a variety of factors, the demand of drivers being only one. But always, major works projects are promoted as solutions to defined extant or anticipated problems.

If we attend to the cyclic nature of transportation and road development over the past 130 years we see the same problems arising from the same "solutions." The problems begin with a redefinition of the purpose of roads that started in the 1870s. Prior to 1870, the year the first asphalt road was constructed in North America, urban streets were primarily an extension of the yard, a place for recreation and social gathering. The *Oxford English Dictionary* cites an 1890s engineering periodical as the first usage of "artery" to mean a street.[7] From that moment forward there have been essentially two competing goals between community and *commutity*. Commutity demands a shift from a multiple-use extension of the contiguous community to a single-use conduit largely independent of the contiguous community.

There are two prongs to my thesis. First, there is clear evidence that over the past 130 years additions or improvements to roads have not provided an overall net reduction in traffic problems. Second, during the same period it is also clear that roads have served specific communities of people in different ways. The broadest division is between those for whom roads are an extension of stationary and local life and those for whom they are a means of transit. This division most naturally applies to the difference between intra-city and inter-city roads. However, a conflation of this difference has meant that urban roads are often treated equivalently to inter-city links.

Humans seem adept at drawing extremely varied lessons from history. Given the abundant evidence of the environmental and health hazards of the car, it might seem unconscionable that there are proponents of both cars and roads designed for cars. Of course, roads are useful for cars, trucks, and buses. However, each of these uses could be shifted to other transport networks. In my discussion I will focus primarily on the rationale for roads for cars. There are three possible explanations for our continued support of the road:

- ignorance or unconsidered repetition of myths and misinformation;
- self-interest; and
- alternative interpretations of evidence, background assumptions, or theories resulting in different weighting of advantages and disadvantages.

To explore these three explanations in what follows, I will focus on a specific road project, the Brantford Southern Access Road. In considering the specific history of this project I will draw out these three models of historical interpretation. The ethical component of my analysis, which I treat at the end of this chapter, is guided by an assumption of the propriety of a policy of non-maleficence. As the practice of any community is harmful to the livelihood of another the first must always give way to the second. My overarching aim throughout is to underline the subtle relationship between past, present and future. Often, in our efforts to be prepared for a future whose contours we are, at best, only vaguely able to discern, we marshal historical evidence in a way clearly dictated by present concerns. This is evident in our response to technological change generally and to the demands of that icon of progress – the car – more specifically. The manner in which we have constructed roads reveals the dangers of wielding an imaginary past to justify present policy designed to meet a future that may never arrive.

¶ The Brantford Southern Access Road

Brantford is a small, southwestern Ontario city with a population under one-hundred thousand. The Brantford Southern Access Road was first conceived in 1958, at the height of the third wave. The actual design was developed in the late 1960s, and in 1973 the citizens of Brantford roundly rejected the proposal. The engineers responded in two ways. First, the design was altered from a full expressway, with cloverleaf interchanges, to a limited access road, with signal-light interchanges. Second, they kept quiet about the continued development of the plan. In the early 1990s, when word of its ongoing progress reached the public, protest was again mounted. A special environmental hearing, called by the provincial Environment Minister, chastised the City for not adequately notifying citizens.[8] The report also criticized the plan itself. The design has remained all but unchanged over the past thirty years, and while specific justifications have varied over those years, the general justification has remained the same. The BSAR was expected to provide for the more efficient movement of vehicles; it would alleviate congestion.

The configuration of the road is a semi-circle, lying south of, and connecting in the east and west with, the inter-city Highway 403. The road lies completely within the city. It is intended to provide the final connection between inter-city lines and intra-city destinations and it is funded jointly with the province. However, as the name makes clear, the road was principally designed to open up access to new suburban lands south of the city. The BSAR cannot be viewed as a commercial or industrial right-of-way, but as a domestic and commuter corridor. Over 130 years of suburban expansion have shown that the new suburban connecting roads do not alleviate congestion on existing roads, and generate their own traffic. Further, since the BSAR connects suburban lands with the main inter-city road, it would facilitate inter-city commuting. Measured against its own objectives of linking suburbs with the urban centre, alleviating congestion and promoting the easy movement of vehicles, the BSAR is self-defeating.

There are two independent components to infrastructure design: a demonstration of need and a determination of placement. In the case of a road, this latter means the alignment of the road between two points. These components are independent as a need could be demonstrated yet a permissible or acceptable alignment might remain unattainable. Impediments to success might include the cost due to the unsuitability of terrain to be traversed or the cost of lands that must be expropriated. Cost may outweigh need. Another impediment may be non-monetary costs. All best routes may traverse inviolable lands or cause other unacceptable social and cultural damage. Need is always weighted against monetary and social costs, and evaluation of alternatives always includes a "do nothing" scenario.

I will focus on the design of one section of the BSAR. En route from Highway 403 to the future suburbs, the design takes the road through an older, established neighbourhood of the city. Here we have a perfect example of the confrontation between community and *commutity*. The design calls for the demolition of existing houses, the realignment and closure of existing streets, and, because of its limited access and high speeds, the road itself acts as a barrier, severing the neighbourhood into portions which would then lie on either side of it. This barrier effect is emphasized by the restriction of pedestrians and bicycles, and by the limiting of access points for automobiles. This segment of the BSAR does not serve the community in which it lies; rather, it has a negative impact. This provides a locus for evaluating the strengths of the justification of the BSAR against real social costs.

The BSAR was initially proposed as a necessary preemptive response to expected overall population increases of the city and resulting shifts in transportation patterns. In its 1993 submission to the Environmental Assessment Advisory Committee, the City submitted that the BSAR would "reduce congestion and travelling time, provide a major access route into and through the city, and provide access to areas planned for new development, specifically the Southwest and eventually the Northwest."[9] Initial and revised population predictions on which the BSAR was based were consistently overly optimistic and the areas of planned new development had not been proposed at the time the BSAR was designed. But the general justifications for the BSAR, congestion and access, belie the three problems of pervasive mythologies, self-interest, and alternative interpretations. I turn to a consideration of these next, as a precursor to drawing some conclusion about the BSAR.

¶ You Can't Get There from Here: Two Myths about Transportation

Engineer and futurist Buckminster Fuller was an enthusiastic chronicler of how technology increases human mobility:

In 1914, American man was averaging 1640 miles per year total travel. Thirteen hundred miles [about 2,100 kilometres] were accomplished by his legs, and 340 additional miles were accomplished by his vehicles.... As a consequence of mass production of the equipment of mobilization during World War 1, in 1919 U.S. man covered 1,600 miles by vehicle alone – in addition to his continued 1,300 miles per year walking – a total of 2,900 miles per man. By 1942 U.S. man was averaging 4,500 miles per year by vehicles plus 1,300 miles per year by legs or an annual total ecological sweep out of 5,800 miles per year.[10]

While his father's lifetime mobility would have been about 50,000 kilometres, his own was over 5 million kilometres.[11] Constant in this increase is the 2,100 kilometres we walk, regardless of how many kilometres we ride. Fuller concluded that technological innovation makes us not only increasingly mobile but exponentially more mobile. Another conclusion may be drawn. The distance each of us walks and the time spent walking has remained constant. Since we ride more, we spend more time riding – even allowing for the increased speeds at which we ride. Hence, ad campaigns that make a virtue of being in your car.

Fuller's statistics also rely on broad notions of mobility and technology. Nonintegral vehicles include bicycles, skateboards, dog sleds, and horses. Technologies of mass production and the technologies mass-produced refer, not only to automobiles, but also to pneumatic tires, wagons, horseshoes, steam trains and rails, and the technologies of road surfacing. All of these technologies change the way we move and the tendency has been to keep only those technologies that allow us to move further and faster. Fuller also demonstrates the thoroughly modern desire to travel further and faster under ideal conditions. If we measure our technological and social success by distance travelled, we clearly do better than ever before. But there is a cost to such travel. Time spent travelling, across the planet or across town, is not necessary time well spent. Travel as an end in itself has only recently attracted large numbers. Purposeless travel is even less popular. Prior to 1950, most – though certainly not all – travel was commercial. And as we ought to know now, there are even greater costs.

The first real change for North Americans came in the years following the American Civil War. The population boom felt by most U.S. cities was accompanied by rapid developments in technology. Before the rise of technologies of transportation, cities had a natural limit in area and density. Increasing density meant increasing the likelihood of disease, which would cap or reduce population. The area of a city could not increase beyond the distance that essential goods such as food could be moved. Previous societies dealt with population growth in a variety of ways. Warfare offered two advantages. It inevitably decreased populations, and, for the victors, afforded new lands on which to expand. Certainly, the Roman Empire never experienced over-population. The industrial revolution offered, for the first time in history, non-violent technological solutions for increased growth. Cities could grow larger than ever before. Outward expansion of cities may not have been a well-considered solution, but it was a deliberate one. It began with the completion of the railroads, was pushed by congestion and overcrowding in cities, and was facilitated by developments in road surfaces, automobility, and the bicycle. The period 1870 to 1900 also marked the shift in defining roads from a multi-use part of the contiguous community to a single-use passageway.

¶ Myth #1: Roads Reduce Congestion

That congestion on city streets slows the flow of traffic was not a new revelation in 1869, the year the last spike was laid in the U.S. linking the east-west rail lines. Nor was it sixteen years later, in 1885, when the Canadian rails were linked. The thirty years from 1870 to 1900 saw the ten largest American cities double in population.[12] This period marked the height of rail transportation. In 1880, U.S. trains hauled 327 million tons of freight; in 1890 that number increased to more than 640 million tons.[13] Oddly, the success of the train, particularly in the United States, was instrumental in its ultimate decline. Growth following the Civil War set the pre-conditions for the first wave of the automobile. In 1875, it cost $7.50 a ton to ship freight from New York to Chicago, but to deliver it from the rail yards to the factory or store cost an additional $5.00.[14] The increased ease of moving goods by rail, along with the mounting demand for goods, placed an increased burden on city streets.

Local delivery was made by horse drawn vehicles. Flesh horses were far less efficient than their iron cousins. In the census of 1900, there were 130,000 horses in Manhattan, 74,000 in Chicago, and 51,000 in Philadelphia. On average, in large cities there was one horse for every twenty-three people.[15] These are horses that lived and worked in the city. Very few were privately owned for riding or leading private carriages. Most were owned by the inter-city and urban street railways, the police and fire departments, and shipping companies. Like cars after them, horses tended to kill people, damage the social fabric of communities, waste energy and natural resources, and cause pollution.

Horses, especially on crowded, noisy streets, might kick, bite, fall over, or drop dead. In the 1880s, the New York Sanitation Department was removing on average 15,000 dead horses per year. In addition, it removed over 150,000 tons of manure annually.[16] In 1880, the Kansas City Sanitation Department announced it would only clean streets with an accumulation of three inches or more.[17] Manure, both wet and dry, was a health hazard. The rise of centralized street engineering in the 1890s was motivated in large part by a concern for public health.[18] The problem, then, seems not to be specifically that cars are unhealthy, but that our design of cities and use of streets is. Whatever the form, increased traffic means poorer conditions for travel and traffic always exceeding the capacity of roads.

The primary reason offered for building the BSAR, and for building and improving most roads is congestion. But one of the lessons we may draw from history is that more and better roads do not alleviate congestion. We need to remind ourselves of the differences between inter-city and intra-city movement. Rail lines are rarely congested; during each wave of the car inter-city lines were not congested. Congestion occurred not between cities, but within them, when goods were transferred from the efficient rails to the inefficient roads. Inter-city, inter-state, and inter-province roads were not built to aid in the movement of goods – though such a justification was often advanced, and such a function is now entrenched.

Before and after each wave of automobility and road expansion, there is statistical and anecdotal evidence of at least equivalent congestion. Describing New York streets in 1867, *Scientific American* reported that "Streets in the lower part of the city are completely blocked three or four days out of the week."[19] In 1929 the average automobile journey between Chicago's Loop and suburban Evanston was only five minutes shorter than the scheduled trip on the elevated railroad fifteen years earlier. In other words, traffic jams were eroding the advantages of the new technology.[20] The economist, urban planner, and transportation expert Wilfrid Owen, appointed to the newly formed National Resources Planning Board in 1939, wrote in the late 1950s: "Where all-out efforts have been made to accommodate the car, the streets are still congested, commuting is increasingly difficult, urban aesthetics have suffered, and the quality of life has been eroded. In an automotive age, cities have become the negation of communities – a setting for machines instead of people."[21] As one editorial writer in 1930 put it: "When Mr. Henry Ford, his successors and predecessors ... put some kind of automobile within easy reach of almost everybody, they inadvertently created a monster that has caused more trouble in the larger cities than bootleggers, speakeasies, and alley bandits."[22]

The average travel speed in urban London 130 years ago was 10 kph; today it is 8 kph. For all their other shortcomings, horses managed to travel at a greater speed than cars. The statistics are comparable for New York. Importantly, the population densities for both cities remain stable from 1880 to 2000.[23] While the phenomenon of congestion is exacerbated on intra-city roads, it occurs on all roads. The credo is that demand increases to meet capacity. As roads are widened or new roads opened, congestion is eased and traffic initially moves more quickly. This in turn encourages more frequent and longer commutes, which in turn results in overall increases in traffic, greater congestion, and a return to the original slow speeds. As traffic levels increase, the attraction of commuting decreases and the traffic use levels off. Of course, many factors specific to the road and community determine how quickly and how great a reduction in mobility results. Recently, physicists have been applying the principles of the behaviour of gases and chaos theory to describe, analyze, and predict traffic flow and congestion.[24] As water seeks its own level, roads appear to seek their maximum capacity.

¶ Myth #2: Cars Move People More Efficiently

There are three components to this myth. First, cars rather than buses, trains and other mass transit are more efficient in getting people from place to place. Second, roads should be constructed to facilitate the mobility of cars, rather than horses, bicycles or pedestrians. Third, because roads are the efficient movers of people, they should have right-of-way over sidewalks, paths, rail lines and other transit corridors. The second and third components require the first. Given my first myth, the merit of myth 2.1 seems immediately suspect. In calculating traffic counts and vehicle capacity, the ratio of buses to cars and multiple occupancy cars to single occupancy cars is always a significant determining factor.

Two things had to happen to make way for *commutity*: 1) the means of travel had to be improved and 2) roads had to be built or upgraded to satisfy the specific needs of travellers. The decision to expand cities outward and to develop suburbs, placed not only a greater burden on the industrial use of roads, but, as with cities today, also meant that a wider spectrum of citizens had to commute in order to work, to shop or to play. When introduced, the automobile was seen as a solution to an existing problem. Before the completion of the railway there were calls for "a cheap mechanical substitute for the horse."[25] This was a call to replace work horses, not private horses. Yet it was private citizens who turned the tide, with bicyclists initially leading the way.

Two years after the linking of the railways in the United States, the safety bicycle was imported from Britain, replacing the high-wheeler. This, the first generation of the modern bicycle, was enormously successful. It was also stable enough that riders could imagine riding on streets. With improvements in bicycle technology came demand for technology-specific improvements in roads. In 1880, the League of American Wheelmen was formed, with the express intention of campaigning for state funding for local road improvements.[26] In that year, 62 per cent of roads were unpaved, 36 per cent were macadam, cobblestone, granite, brick, or wood, and less than 1 per cent asphalt. The non-asphalt paving was designed for horses, who needed a rough surface for traction. If the horse – the engine of mobility – couldn't get a foothold, the whole vehicle would not move. Rough rides, then, were an essential co-factor of transportation. The existing paved roads were completely unsuited for the bicycle, and provided a rough ride for other wheeled transportation. At this time, commuter transportation within cities was almost exclusively on designated, and smooth, rails. The best surface for cyclists was asphalt. It was also the most costly. But advances in the processing and laying of asphalt, along with the lobbying of the Wheelmen, meant that by 1900 about 7 per cent of roads were so paved; by 1930 almost 40 per cent were asphalt.[27]

This was hardly all the work of a bicycle lobby group. What the Wheelmen did was either allay or successfully meet the initial concerns and challenges of farmers, concerned that improvements for the idle rich would mean increased property taxes, and urban dwellers, concerned that improvements would mean more and different vehicles making their streets less safe. The first concern was allayed; the second was met with legal victories. The success of bicycle enthusiasts at gaining the financial support of upper-tier governments had three important impacts. First, this cleared the way for the successful introduction of the car, since both cars and bicycles required the same quality roads. The first car users were the idle rich, and the first use of cars – even by the less affluent – was leisure. In order for people to want to ride, rather than need to ride, the activity had to be enjoyable. Roads designed for horses deflated tires, broke axles, shook loose hoses and bolts, and caused physical discomfort for the rider. Where the roads went, how they were connected, and how direct their routes happened to be were all secondary concerns for the leisurely rider.

Second, the involvement of upper-tier governments ensured greater connectivity and uniformity of roads. Prior to this change in management, roads were the responsibility of the abutting property owners. Paving choices, standards of upkeep, even alignments changed from block to block within cities. But a more centralized control within cities had begun in the 1870s under the urging of transport companies and fire departments. This process had continued with the creation of street cleaning departments, following the increased health concerns arising from increased horse traffic. Now, through the Office of Road Inquiry (ORI) and the National League of Good Roads (NLGR) – both created through the activities of the Wheelmen – the control of roads, from planning through to maintenance, was being centralized.[28] For the first time, a national vision was considered.

Third, the efforts of bicycle, and shortly thereafter automobile, enthusiasts established a new conception of the purpose of roads. Roads could be used by the idle – rich or otherwise. But the evolution of centralized engineering is a major factor in the polarization of community and *commutity*. Today, final decisions are removed from the communities in which the roads exist. Increasingly, the basis for decision-making is the need of those who *move through* the community, not those who *reside in* the community. Centralization cements the view that roads, rather than being a part of the community in which they physically exist, are a part of the communities which they connect. Roads were not merely an extension of the yard, occasionally cleared for the arrival of a delivery vehicle; what was once your yard was now a passageway shared with someone else.

¶ Self-Interest: The Road to *Commutity*

Most major new road developments are officially justified on the twin grounds of congestion and access. But repeatedly other interests play an equal or greater role in decision making. The initial pressure on roadways arose from the burgeoning use by transport companies and was fuelled by economic costs. Four sectors of society consecutively began pushing for better roads. The railroads first raised the idea, with the hope of cheaper depot to destination costs. Next, bicyclists and sport auto enthusiasts advocated new roads with the hope of saving their kidneys and expanding interest in their activities. Finally, years after the railroads began the push, truckers joined in, not with the hope of assisting the railroads on inter-city roads, but with the aim of taking away the railroads' business on intra-city roads. As a force in the creation and improvement of roads, truckers did not emerge until, in preparing to enter the First World War, the U.S. government took over all rail shipping for the war effort. Trucking was still short haul, depot to destination, until 1917, when hauling consumer goods between cities became a viable enterprise. Prior to 1920, less than 10 per cent of street traffic was comprised of trucks.[29]

The political pressure for funding road improvements came from the leisure sector. The Wheelmen, ORI, and NLGR were smart lobbyists, parlaying limited finances into broad-based support. The railroads were won over with the argument that all roads were essentially feeder links to the rail lines. Short, sample roads were built throughout the country to demonstrate to farmers and rural citizens the benefits of better roads. In the mid-1890s, the U.S. Federal government was persuaded to begin rural free mail delivery (RFD), and at the same time, carriers were allowed to stay home if roads were not negotiable.[30] As Stephen Goddard sums up the interconnected progress of mobility: "The railroad had broadened people's perspectives, the bicycle had let its rider choose his or her course, and RFD had created a reason for rural folks to write their congressmen. But it was the demand in Europe and America for the horseless carriage that pushed the movement to critical mass."[31] All of this activity was undertaken by the bicycle lobby not for the betterment of the general citizenry, but with the express, if often unstated, goal of creating better bicycle roads.

At the first meeting of the American Automobile Association, in 1903, automobiling was acknowledged as a sport, and the group truly became an important club. At the end of its first year, the AAA had fifty affiliates around the country and 35,000 cars had been purchased.[32] It was street congestion, adding to transportation costs, that got the railroad owners excited about improving streets and the vehicles hauling goods on them. But it was those who loved to ride who convinced politicians and other citizens to invest in roads, and it was leisure vehicles, not work vehicles, that filled those roads. The call for road and vehicle improvements put out by the railroads was based on a sound analysis of city streets and the necessity of moving goods. But the alleviation of congestion was the real object of only a small minority of those who advocated more and better roads, and more extensive use of the automobile. The real motivation was the desire to go farther, more comfortably.

The separate issues of inter-city and intra-city roads were conjoined during the third wave of the car. The highest official stamp of this historicist myopia came in 1956, when President Eisenhower enacted the Federal-Aid Highway Act. In 1954, he sweepingly called for "a grand plan for a properly articulated system that solves the problems of speedy, safe transcontinental travel, inter-city transportation, access highways and farm-to-farm movement, metropolitan area congestion bottlenecks and parking."[33] Thus, highways and limited-access roadways were seen as a solution to intra-city traffic problems.[34] While Eisenhower had long been a supporter of road improvements, it is clear that the combined lobbying efforts of a broad base of vested interests enticed him to push the matter onto the agenda of Congress. Since the 1920s, the efforts of the railroads, the Wheelmen, and the AAA had grown into "a loose association of road contractors, state and federal highway officials, automobile clubs, trucking associations, automobile manufacturers, producers and suppliers of construction equipment and materials, engineers, oil companies, investment bankers and financial organizations, as well as many political figures with deep commitments to highway construction interests."[35]

No longer was the express goal of road construction the alleviation of congestion, nor even improved access to distant places. Part of the Highway Act was a self-perpetuating mechanism, a trust fund, maintained by taxes on gas and oil, which could only be used for new road construction. Use of highways ensured more highways to use. The philosopher Lewis Mumford wrote of Congress passing this legislation: "The most charitable thing to assume about this is that they hadn't the faintest notion of what they were doing."[36] For the leisure and sport advocates, new roads meant new vistas. This marked the functional separation of roads from automobiles. The improvement of surface technologies and the construction of roads were increasingly undertaken for the sake of having roads rather than merely as a necessary co-factor of having automobiles.

For many in this "loose association," design and construction was the end in itself. But the public justification of urban and suburban roads was still the need to alleviate congestion and increase commuter efficiency by decreasing travel times. Still, the actions of the various proponents of expansion belied this justification. In the 1940s a company called National City Lines systematically bought up and dismantled over one hundred streetcar systems in over forty-five U.S. cities. National City Lines was created by General Motors, Firestone, Standard Oil, and Mack Truck.[37] Streetcars did ease congestion, moving more commuters in less space. Moreover, passenger rail service was comfortable. The push for smooth asphalt indirectly forced horses out of the commercial transportation industry. Roads either provided sufficient friction for horses or they did not. Two transportation systems provided the most efficient movement of commercial goods and people. But one system, which would necessitate the replacement of both older systems and would need more ongoing maintenance, offered the greatest profits.

¶ Alternative Interpretations and an Ethics of Mobility

How should we guide decisions about where and when roads should be built? There is room for alternative interpretations of some of the evidence, background assumptions, and theories underlying the justifications of roads. But the role of interpretation cuts the issues at different joints than does the received interpretation of this history. Roads provide access, but they do not necessarily represent the best alternatives. Trains, planes, and the Internet also provide access to distant places. Roads, *per se*, do not alleviate congestion. To do so, decisions about roads and vehicles must be conjointly made.[38] Historically, decisions to construct roads suitable for motor vehicles rather than horses and to encourage private automobiles have not alleviated congestion or reduced travel times. Despite the repeated claims to the contrary, there seem to be three real functions of roads: the movement of goods, commuting, and pleasure. The second and third functions may be designated, respectively, a necessary and an unnecessary evil. The structural features of our cities and communities now make necessary increased transportation from home to work to market. This is the aspect of cars the ad agents attempt to subvert. But the leisure activity that raised concerns in the late nineteenth century is now widely understood as seriously destructive.

One factor in a land use cost-benefit analysis is the type of vehicle traversing the road. Horses pollute city streets, though this can be ameliorated. Horses rarely collide with people, and when they do it is seldom fatal. Philosopher Louis Pojman asks us to consider the following thought experiment: "Imagine that we invented a mighty Convenience Machine that would make our lives wonderfully more enjoyable and enable us to reach more of our goals. Unfortunately, using the machine would cost about 43,000 lives per year, more casualties than eight years of the war in Vietnam. Would you use the machine? Should we allow it to be sold on the market?"[39] He is, of course, asking us to think about the car. All technologies bring gains and losses. Often, with the ability to produce more, more quickly, comes an increased risk of more serious personal injury. But, in addition to being cheaper and more plentiful, mass produced goods may be inferior in a variety of ways to hand crafted ones. Pojman balances a multitude of conveniences against only one inconvenience. But there are others. How do we negotiate the two competing goals between community and *commutity*?[40]

I assume that our actions ought to be guided by a principle of nonmaleficence. More specifically, we want to maximize the benefit to the most people while not violating minimal side-constraints on our treatment of people. Generally, one should leave a person significantly worse off in order to trivially benefit any number of others. Since the benefit of private automobiles is almost always trivial – a convenience rather than a necessity – they will almost always lose out. The neighbours contiguous to the road are, in this sense, innocent bystanders. The road itself has a negative impact, both on them and on those more remote, including those who would use it the most. Given the history of roads – only sketched here – the more exclusive the use and the more distant the accrued benefits, the more damaging the road.

The older model of the road was as an extension of the yard as a multi-purpose part of the neighbourhood, providing access for the contiguous inhabitants both to move around and out of the neighbourhood and to receive goods and visitors into the neighbourhood. Roads used to benefit those adjacent to them. Such roads still exist. But more prevalent is the modern model – the road as artery, as conduit, as a single-purpose imposition on the neighbourhood. To illustrate: if teleportation replaced vehicular transportation, arterial roads would disappear, but not multi-purpose community roads.

A stronger argument can be made. Given that roads do not alleviate congestion, but do increase pollution, death, and suffering, they must be given a low priority. The economist Herman Daly has pointed out that sustainable growth on a finite planet is an oxymoron. He argues for a consistent distinction between "growth" and "development," based on their standard dictionary meanings, and cautions against the common equivocation surrounding these terms. To grow, he points out, means "to increase naturally in size by the addition of material through assimilation or accretion." Meanwhile, to develop means:

> … to expand or realize the potentialities of, to bring gradually to a fuller, greater, or better state.… Politically it is very difficult to admit that growth, with its almost religious connotations of ultimate goodness, must be limited. But it is precisely the non-sustainability of growth that gives urgency to the concept of sustainable development.… Sustainable development is a cultural adaptation made by society as it becomes aware of the emerging necessity of non-growth.[41]

The upshot is that sustainable development is only meaningful when it realizes an improvement or efficiency in ways and means. On a finite planet, nearing its upper carrying capacity, a policy of non-growth is the only defensible one. The history of road construction demonstrates a failure to attain development over growth. At a point of conflict between development and growth, between a benign human activity and a destructive one, between community and *commutity*, the former of each pairing must take precedence.

The road to this ethical conclusion has been to challenge, by demonstration, the assumptions of historical determinism. I am particularly critical of the twin assumptions that progress is inevitably good and immune from human intervention. The repeated justifications for road expansion that mythologize the alleviation of congestion and the movement of people demonstrate how history is malleable, how it is interpreted and used for specific human ends. My cautionary tale also demonstrates the importance of a critical knowledge of history. Willful ignorance and self-interest are dishonest, but together with genuine ignorance can only be met with the complex and messy business of recovering and interpreting history.

Endnotes

1 See J. H. Crawford, *Carfree Cities* (Utrecht: International Books, 2000); available at <http://www.carfree.com> (10 August, 2004).
2 Some early criticism of the effects of automobiles on street life can be found in Jane Jacobs, *The Death and Life of Great American Cities* (New York: Vantage Books, 1992, first published 1961); World Health Organization, *Urban Air Pollution with Particular Reference to Motor Vehicles* (Geneva: World Health Organization, 1969); Richard O. Zerbe, *Urban Transportation for the Environment* (Cambridge, MA: Ballinger, 1975). The criticism has continued more recently in Donald Appleyard, *Livable Streets* (Berkeley: University of California Press, 1981); David Engwicht, *Reclaiming Our Cities and Towns: Better Living with Less Traffic* (Philadelphia: New Society Publishers, 1993); Katie Alvord, *Divorce Your Car! Ending the Love Affair with the Automobile* (Gabriola Island, BC: New Society Publishers, 2000). Frank Coffey and Joseph Layden, *America on Wheels: The First 100 Years, 1896–1996* (New York: General Publishing Group, 1996) contains some of the earliest dissenting opinions about the utility of the automobile.
3 Recent efforts at debunking technological determinism include those of Ian Barbour, *Ethics in an Age of Technology* (Toronto, Harper Collins, 1992) and Andrew Feenberg, *Questioning Technology* (London: Routledge, 1999). For challenges to historical determinism see William H. Dray, *Philosophy of History* (Englewood Cliffs, NJ: Prentice-Hall, 1964), Karl Popper, *The Open Society and Its Enemies* (Princeton: Princeton University Press; 5th revised edition, 1971, first published 1945), and Georg Lukacs, *History and Class Consciousness*, trans. Rodney Livingstone (MIT Press, 1988).

4   Clay McShane, *Down the Asphalt Path: The Automobile and the American City* (New York: Columbia University Press, 1994), 104.
5   Bruce E. Seely, *Building the American Highway System: Engineers as Policy Makers* (Philadelphia: Temple University Press, 1987), 72.
6   Jon C. Teaford, *The Twentieth-Century American City* (Baltimore: Johns Hopkins University Press, 1986), 62.
7   McShane, *Down the Asphalt Path*, 57.
8   Philip H. Byer, et al, *Environmental Assessment Advisory Committee Report No. 52: Brantford Southern Access Road* (18 January 1993), 7–9.
9   Ibid., 10.
10 R. Buckminster Fuller, *Utopia or Oblivion: The Prospects for Humanity* (New York: Bantam Books, 1969), 50.
11 Fuller was an atypically mobile traveller: the Buckminster Fuller Institute claims he circled the globe 57 times in his life. See <http://www.bfi.org/index.html> (10 August, 2004).
12 McShane, *Down the Asphalt Path*, 22.
13 Ibid., 42.
14 Ibid., 45.
15 Ibid., 43–44.
16 Ibid., 48–49, 51–52.
17 Ibid., 53.
18 Ibid., 52–53.
19 Quoted in McShane, *Down the Asphalt Path*, 50.
20 Teaford, *The Twentieth-Century American City*, 63.
21 Quoted in Richard O. Davies, *The Age of Asphalt. The Automobile, the Freeway, and the Condition of Metropolitan America* (Philadelphia: J. B. Lippincott, 1975), 25.
22 Quoted in Teaford, *The Twentieth-Century American City*, 64.
23 Manhattan's population density increases from 20,446 per square kilometre in 1880 to 26,978 in 2000, while urban London's population density decreases from 32,488 in 1881 to 23,460 in 2001.
24 Dirk Helbing and Bernardo A. Huberman, "Coherent moving states in highway traffic," *Nature* 396 (1998): 738–40; Dirk Helbing and Martin Treiber, "Gas-kinetic-based traffic model explaining observed hysteretic phase transition," *Physical Revue Letters* 81 (1998): 3042–5; see also Michael Schreckenberg, Andreas Schadschneider, Kai Nagel, and Nobuyasu Ito, "Discrete stochastic models for traffic flow," *Physical Revue E* 51:172 (1995): 2939–49.
25 McShane, *Down the Asphalt Path*, 44.
26 Seely, *Building the American Highway System*, 11–12.
27 McShane, *Down the Asphalt Path*, 59.
28 Stephen B. Goddard, *Getting There: The Epic Struggle between Road and Rail in the American Century* (New York: Basic Books, 1994), 46–47; See also Seely, *Building the American Highway System*, 11–16.
29 McShane, *Down the Asphalt Path*, 192.
30 Goddard, *Getting There*, 48.
31 Ibid., 48.
32 Ibid., 50.
33 Quoted in Davies, *The Age of Asphalt*, 18.
34 Davies, *The Age of Asphalt*, 18–19.
35 Ibid., 16.

36 Lewis Mumford, *The Highway and the City* (New York: Harcourt, Brace and World, 1963), 234.
37 Jane Holtz Kay, *Asphalt Nation: How the Automobile Took Over America, and How We Can Take It Back* (New York: Crown Publishers, 1997), 213, 241.
38 In what follows, I'm leaving aside the separate issue of vehicle type; buses (just as inner city street cars) move more people, more efficiently on the current road systems, and thus could alleviate congestion.
39 Louis P. Pojman, *Global Environmental Ethics* (Mountain View, CA: Mayfield Publishing, 2000), 292.
40 It seems to me that the necessary negotiation that must occur between these two competing visions of shared living space is similar to the one that is needed between aboriginal and non-aboriginal people over land use and ownership (see John McLaren, Nancy Wright and Andrew Buck's essays in Section II of this volume "'Sharper Than Any Two Edged Sword': History, Colonialism and Land").
41 Herman E. Daly, "Sustainable Growth: An Impossibility Theorem," in Joseph DesJardins, ed. *Environmental Ethics: Concepts, Policy, Theory* (Mountain View, CA: Mayfield Publishing, 1999), 424.

Bibliography

Alvord, Katie. *Divorce Your Car! Ending the Love Affair with the Automobile*. Gabriola Island, BC: New Society Publishers, 2000.
Appleyard, Donald. *Livable Streets*. Berkeley: University of California Press, 1981.
Barbour, Ian. *Ethics in an Age of Technology*. Toronto: Harper Collins, 1992.
Byer, Philip H., et al. *Environmental Assessment Advisory Committee Report No. 52: Brantford Southern Access Road*.
Coffey, Frank, and Joseph Layden. *America On Wheels: the first 100 years, 1896–1996*. New York: General Publishing Group, 1996.
Crawford, J. H. *Carfree Cities*. Utrecht: International Books, 2000.
Daly, Herman E. "Sustainable Growth: An Impossibility Theorem." In *Environmental Ethics: Concepts, Policy, Theory*, edited by Joseph DesJardins, 423–27. Mountain View, CA: Mayfield Publishing, 1999.
Davies, Richard O. *The Age of Asphalt. The Automobile, the Freeway, and the Condition of Metropolitan America*. Philadelphia: J. B. Lippincott, 1975.
Dray, William H. *Philosophy of History*. Englewood Cliffs, NJ: Prentice-Hall, 1964.
Engwicht, David. *Reclaiming our Cities & Towns: Better Living with Less Traffic*. Philadelphia: New Society Publishers, 1993.
Feenberg, Andrew. *Questioning Technology*. London: Routledge, 1999.
Fuller, R. Buckminster. *Utopia or Oblivion: the Prospects for Humanity*. New York: Bantam Books, 1969.
Goddard, Stephen B. *Getting There: The Epic Struggle between Road and Rail in the American Century*. New York: Basic Books, 1994.
Helbing Dirk and Bernardo A. Huberman, "Coherent moving states in highway traffic." *Nature* 396 (1998): 738–40
Helbing Dirk and Martin Treiber. "Gas-kinetic-based traffic model explaining observed hysteretic phase transition." *Physical Revue Letters* 81 (1998): 3042–45.

Jacobs, Jane. *The Death and Life of Great American Cities.* New York: Vantage Books, 1992.

Kay, Jane Holtz. *Asphalt Nation: How the Automobile Took Over America, and How We Can Take It Back.* New York: Crown Publishers, 1997.

Lukacs, Georg. *History and Class Consciousness.* Trans. Rodney Livingstone. Cambridge, MA: MIT Press, 1988.

McShane, Clay. *Down the Asphalt Path: The Automobile and the American City.* New York: Columbia University Press, 1994.

Mumford, Lewis. *The Highway and the City.* New York: Harcourt, Brace and World, 1963.

Pojman, Louis P. *Global Environmental Ethics.* Mountain View, CA: Mayfield Publishing, 2000.

Popper, Karl. *The Open Society and Its Enemies.* Princeton, NJ: Princeton University Press. 5th edition, 1971.

Schreckenberg, Michael, Andreas Schadschneider, Kai Nagel, and Nobuyasu Ito. "Discrete stochastic models for traffic flow." *Physical Revue E* 51:172 (1995): 2939–49.

Seely, Bruce E. *Building the American Highway System: Engineers as Policy Makers.* Philadelphia: Temple University Press, 1987.

Teaford, Jon C. *The Twentieth-Century American City.* Baltimore: Johns Hopkins University Press, 1986.

World Health Organization, *Urban air pollution with particular reference to motor vehicles.* Geneva: World Health Organization, 1969.

Zerbe, Richard O. *Urban Transportation for the Environment.* Cambridge, MA: Ballinger Pub. Co., 1975.

II

Predictions of Global Catastrophe: Just Another Chicken Little?[1]

STEPHEN F. HALLER

More than a few scientists and environmentalists have claimed to have shown that, should present habits of production and consumption continue, we will soon reach the limits of the earth's capacity to support its inhabitants. Population, food and resource consumption, and industrial emissions have been increasing at exponential rates, and the speed of the increase has resulted in environmental and social problems on a scale far surpassing anything we have encountered previously. Potential crises are global in scope and the possible consequences are catastrophic. We are risking the very capacity of the Earth to support any life, or at least our own capacity for survival as a species. In *It's a Matter of Survival*, David Suzuki and Anita Gordon declare that "we are the last generation on earth that can save the planet."[2] If these claims are correct, any humans lucky enough to survive the impending juggernauts of, say, overpopulation, global warming, nuclear winter or ozone-layer depletion, will, it is asserted, find themselves in a world irreversibly damaged – a sun-baked, tornado-swept and life-impoverished planet.

These warnings are not new. In 1798 Thomas Malthus claimed that the earth was already overpopulated and could not possibly support more inhabitants. Obviously, he was mistaken. In 1972, an influential book *Limits to Growth* warned of impending catastrophes related to population and resource depletion. They did not come to pass. Similar warnings were made again in 1992 when a twentieth-year anniversary update called *Beyond the Limits* was published. Why should we believe it this time? Indeed, the history of global catastrophe prediction has been a record of exaggeration and failure.[3] Why should we believe any of these warnings? Haven't we met these Chicken Littles too often to believe any longer that the sky is falling? Chicken Little's screams of "The sky is falling!" caused a panic among his barnyard companions, and destruction or tragedy ensued as a result of the panic. Chicken Little wasn't right, and the moral of the story is not to panic at the arrival of bad news.

We have heard environmental doomsday predictions too many times before. How should this history affect our decisions? We might take the lesson of Chicken Little to heart, and view warnings of global catastrophe with a grain of salt. In that case, we should demand that Chicken Little come up with evidence that his fears are justified. This is, in fact, how science proceeds. The burden of proof is usually on those who make assertions of possible harm. I will argue for a reversal of the burden of proof and in favour of what has come to be known as the precautionary principle. As Jim Gerrie implies in his contribution to this volume, too programmatic a response to technological change accomplishes little.[4] The magnitude of the stakes facing us when it comes to environmental concerns bolsters the case for a more flexible response. And the history of environmental degradation gives us reason to take the warnings of catastrophe more seriously than we might if they were considered on their merits alone.

¶ The Challenge of Assessing the Threat

Jonathan Swift, in his description of Laputa in *Gulliver's Travels*, poked fun at those who are in a perpetual state of anxiety over potential doom.

The cloud-dwelling Laputians were incessant doomsayers, inventing theories about how the sun might become encrusted in its own effluvia and, thus, cease to warm and light the earth. The Laputians would greet each other each morning with worries about the possibility of destruction, and were continually estimating the odds of a comet crashing into the earth, or of the earth's orbit decaying soon and our planet crashing into the sun. It might seem that we are in much the same position today. We also have predictions of a catastrophic end to our environment and ways of life, and are greeted daily in our magazines and newspapers with discussion of potential environmental disaster. We do not want to make the same mistake as the Laputians and worry unnecessarily about things that may not come true, nor do we want to take drastic action and make sacrifices today for the sake of avoiding a phantom future.

How can we tell whether current fears of catastrophes are any less unfounded than those satirized by Swift? If we are to understand whether claims of potential catastrophe are credible, and also whether it is possible to intervene, we need an understanding of the mechanisms by which the catastrophes would befall us. We create computer models to supply us with this understanding. A good model is an idealized representation of some system, a representation able to reveal general patterns in that system's behaviour and to provide predictions of what will happen when certain changes occur in the system. Thus, for example, one well-constructed global circulation model of the earth's climate predicts that the global average temperature will rise with increasing concentrations of carbon dioxide and other "greenhouse gases."

Unfortunately, we have little reason to place much confidence in the ability of current models of global systems to make reliable predictions. The reliability of the predictions generated by these models is questionable because, unlike models of smaller systems, models of global systems cannot be tested against their predictions and improved by trial and error. Unlike models of local systems, these global models cannot be 'tuned' by experiment. We cannot, for example, perform experiments on global systems to see whether the predictions made by models of nuclear winter are accurate. Because of this limitation, the history of catastrophe prediction has largely been a matter of luck. Let me illustrate, briefly, with two examples.

¶ Nuclear Winter

Just in case anyone needed a further reason for avoiding nuclear warfare, various scientists were warning in the early 1980s of the possibility of a new and previously unimagined disaster – nuclear winter. They conjectured that in the aftermath of a nuclear exchange, explosions and fires would inject many particles of soot and dust into the atmosphere. These particles would then reflect so much sunlight back into space for such a long period of time that the earth would be plunged into a winter that would have catastrophic effects on the planet's life. Thus, they urged that the global nuclear stockpile be reduced to a level below that which would trigger this potential catastrophe. Later, the conclusions had to be modified. It turned out that the nuclear winter models were not "robust"; that is, small changes in the initial conditions and assumptions would result in wide variations in the predictions of temperature decreases and duration of the dust cloud. The models were extremely sensitive to minor changes in the estimates of the amount of combustible material in cities, the amount of soot produced, whether the nuclear exchange took place in the summer or winter, and the 'spottiness' of the cloud formation.[5] This sensitivity of the model to small changes in assumptions is a serious defect. For example, if the nuclear exchange takes place in the winter instead of the summer, the temperature drop is smaller by one order of magnitude.[6]

S.L. Thompson and S. H. Schneider argue that, as a result of these considerations, the deep-freeze interpretation of nuclear winter is now dismissed by most scientists as unlikely. Instead, these authors suggest that we think in terms of a nuclear autumn rather than a nuclear winter.[7] While not suggesting that nuclear war will have no other lasting environmental effects, Thompson and Schneider nonetheless argue that "on scientific grounds the global apocalyptic conclusions of the initial nuclear winter hypothesis can now be relegated to a vanishingly low level of probability."[8]

The fact that nuclear winter might not ensue should a nuclear exchange take place in, say, the fall does not bankrupt the theory that we are at risk of having a nuclear winter, as, for one thing, the nuclear exchange might indeed take place in the summer. The fact that a model specifies conditions under which some catastrophe would occur, conditions that do not always hold, does not make the model any less respectable. However, a conclusion that is dependent on many questionable assumptions is not as strong as one that is independent of these assumptions or has a wider margin of error. The nuclear winter hypothesis has not been falsified by its lack of robustness, but confidence in its predictions has been considerably weakened by its dependence on questionable assumptions about initial parameters.

Unfortunately, such sensitivity analysis reveals that most global models are not robust. The complexities created by complicated feedback processes are especially difficult to model. Very small changes in assumptions about the nature of these feedback loops can completely reverse a behavioural trend.[9]

¶ Ozone Layer Depletion

What is interesting about the history of models of ozone layer depletion is that the fear they generated was sufficient to initiate world-wide preventive action *before* any consensus was reached about the plausibility of the models and before there was any measurable damage.[10] In this case, the causal evidence was not discovered until afterwards. Action was taken to reduce the use and release of CFCs as early as 1978. However, it was not until 1988 that a study of the Antarctic atmosphere was published that revealed that there was a direct correlation between increased concentrations of chlorine and decreases in ozone.[11]

The effective political actions of a strong environmental movement led to preventive action being taken as early as 1978 with a ban on aerosol sprays in the United States, Canada, Norway and Sweden.[12] However, the production of CFCs for other uses continued to grow. It was not until 1984 that the ozone hole over Antarctica was first noticed. A 40 per cent decrease in ozone over ten years had gone previously unnoticed because researchers had rejected low readings as anomalous.[13]

The nature of the phenomenon was yet to be understood. Explanations and evidence would not come until three years later. Nonetheless, international political agreements were reached in 1987 to limit production and use of CFCs. An international agreement to reduce CFC use, known as the "Montreal Protocol," was signed in 1987. Soon after, the results of a crucial experiment were published. A NASA research plane had flown over the Antarctic taking measurements of the relevant variables. The measurements revealed that decreases in ozone concentration were directly proportional to concentrations of chlorine present.[14]

¶ Factors in the Acceptance of Models

These two examples show that, in the past, decisions about how to respond to possible global threats were made for reasons other than merely the strength of the scientific models involved. Policy-makers sometimes used the bare possibility of what they deemed undesirable outcomes to justify action meant to forestall those outcomes. In some cases, decisions about global risks have been made largely on the basis of political commitments and despite the absence of convincing evidence. Models found wanting scientifically were nevertheless accepted as providing sufficient grounds for decision-making. In hindsight, whether the resulting decisions turned out to be the correct ones or not has largely been a matter of luck.

The models both of ozone depletion and of nuclear winter were accepted in their early stages as revealing significant global risks. The general consensus now is that, in the ozone depletion case, fear of the risk turned out to be justified, while in the case of nuclear winter, faith in the model turned out to be unjustified. The effects of dust kicked up by a nuclear war would still be serious, but it is now generally thought that these effects would be much less serious than first portrayed in earlier nuclear winter models. In the case of neither of these models was there sufficient evidence for thinking that its predictions of catastrophe were reliable, yet people did accept them and thought that they provided sufficient reasons for action.

If the models' predictions were unsupported by convincing evidence, why were they nonetheless accepted? More than a few observers have suggested that they were accepted for political reasons. As John Hill argues persuasively elsewhere in this volume,[15] the lessons that humanity has often chosen to draw from its history are frequently guided not by a pursuit of the truth so much as by political expediency. This rule applies equally to science as it does international relations.

Despite their weaknesses, nuclear winter models gained a great deal of support, and were taken as supplying one more reason for limiting and reducing nuclear armaments. The rapid acceptance of the nuclear winter vision might have been a result of researchers' concerns to be politically correct. In "A Memoir of Nuclear Winter," Tony Rothman reports on his interviews with some major participants in the debate, and concludes that this widespread acquiescence in the promotion of a suspect model was a result of the noncritical stance that most scientists adopted for political reasons.[16] Rothman argues that the theory of nuclear winter gained wide support because of the politics involved rather than the science behind the theory. Specifically, nuclear winter models were quickly adopted because they gave support to a policy of weapons reduction. Rothman describes how many scientists uncritically supported these weak models because they thought that it would be immoral not to support a theory that furthered their political aims of nuclear disarmament. Rothman laments that current, better models of nuclear winter would have more influence on policy today had more moderate conclusions been publicized in the first place, rather than the apocalyptic versions that later had to be withdrawn.

Models of ozone layer depletion were also able to generate confidence in the predictions of catastrophe despite the absence of direct evidence that CFCs were actually causing any damage. The confidence in the models was sufficient to initiate world-wide preventative action *before* there was any measurable evidence.[17] As mentioned above, action was taken to reduce the use and release of CFCs as early as 1978. However, it was not until 1988 that a study of the Antarctic atmosphere was published that revealed that there was a direct correlation between increased concentrations of chlorine and decreases in ozone.[18] In *Beyond the Limits*,[19] Meadows et al. speculate that the decision to reduce CFC use was made because of the general climate of environmentalism.

Paralleling the nuclear winter case, the model was accepted before the evidence was convincing. Also analogously with the case for the nuclear winter model, the model's predictions were accepted for political reasons rather than based purely on the model's scientific merits. Supporters were proved correct about the existence of ozone depletion. In fact, it now appears that they had even vastly underestimated the magnitude of the problem. In the nuclear winter case, however, the models portrayed a catastrophe that is now believed to be exaggerated. How do we know which error we are likely to commit next time? Models of global warming and models of overpopulation and limits to growth are also unable to provide convincing evidence of the likelihood of catastrophe. How, then, should we react to them? Should we follow the example of the ozone layer depletion case, be cautious and act on the assumption that predictions of catastrophe will turn out to be correct? In this case, policy-makers took early action which later proved warranted. Or has the nuclear winter example taught us not to respond to the cries of Chicken Little? After all, there is almost no end to speculations about possible catastrophic futures.[20] Should we assume them all to be true and take the immediate precautionary actions that supporters of the models of global catastrophe say are necessary? Or should we remain sceptical, and take minimal action, or no action at all? How are current dilemmas about global risk being decided?

Suppose one accepts the thesis that models of global systems cannot provide any definite reason for thinking that human activities are contributing to some imminent global catastrophe. Does one's acceptance mean that one should support the claim that there is no good reason to act on the recommendations for avoiding catastrophe supplied by these models? Not necessarily. Despite the uncertainty of predictions generated by models of global systems, it turns out that the threats to biodiversity, to resources, and to coastal cities and agriculture, posed by global warming, ozone depletion, population increase, or nuclear winter, though not firmly established, have a non-negligible degree of probability. While global models might not be able to provide definitive reasons for thinking that catastrophe is *likely*, they do make us aware of frightening *possibilities* and, moreover, supply us with guidance on how to eliminate them. Global catastrophe, however unlikely, *is* possible.

At the same time, the stakes are high. The earth might be at risk, and, perhaps, something should be done. However, what those who design the models advise us to do is usually very costly. To prevent global warming, we are told, we must change our transportation and agricultural practices. To prevent economic or agricultural collapses we must find ways of reducing population growth. To address the problem of global catastrophic risks then, one needs to know both what these risks are, and what we are willing to do about them. Thus, the problem can be divided into two, separable questions – what to believe and what to do. Even if we are uncertain about the possibility of global catastrophe, this is a separate question from how we are to act.

The visible, palpable degradation of the environment, the exponential rise in population, the loss of forests, the high rate of species extinction, the decline of fisheries, the fouling of rivers – all generate, for many people, a fear of catastrophic environmental collapse. Many authors who are critical of models of global risk nonetheless conclude that we should be concerned with the state of the natural environment because of the history of environmental crises and the apparent trend towards increasing environmental stress. We know from measurements of ozone depletion that human action is capable of causing global changes quickly, and it is possible that the environment is not as resilient as many people might once have assumed it to be. We have seen that it is possible that some activities are putting the earth at risk of catastrophe. Given the conflicting influences of scientific uncertainty and the need to decide what to do about the risk of global catastrophe, there is a need for some strategy of decision-making.

¶ The Precautionary Principle

The history of environmental disasters has prompted in many an attitude of caution and a desire for preemptive action. Our experiences with chemicals such as mercury, PCBs, DDT, and CFCs have shown that we are capable of causing large, persistent, expensive, and harmful damage to the environment. The disposition to prefer to err on the side of caution when the stakes are high is becoming more common in international agreements concerning possible threats to the global environment. It has come to be known as the *precautionary principle.*

The precautionary principle states that scientific proof of a crisis is not needed to justify preventative action. What the precautionary principle attempts to do is provide a philosophical ground for preemptive action in cases of uncertainty. Adopting a cautious attitude reverses the burden of proof that is usually on those who make assertions, and instead takes warnings of catastrophe seriously until proven otherwise. Since irreversible catastrophes cannot be compensated for after the fact, it is argued that they should be completely avoided. Nicholas Rescher explains his reasoning on the subject, observing "With catastrophes we give way to the cautious pessimism of 'worst possible case' thinking. Here we do not calculate risks; we do not weigh probabilities; we simply note that there is a real chance of an absolutely disastrous outcome and turn to other alternatives, however unappealing in various ways."[21]

Of course, this strategy forgoes the possible benefits involved with taking risks, and we will never know what would have happened had we taken some other action, some other road. We might never know for sure whether our precautionary action is meeting a genuine need or whether it is but vain effort. The investment in possible catastrophe avoidance may make fools of us all. This reversal of the burden of proof is also difficult to defend against objections that it is vague and anti-scientific. The precautionary principle still stands in need of strong, supportive arguments. The lessons of history might provide one such justification for the precautionary principle that is based on culpable ignorance.

We should be expected to know in general what kinds of effects will result from familiar types of actions, even if we can't predict the exact details. The history of large-scale technology provides enough examples to give rise to a belief in the possibility of harm resulting from new and unfamiliar technology. It is the record of historical failures that justifies precautionary action. Historical experience gives rise to expectations of harm. We know that we have the ability to make large-scale changes in the planet. For example, we know that the ozone layer has been depleted. These experiences provide a justification for reversing the burden of proof that is normally on those who make predictions.

¶ Culpable Ignorance

Annette Baier thinks that our moral decisions are structured around "what maddens us" rather than around the most effective way of preserving lives.[22] She claims, for example, that we focus on deviant and malicious behaviour rather than on pollution even though pollution is probably the cause of more deaths.

Negligence and culpability "madden" us in this sense, and, perhaps, provide the strongest reason for precaution. The basic notion of moral culpability is that if a harm occurs, a harm that should have been foreseen and could have been avoided, then a basic moral obligation has been violated. K. R. Blair and W. A. Ross have argued that our continued production of greenhouse gases is a case of morally culpable negligence. Since suffering would result if the models of global warming are accurate, then "all action that can be taken to avoid global warming is ethically required."[23] René Dumont blames the greenhouse effect for droughts causing one million deaths from starvation each year.[24] He then goes on to accuse suspected greenhouse offenders of murder. Peter Danielson argues that while we may be excused for greenhouse gas emissions to date, we are "no longer innocent" of the potential effects of our actions, and are morally responsible for any harm that might result.[25] Danielson thinks that the awareness of a plausible model that predicts harm is sufficient to make us morally responsible. In one sense he is right. If we pursue activities, knowing that they might result in harm to others, we are morally culpable. However, Danielson begs the question with respect to global warming. Whether the emission of greenhouse gases is a risky activity is the very issue in question. Can people ignorant of the complicated, long-term effects of their actions really be held morally responsible?

Ian Hacking has developed an argument about "culpable ignorance" that could be used as a measure to determine when precaution is morally required and when it is not.[26] He argues that acting in a state of ignorance is morally culpable if harm is likely to result and the agent *could have* found out about the likely consequences of the action. However, an agent is not morally culpable if no reasonable person could be expected to know these consequences. We cannot be expected to know all the harms to which some of our current actions might be linked. Hacking's criterion of culpable ignorance prevents both excessive caution and total inaction when faced with ignorance. Obviously, many of our actions will have negative consequences of which we remain ignorant, so we will cause harm. However, only some of this ignorance is morally culpable.

Adapting arguments from Aristotle and Aquinas, Hacking argues that culpability involves universals rather than particulars.[27] There are universal generalizations about car brakes, for instance, that one should be expected to know. However, one cannot be expected to know the particular details of any one set of brakes that might result in harm. Thus, I am morally blameworthy if I drive a car without getting the brakes checked regularly, but not if some unusual mechanical defect affects my particular car. We should be expected to know in general what kinds of effects will result from familiar types of actions, even if we cannot predict the exact details, but ignorance of the future is too widespread to be allowed as a general reason for inactivity. Thus, we should not limit our activities except in cases where our actions would be culpable. To think otherwise and to behave with maximum caution, constantly worried about what disaster might occur, is to assume, unreasonably, an unlimited responsibility for all world events resulting from human activity.

However, there is a type of situation where an agent is blameworthy for acting under ignorance even when the ignorance is unavoidable. Hacking argues that the history of large-scale technology provides enough examples to give rise to a universal belief in the possibility of harm resulting from new and unfamiliar technology. It is the record of historical failures that justifies precautionary action and nullifies the excuse of ignorance in any particular case. In this particular instance at least, history provides a fairly unambiguous object lesson.

To illustrate, he discusses "interference effects," which are those that result from the combination of technologies. For example, while we might know how two medicines work individually, we do not know what interference effects will result when these medicines act in concert. Hacking supposes that it might be "in the nature of rapidly expanding deployment of new technologies to produce such [harmful] effects by unforeseeable universal facts."[28] There is enough regularity to such harm that it should now be expected. A universal expectation would provide grounds for precaution even though it is impossible to find out whether any particular new technology is likely to result in harm. Hacking claims that his argument provides "a new kind of reason for being leery of new technology."[29]

The precautionary principle is founded on similar expectations of harm resulting from actions that have global effects – expectations formed from historical experience. What Hacking's reasoning implies is that actions that have potentially catastrophic consequences can be morally culpable even if we cannot foresee the specific consequences. They are culpable because experience has shown that we should expect harmful consequences from certain kinds of activity. We know from experience that lack of precaution will cause the continued degradation of the environment. PCBs, CFCs, and DDT were all assumed to be harmless. We now know that scientists were wrong in all three cases. Hacking's argument for culpability takes into account the pervasiveness of these errors. Although we might not be able to justify precaution in any one instance, precaution is justified as a general strategy because it is based on our previous experiences. By demanding proof of environmental risk before we take action, we are culpable because this makes it more likely that we will eventually make an error and fail to take precautionary action when it is necessary.

Hans Jonas, too, uses the notion of culpable ignorance to argue for precaution. In normal situations, we have a duty to find out what are the likely effects of our actions. However, he writes, "a novel moral problem" is created when our ability to predict the consequences of our actions is weak, and the potential effects of those actions are global, irreversible and cumulative. In unprecedented situations, he continues, the "recognition of ignorance becomes the obverse of the duty to know."[30]

Endnotes

1. A fuller treatment of this topic can be found in my *Apocalypse Soon?: Wagering on Warnings of Global Catastrophe* (Montreal: McGill-Queen's University Press, 2002).
2. Anita Gordon & David Suzuki, *It's a Matter of Survival* (Toronto: Stoddart, 1990), 3.
3. See especially "Environmental Scares" *The Economist*, 20 December 1997, 19–21.
4. Jim Gerrie, "Canada's Lost Tradition of Technological Criticism," especially 235–36.
5. Tony Rothman, "A Memoir of Nuclear Winter," in *Science à la Mode* (Princeton, NJ: Princeton University Press, 1989), 124–32.
6. S. L. Thompson and S. H. Schneider, "Nuclear Winter Reappraised," in *Foreign Affairs* 4:5 (Summer 1986): 987.
7. Ibid., 993.
8. Ibid., 983.
9. H.S.D. Cole, ed., *Models of Doom* (New York: Universe Books, 1973), 133.
10. D. H. Meadows, D. L. Meadows, and J. Randers, *Beyond the Limits* (Toronto: McClelland & Stewart, 1992), 141–60.
11. Ibid., 152–53.
12. Ibid., 150.

13　Paul Brodeur, "Annals of Chemistry: In the Face of Doubt," *New Yorker*, 9 June 1986, 71.
14　Meadows et al., *Beyond the Limits*, fig. 5-5, 152.
15　Hill concentrates on American and German falsifications of the historical record surrounding the outbreak of the Great War (see John S. Hill, "Historical Fictions: The Invention of Historical Events for Political Purposes," in this volume).
16　Rothman, "A Memoir of Nuclear Winter," 109-47.
17　Meadows et al., *Beyond the Limits*, 141-60.
18　Ibid., 152-53.
19　Ibid., Chapter 5.
20　See especially, John Leslie, *The End of the World* (London: Routledge, 1996).
21　Nicholas Rescher, *Risk: A Philosophical Introduction to the Theory of Risk Evaluation and Management* (Washington: University Press of America, 1983), 73.
22　Annette Baier, "Poisoning the Wells," reprinted in D. MacLean ed., *Values at Risk* (New Jersey: Rowan and Allanheld, 1986), 49-74.
23　K. R. Blair and W. A. Ross, "Energy Efficiency at Home and Abroad," in Harold Coward and Thomas Hurka, eds., *The Greenhouse Effect: Ethics & Climate Change* (Waterloo, ON: Wilfrid Laurier University Press, 1993), 9.
24　René Dumont, in Kent A. Peacock, ed., *Living with the Earth: An Introduction to Environmental Philosophy* (Toronto: Harcourt Brace Canada, 1996), 35.
25　Peter Danielson, "Personal Responsibility," in Coward and Hurka, *The Greenhouse Effect*, 87-88.
26　Ian Hacking, "Culpable Ignorance of Interference Effects," reprinted in *Values at Risk*, D. MacLean, ed. (New Jersey: Rowan and Allanheld, 1986), 153.
27　Ibid., 137-39.
28　Ibid., 143.
29　Ibid., 152.
30　Hans Jonas, *The Imperative of Responsibility: In Search of An Ethics for the Technological Age* (Chicago: University of Chicago Press, 1984), 8.

Bibliography

Baier, Annette. "Poisoning the Wells." Reprinted in *Values at Risk*, edited by D. MacLean, 49-74. New Jersey: Rowan and Allanheld, 1986.
Blair, K. R., and W. A. Ross. "Energy Efficiency at Home and Abroad." In *The Greenhouse Effect: Ethics & Climate Change*, edited by Harold Coward and Thomas Hurka, 149-69. Waterloo, ON: Wilfrid Laurier University Press, 1993.
Brodeur, Paul. "Annals of Chemistry: In the Face of Doubt." *New Yorker*, 9 June 1986, 70-87.
Cole, H.S.D., ed. *Models of Doom*. New York: Universe Books, 1973.
Danielson, Peter. "Personal Responsibility." In *The Greenhouse Effect: Ethics & Climate Change*, edited by Harold Coward and Thomas Hurka, 81-98. Waterloo, ON: Wilfrid Laurier University Press, 1993.
"Environmental Scares." *The Economist*, 20 December 1997, 19-21.
Gordon, Anita, and David Suzuki. *It's a Matter of Survival*. Toronto: Stoddart, 1990.
Hacking, Ian. "Culpable Ignorance of Interference Effects." Reprinted in *Values at Risk*, edited by D. MacLean, 136-54. New Jersey: Rowan and Allanheld, 1986.

Haller, Stephen. *Apocalypse Soon?: Wagering on Warnings of Global Catastrophe*. Montreal: McGill-Queen's University Press, 2002.

Jonas, Hans. *The Imperative of Responsibility: In Search of An Ethics for the Technological Age*. Chicago: University of Chicago Press, 1984.

Leslie, John. *The End of the World*. London: Routledge, 1996.

Meadows, D. H., D. L. Meadows, and J. Randers. *Beyond the Limits*. Toronto: McClelland and Stewart, 1992.

Peacock, Kent A., ed. *Living with the Earth: An Introduction to Environmental Philosophy*. Toronto: Harcourt Brace Canada, 1996.

Rescher, Nicholas. *Risk: A Philosophical Introduction to the Theory of Risk Evaluation and Management*. Washington: University Press of America, 1983.

Rothman, Tony. "A Memoir of Nuclear Winter." In *Science à la Mode*. Princeton, NJ: Princeton University Press, 1989.

Thompson, S. L., and S. H. Schneider. "Nuclear Winter Reappraised." *Foreign Affairs* 4:5 (Summer 1986): 981–1005.

Index

Note: Page references in *italics* refer to photographs and maps.

A

Aboriginal peoples, colonialism and land, 19–20
   in Australia, 79, 81, 82, 86–89, *87, 90–91, 92,* 97–98, 103–20, 125–42
   in Canada, 79, 81–82, 83–85, *84,* 89–90, *91*–98, *93, 94, 95*
Adorno, Theodor, 3
African diaspora, 195–211
al-Ghazali, Abu Hamid, 63–64
Alcoholics Anonymous, 173–74, 189n32
Alliance Atlantis Communications Inc., 40–41, 46–48, 55n30
Alliance Broadcasting, 38–39
Alliance Communications, 40, 54n14
Allward, Walter, 13
America, 162
American Automobile Association, 261
American Historical Association, 155
American History Illustrated, 36

Angus Reid, 49
Anzaldúa, Gloria, 199
Appleby, Joyce, 10–11
Aristotle, 63, 66
Arts & Entertainment (A&E), 36
Atlantis Communications, 40
The Atlas, 131
Auden, W. H., 23
Australia, colonialism and land, 79, 81, 82, 86–89, *87,* 90–91, *92,* 97–98, 103–20, 125–42
Australian National University, 80

B

Baier, Annette, 278
Barbour, Ian, 265n3
Barwick, Diane, 104
BBC (British Broadcasting Corporation), 5, 36
Beard, Charles A., 162, 170n59

285

The Beaver, 39
Beaver people, mapping of hunting grounds, 89–90
Bell, Richard, 65
Benitex-Rojo, Antonio, 202
Benz, Karl, 249
Berger, Carl, 220
Bergson, Henri, 180, 181–82
Berlin, Isaiah, 18
Berton, Pierre, 19, 55n35
Bethmann-Hollweg, Theobald von, 153
Beyond the Limits (Meadows et al.), 270, 275
Bitter Springs (film), 126–29, 141–42
Blackstone, William, 117
Blair, K. R., 279
Bolen, Norm, 39, 43, 44, 45, 48, 49
Bowne, Borden Parker, 180
Box, Ian, 220
Boxer Rebellion, 20–21, 164–65
Brand, Dionne, 196, 205, 207–10
Brand, Stewart, 23
British Columbia
  mapping of native hunting grounds, 89–90
  Sons of Freedom, 96
Broadcasting Act (Canada), 40, 45
Brody, Hugh, 89–90
Brooke, Rupert, 11
Brown, Jeffrey Scott, 20
  "Being Present, Owning the Past, and Growing into the Future: Temporality, Revelation and the Therapeutic Culture," 173–93
Buck, Andrew R., 19, 98, 167n2
  "Understanding Property in Australian History," 125–46
Bullock, Alan, 4
Burns, Ken, 19, 36

C
Canada
  Canadians' familiarity with national history, 16
  colonialism and land, 79, 81–82, 83–85, *84*, 89–90, *91*–98, *93, 94, 95*
  Doukhobors, 92–96, *93, 94, 95*
  historical television programming, 35, 38–53
  mapping and surveying of land, 83–85, 89–91, *90, 91, 94*–95
  Red River Settlement, 83–85, *84*
  technological criticism in, 217–39
Canada: A People's History (TV program), 10, 16, 27n22, 52–53
Canadian Association of Broadcasters Specialty Board, 41–43
The Canadians (TV program), 43
Cardoso, Andrew, 44, 45, 48, 49
Carpenter, Humphrey, 114
Carter, Paul, 88
cartography, 83–85, 89–91, *90, 91, 94*–95
Castles, Alex, 97
CBC (Canadian Broadcasting Corporation), *Canada: A People's History*, 10, 16, 27n22, 52–53
Chamberlin, John, 67
Chaney, Fred, 91
China, Boxer Rebellion, 20–21, 164–65
Chrétien, Jean, 61–63
Chrisholm, Caroline, 106
Christian, William, 220–21
Cicero, 63
CIFC (Canadian Independent Film Caucus), 47, 48, 50, 51, 55n28
The Citizen, 133, 135
Clark, Ian, 65
Cline, Catherine, 168n11
Cohen, Paul, 20–21, 164, 165
collective memory, 163–65
Colonial Magazine, 132–33
colonialism, impact on property and property rights, 19–20, 79–99, 103–20, 125–42
Combat! (TV program), 44, 51
commemoration, rites of, 14
Coughlin, Father, 160
Cowper, Charles, 107
Cristi, Renato, 73n23
Crowe, Sir Eyre, 88, 168n16
CRTC (Canadian Radio-Television & Telecommunications Commission), 38, 40, 41–43, 45–47, 48, 52
CTV (Canadian Television Network), 38
Curr, Edward, 103–4

D
Daly, Herman, 264
Danielson, Peter, 279
Dass, Ram, 182
Davids, Dan, 36
Davies, Carole Boyce, 202–3

De Kerckhove, Derrick, 234–35
Deniehy, Daniel, 106
Descartes, René, 63–64, 72n8
Die Grosse Politik der Europaischen Kabinette, 152–57, 166–67, 167n11
Discovery Channel, 36
Dominion Institute, 16, 49
Doukhobors, 92–96, *93, 94, 95*
Drache, Daniel, 219
Dresser, Horatio, 189n20
Driesch, Hans, 180
Duffy, Dennis, 234
Duguid, Leslie, 131
Dumont, René, 279
Duncan, Carol B., 20, 99n10, 100n16, 189n31
  "*Travessao*: African Diasporic Migratory Subjectivity and the Making of History," 195–213

E
Eastwood, Janet, 39
Edna, NWT (now Alberta)
  map of homestead divisions, 90, *91*
education
  OZCAN legal history program, 79–99
  relevance of philosophy, 63–64
  teaching history, 17, 59–72
Eisenhower, Dwight, 261
Empire, 135, 140–41
environmental crisis. *See* global catastrophe predictions
Espmark, Kjell, 52
Eucken, Rudolf, 180
Evans, Richard, 9
Ewing, Karen, 100n16

F
fabrications. *See* historical fictions
Farrugia, Peter, "Introduction: Navigating the River of History," 1–31
Fay, Sidney Bradshaw, 153–58, 165, 169n37
Feenberg, Andrew, 237–38, 265n3
Feyerabend, Paul, 66
films, 19, 37–38, 50
Firestone, 262
First World War. *See* World War I
Fischer, Fritz, 18, 157–58, 169n38
Fong, Jennifer, 43

Fortune, 160
Foster, Hamar, 97
Foucault, Michel, 226
4 Little Girls (film), 50
Fox, Richard, 188n9
Frye, Northrop, 220
Fukuyama, Francis, 61
Fuller, R. Buckminster, 253–54, 266n11
Fussell, Paul, 13

G
Gates, Henry Louis, 198
Geertz, Clifford, 104
General Motors, 248, 262
Germany
  reclaiming of past, 14–16, 24
  view of origins of WWI, 20, 150–58
Gerrie, James, 21, 270
  "Canada's Lost Tradition of Technological Criticism," 217–45
Gipps, Governor, 130, 136
global catastrophe predictions, 269–81
  acceptance of scientific models, 274–77
  assessing the threat, 270–71
  culpable ignorance, 278–81
  nuclear winter, 272–73
  ozone layer depletion, 273–74
  the precautionary principle, 277–78
Globe & Mail, 16
Goddard, Stephen, 260
Gooch, G. P., 153, 155
Gordon, Anita, 269
Goyder, John, 218–19
Granatstein, J. L. (Jack), 9–10, 15–16, 35–36, 49, 219
Grant, George, 21, 22, 217–39, 241n65
Grass, Günter, 28n39
Great War. *See* World War I
Greenberg, Cary, 190n38
Grierson, John, 55n28
Groarke, Leo, 17–18, 53n2, 72n8, 73n11, 196
  "Teaching History: The Future of the Past," 59–75
The Guardian, 132
Guzman, Jaime, 73n23

H
Hacking, Ian, 181, 279–81
Halbwachs, Maurice, 163, 164
Haller, Stephen F., 21, 22

Index 287

"Predictions of Global Catastrophe: Just Another Chicken Little?", 269–83
Hamilton, Paula, 108
Hanson, Philip, 225
Hargraves, John Fletcher, 139
Harris, Mark Jonathan, 50
Harris, Michael, 97
Heaven, Edwin and David, 221
Heidegger, Martin, 218, 238
Heraclitus, 3, 25
Herwig, Holger, 168n11
Hilgartner, Stephen, 65
Hill, Draper, 63
Hill, John S., 13, 18, 20, 211n3, 274, 282n15
"Historical Fictions: The Invention of Historical Events for Political Purposes," 149–72
Hiroshima, 50
historians
  J. L. Granatstein's criticism of, 9–10
  media and the historian/celebrity, 5–6
  and objectivity, 11, 12
  responsibility of, 71
  role and importance of, 2, 218
  specialized expertise of, 17–18, 67–70
  suspicion of, 2
  and television history, 49, 70–71
  traits of mid-twentieth-century historians, 4
historical consciousness, 2, 4, 7, 60, 66
historical determinism, 248, 265
historical education
  importance of, 60–72
  interdisciplinary approach to, 70–71
  relevance of philosophy in, 63–64
  value of historical reflection, 64–65
historical fictions
  consequences of, 166–67
  defined, 167n1
  and origins of WWI, 20, 149–67
historical research
  "local reading" of sources, 19, 100n10, 104–5, 107, 119, 120
  study of primary historical documents, 67, 68
history
  bourgeois and proletarian forms of, 7–8
  "coping" with the past, 24–25
  defined, 2
  fact/fictional divide in construction of, 15, 197, 211. *See also* historical fictions
  importance of, 2, 14–16, 59–72, 99
  influence on individuals and collectives, 22–23
  irony of, 25
  lessons of, 2, 25, 99, 103, 166, 278
  linearity of, 7–8
  meaning of, 8
  popularization of, 17, 19. *See also* infotainment
  post-modernist critique. *See* post-modernism
  provisional nature of, 11
  reductionist approach to, 69–70
  river analogy, 2–3
  role in education, 60–72
  social, 6–7
  specialization of discipline, 17–18, 67–70
  teaching of, 17, 59–72
History Bites (TV program), 44, 50
The History Channel (U.S. cable service), 36–38
history television, 19, 35–57, 70–71
History Television (Canadian cable service), 18, 38–52
Holocaust, 4, 14, 19, 164
Howard, John, 126
Howison, G. H., 180
Hulme, Peter, 107
Hume, David, 59, 64, 68, 73n11
Hunt, Lynn, 10–11
Hynes, Samuel, 13

I
Iggers, Georg, 6
Indigenous peoples, colonialism and land, 19–20
  in Australia, 79, 81, 82, 86–89, *87, 90–91, 92,* 97–98, 103–20, 125–42
  in Canada, 79, 81–82, 83–85, *84,* 89–90, 91–98, *93, 94, 95*
infotainment, 35–57, 70
Innis, Harold, 21, 22, 217–39
It Seems Like Yesterday (TV program), 44, 50, 51

J

Jacobs, Jane, 237
Jacobs, Margaret, 10–11
James, William, 180
Jay, Elisabeth, 114–15
Jonas, Hans, 281
Jonas, Joyce, 198
Jung, Carl, 189n29

K

Kaminer, Wendy, 183
Kantorowicz, Hermann, 167n11
Katz, Stan, 183
Kautsky, Karl, 151
Kercher, Bruce, 97
Kroker, Arthur, 218–19, 226, 233
Kuhn, Thomas, 66
Kurtz, Ernest, 190n40

L

land and colonialism, 19–20
  in Australia, 79, 81, 82, 86–89, *87*, 90–91, *92*, 97–98, 103–20, 125–42
  in Canada, 79, 81–82, 83–85, *84*, 89–90, *91*–98, *93*, *94*, *95*
  mapping and surveying of land, 83–85, 89–91, *90*, *91*, 94–95
Lang, Gideon Scott, 134
Lang, John Dunmore, 107
Langer, William L., 155
Lasch, Christopher, 175, 176
Lassner, Franz, 167n11
League of American Wheelmen, 258–59, 260, 261
The Learning Channel, 37
Lears, Jackson, 175–76, 177
Lee, Dennis, 221
Lee, Spike, 50
legal history program, OZCAN, 79–99
lessons of history, 2, 25, 99, 103, 166, 278
Levi, Primo, 14
Lewes, Henry, 64
Leys, Ruth, 181
Limits to Growth (Meadows et al.), 270
Littlewood, Alan, 237
Liu, Aimee, 183
Long, Huey, 160
"The Long Now" Foundation, 23
The Long Way Home (film), 50

Lowe, Robert, 135–36
Lowenthal, David, 99

M

Maday, Charles, 37
Madeary, G., 121n13
Maeterlinck, Maurice, 181–82
Malouf, David, 85–86
Malthus, Thomas, 270
Mandela, Nelson, 23–24
Marchand, Philip, 220, 234, 235
Marcuse, Herbert, 218
Marshall, Paule, 196, 205–7
Martin, Chester, 99n8
Mates, Benson, 64
May, Tommy, 91
McFarlane, Peter, 39
McLaren, John, 19, 20, 66, 128
  "The Memory of Property: The Challenge of Using the Past to Enlighten the Lawyers of the Future," 79–102
McLuhan, Marshall, 21, 22, 217–39
McNabb, Jerry, 47
McNabb and Connolly, 47
media. *See also* history television; movies; radio
  influence on history, 4–6
Medina, Ann, 50–51
memory and memories
  defined, 2
  and history, 12–14, 163–64, 165
Mercer, Rick, 51, 56n45
Merchants of Death (Engelbrecht, Hanighen), 160
Mill, John Stuart, 140
Mitchell, Thomas, 135–36
monuments, 13
Moore, Christopher, 56n44
Morel, E. D., 153
Morgan, Sally, 86–88
  painting, *87*
Mosley, Oswald, 50
Mosse, George, 13
Mother Yvonne, 200–203, 207
movies, 19, 37–38, 50
Muggeridge, John, 220
Mumford, Lewis, 262
Murray, Gilbert, 153

Murray, Terence, 139
Myers, Jack, 37
Myers Communications, 37

N
Narrative of Olaudah Equiano, 196
National City Lines, 262
National Film Board, 55n28
National League of Good Roads (NLGR), 259, 260
National Non-Partisan League, 159
Neeson, Janet, 97
Nettheim, Garth, 97
New Republic, 160, 162
New South Wales, Australia, history of land issues, 103–20, 129–42
New York Herald Tribune, 162–63
Newman, Peter C., 55n35
Newton, Isaac, 178
Nicholas of Autrecourt, 63, 64, 73n11
Nietzsche, Friedrich, 63, 71–72
Novick, Peter, 164, 165
nuclear debate, historical relevance, 65
Nye, Gerald, 158–63, 165
Nye Committee, 158–63, 165–67

O
O'Connor, Rory, 65
Office of Road Inquiry (ORI), 259, 260
Olney, Justice, 103–4
The Origins of the Second World War (Taylor), 3–4
The Origins of the World War (Fay), 155–57
Orwell, George, 65
Our House (TV program), 43–44
Owen, Wilfrid, 256–57
OZCAN, legal history program, 79–99

P
Pal, Leslie, 225
Paléologue, M., 157
Parent, Gilbert, 43
Paris, Erna, 24
PBS (Public Broadcasting Service), 19
Peele, Stanton, 183, 184
personal history, and therapeutic culture, 173–87
Philadelphia Record, 162
philosophy, relevance to general education, 63–64

Piggin, Stuart, 115
Pioneer Quest: A Year in the Real West (TV program), 51
Pitty, Roderic, 104
Plato, 62, 69
Pojman, Louis, 263
The Poor Man, 105, 107–20
popularization of history, 17, 19. See also infotainment
Populist Party, 159
post-modernism
  contentions, 7–8
  impact on study of history, 10–12
  rejection of, 8–10
Press, Gerald, 60
property. See land and colonialism

Q
Queen Mother Ruby, 199–204, 209

R
radio, 5, 26n9, 40, 41, 53
Ramsland, John, 106, 115
Rat Patrol (TV program), 44, 51
Rawlinson, J., 219
Reagon, Bernice Johnson, 203
Red River Settlement, 83–85, *84*
Regina v. Dudley and Stephens, 96–97
Reinarman, Craig, 190n37
relativism, 9, 11
Renouvin, Pierre, 155, 156
Rescher, Nicholas, 278
Reynolds, Henry, 97, 117, 118
Richmond, Rev. Legh, 114–15
Richter, Mischa, 61–63
Rieff, David, 183–84
Rieff, Philip, 174–75, 176–77, 190n42
road construction, 247–65
  alternatives and ethics of mobility, 262–65
  Brantford Southern Access Road, 251–53
  self-interest and road construction, 260–62
  transportation myths, 253–60
Robertson, John, 106–7, 117, 121n13
Robson, Stuart, 29n60
Rose, Deborah Bird, 88
Ross, W. A., 279
Rothman, Tony, 275

Rotstein, Abraham, 220
Rousso, Henry, 164, 170n63
Royce, Josiah, 180
Ryan, Simon, 82

S

Saskatchewan, Doukhobors, 92–96, *93*, *94*, *95*
Saving Private Ryan (film), 19
A Scattering of Seeds (TV program), 43–44, 45, 47–48, 51, 52, 55n31
Schiller, F. C. S., 180
Schindler's List (film), 19
Schmitt, Bernadotte, 155
Schneider, S. H., 272
science, history of, 66–67
Sebald, W. G., 14–15
Second World War. *See* World War II
Shapiro, Ann-Louise, 4–5, 7, 19
Sharif, M. M., 64
Simpson, Brian, 96–97
Simpson, M. Carleton (Carl), 21, 222
 "Linking the Past to the Future," 247–68
social history, emergence of, 6–7
Solecki, Sam, 235
Solicitor's Journal, 140
Solomon, Graham, 73n11
Sons of Freedom, 96
Sontag, Raymond, 155
specialization of history discipline, 17–18, 67–70
Spielberg, Stephen, 4
The Spirit of Enterprise, 38
Spiritual Baptist Church, 196, 197
Standard Oil, 262
Stanley, Lord, 130–31, 135
Starowicz, Mark, 53
Stephen, Sir Alfred, 134, 138–39, 140
Suissa, Sydney, 48–50, 51–52, 55n30, 55n35, 55n39
Susman, Warren, 175–76, 177
sustainable development, 264–65
Suzuki, David, 269
Swift, Jonathan, 270–71
Sydney Morning Herald, 105, 118, 125, 135, 136–37, 138
Sykes, Charles, 183

T

Taylor, A. J. P., 3–4, 5–6, 26nn5, 6, 9
teaching history, 17, 59–72
technological determinism, 248, 265n3
technology
 Canadian technological criticism, 21, 217–39
 environmental catastrophe predictions, 21–22, 269–81
 highway construction, 21, 247–65
 Telefilm's Equity Investment Program (TEIP), 45–46
television. *See* history television
Temperley, Harold, 155
testimonies, 14
therapeutic culture, 173–87
Thompson, E. P., 97
Thompson, S. L., 272
Thomson, Edward Deas, 139
Thomson, Iain, 238
time, framework of, 17, 20, 23, 100n16, 180, 181, 182, 203, 211
Tosh, John, 12
transportation. *See* road construction
travessao (spirit traveler), 196–211
Trevor-Roper, Hugh, 4
Troitzkoe, Saskatchewan, 95
truth, historical, 8, 9, 10–11, 12, 24, 149, 156, 166, 274
twelve-step programs, 21, 173, 183–87, 189n32, 190nn37, 38, 42
Twomey, Christina, 106, 120

U

United States
 9/11 terrorist attacks, 22–23
 American familiarity with, 16
 historical television programming, 35, 36–38
 Ken Burns' Civil War documentary, 19, 36
 view of origins of WWI, 158–63
University of British Columbia, 80
University of Victoria, 80

V

Vandenberg, Arthur, 160
Vittert, Mark, 37
Voskrisennie, Saskatchewan, *94*

Index   291

W

Wainburranga, Paddy Fordham, 88–89
Wakefield (colonial reformer), 108, 119
Walser, Martin, 15
Washington Post, 22, 160
Watson, John, 223, 227
Weber, Max, 176–77, 188n8
The Weekly Register, 131
Weinberg, Julius, 73n11
Welch, Kathleen, 66
Wentworth, William Charles, 129–30, 136
Westfall, William, 223, 229, 233
Wheelmen. *See* League of American Wheelmen
White, Hayden, 7–8, 27n17
White, Richard, 97
Whitehead, Alfred North, 232
Wiesel, Elie, 14
Williams, Robert A., Jr., 97
Wilson, Woodrow, 160–61
Windeyer, Richard, 118
Winter, Jay, 13, 19
Wirth, Joseph, 152
Wiskemann, Elizabeth, 4
Witten, Cindy, 48
Wittgens, Hermann J., 167n11
Woodward, E. L., 167n11

World War I, 13, 19
  historical fictions on origins of, 20, 149–67
  television programming, 39
World War II, 12, 14, 19
  The Origins of the Second World War (Taylor), 3–4
  television programming, 39
  "The World at War" radio broadcast, 5
Wright, Nancy E., 19, 28n30, 99–100n10, 167n2
  "Reading the Past: The Dispossession of the Poor and the Aborigines in Colonial New South Wales," 103–24
Wright, Robert, 10, 17, 18, 27n22, 70, 72n3, 74n27, 196
  "The Way We Were? History as 'Infotainment' in the Age of History Television," 35–57

Y

Yaffe, Phyllis, 43, 45–46
Yorkton, Saskatchewan, *93*
Yorta Yort v. Victoria, 103–4

Z

Znaimer, Moses, 50

www.ingramcontent.com/pod-product-compliance
Lightning Source LLC
Chambersburg PA
CBHW061706300426
44115CB00014B/2586